Understanding Research Methods

An Overview of the Essentials

Fifth Edition

Mildred L. Patten

Pyrczak Publishing

P.O. Box 250430 • Glendale, CA 91225

"Pyrczak Publishing" is an imprint of Fred Pyrczak, Publisher, A California Corporation.

Although the author and publisher have made every effort to ensure the accuracy and completeness of information contained in this book, we assume no responsibility for errors, inaccuracies, omissions, or any inconsistency herein. Any slights of people, places, or organizations are unintentional.

This edition was written in collaboration with Randall R. Bruce.

Project director: Monica Lopez.

Editorial assistance provided by Cheryl Alcorn, Karen M. Disner, Brenda Koplin, Erica Simmons, and Sharon Young.

Cover design by Robert Kibler and Larry Nichols.

Printed in the United States of America by Malloy, Inc.

ISBN 1-884585-64-7

Contents

Continued →

Tables

Index

NOTES

INTRODUCTION TO THE FIFTH EDITION

This book provides you with an overview of basic research methods.

The distinctive features of this book are:

- The division of the material into short sections instead of long chapters will help you take small steps through this exciting—but highly technical—field of study. The long chapters in other research methods books prompt students to take big gulps, which often are not easily digested.

- When one topic builds directly on the previous one, the second one begins with a reminder of what you should have mastered in the previous topic. This helps you keep your eye on the big picture and make a smooth transition from one topic to the next.

- Technical jargon is defined in plain English to the extent possible, and numerous examples make abstract research concepts concrete. Students' reactions in field tests attest to success in the effort to make this book comprehensible.

- The material on statistics is presented at the conceptual level. It shows you how to interpret statistical reports but does not bog you down with computational details.

- The exercises at the end of the topics encourage you to pause to make sure you have mastered one topic before moving on to another. This is important because many topics are cumulative. Thorough mastery of an earlier topic is frequently a prerequisite for mastering a later topic with ease. The first part of each exercise tests your comprehension of factual material. The second part asks you to interpret and apply the material you have mastered. This will help you internalize the concepts as well as stimulate classroom discussions. Finally, the third part provides questions that help you consider major issues in planning a research project.

Why should you have an overview of research methods? Because...

- Leaders in all fields are increasingly relying on the results of research in making important decisions, such as how to help those who are de-

pendent on welfare, which types of educational programs to fund, and how to adjust work environments to improve employees' output and satisfaction. If you hope to become a decision-maker in your field, you must master research methods to be effective in sorting through the conflicting claims often found in the research literature on a topic.

- Many of you will be expected to do simple but important research on the job. For instance, clinical psychologists are expected to track improvements made by their clients, teachers are expected to experiment with new methods in the classroom, and social workers are expected to collect data on their clients.

- All of you will be making lifestyle decisions based on research reported in the media. Should you take vitamin supplements? How should you dress for success on the job? Which make of automobile should you buy if your primary concern is safety? Answers based on research are often offered in newspapers, magazines, and television newscasts. As a result of studying research methods, you will become a knowledgeable, critical consumer of research. For instance, you will consider questions such as "Was the sample biased?" "Is the data analysis misleading?" and "Are the results statistically significant?"

- Finally, you may need to read and report on published research in other classes. You will be more skilled at doing this if you have a solid understanding of basic methods of research.

New to the Fifth Edition

This edition contains a new part (Part H), which expands the coverage on qualitative research. Specifically, Topics 60 and 61 describe sampling in qualitative research, Topics 62 and 63 describe methods used to collect qualitative data, and Topic 64 describes specific techniques qualitative researchers use to ensure the quality of their research. Part H concludes with Topics 65 and 66, which describe two frequently used general approaches to the analysis of qualitative data.

Acknowledgments

Dr. Anne Hafner and Dr. Robert Morman, both of California State University, Los Angeles, provided many helpful comments on the first draft of this book. New material for subsequent editions was reviewed by Dr. Robert Rosenthal of Harvard University and the University of California, Riverside; Dr. Deborah M. Oh of California State University, Los Angeles; and Dr. Richard Rasor of American River College. All these individuals made important contributions to the development of this book. However, errors and omissions, of course, remain the responsibility of the author.

Mildred L. Patten

PART A

INTRODUCTION TO RESEARCH METHODS

This part of the book defines what we mean by empirical research and provides an overview of the characteristics of the major approaches to this type of research. Broad issues that underlie all types of research— such as the nature of research hypotheses, how researchers define the variables they plan to study, ethical considerations in research, and the relationship between theory and research—are also covered in this part.

NOTES

The **empirical approach** to knowledge is based on **observations**.[1] We all use the empirical approach in everyday living. For instance, if a teacher observes students becoming restless during a certain lesson, he or she might say they "know" the lesson is boring. As useful as everyday observations often are, they can be misleading and are often misinterpreted. For example, the teacher may have misinterpreted reasons for the students' restlessness. It might be the time and day, such as a warm Friday afternoon, that is the culprit and *not* the inherent interest of the lesson. Even if the lesson is boring to this teacher's students, the teacher might conclude that the lesson is boring to students *in general*, when it might, in fact, be interesting to other students at other ability levels, with different backgrounds, and so on.

When researchers use the empirical approach, they strive to avoid misleading results and poor interpretations. The key to doing so is careful planning of **why** they want to make observations, **whom** they want to observe, as well as **how** and **when** to observe.

The question of *why to observe* establishes the need for the study. Perhaps a better method for helping students acquire a certain mathematics skill is needed. After considering their own experiences and reviewing related literature on the topic, researchers prepare a formal statement of their research purpose, such as "whether the use of hands-on manipulatives to teach Topic X will result in greater student achievement than a lecture and workbook approach." They might also arrive at a **hypothesis**, which is a statement of what they expect the results to show. For example, they might hypothesize that those who use manipulatives will have higher scores than those who are exposed to the lecture/workbook approach. The question of *why* is explored throughout Parts A and B of this book.

When researchers plan *whom to observe*, they first decide whether to observe an entire population (such as all fifth-grade students in a school district) or just a sample of the population. If a sample is to be observed, which is often the case, they consider how to obtain a sample that is not biased against any types of individuals or subgroups. For example, asking students to volunteer to take a mathematics lesson might result in a sample of students who are more interested in mathematics than the students in the population as a whole. Such a sample would be biased against those who are less interested. Methods of drawing unbiased samples are discussed in Part C of this book.

When researchers plan *how to observe*, they select among available instruments such as objective tests, interviews, and direct observation of behavior, with an eye to selecting the most valid instrument(s). If none is judged to be reasonably valid for their purpose, they develop new instruments. Then, of course, they need to decide *when* they will use the instruments to obtain the most valid results. These issues are explored in detail in Part D of this book.

The observations researchers make may result in **data** in the form of numbers, which are analyzed statistically. Popular statistical techniques are described in Part F of this book. Note that some scientific observations are *not* reduced to numbers but are expressed in words. For example, interview data may be described in a narrative that points out themes and trends. The choice between the two approaches is described in Topics 9 and 10 as well as Part H of this book.

One of the most fundamental distinctions in scientific research is whether research is **experimental** or **nonexperimental**. In *experimental* research, treatments are given for the research purpose, such as treating some students with manipulatives and others with a lecture/workbook approach in order to determine which treatment *causes* greater achievement.[2] Of course, we are not always interested in cause-and-effect questions. For example, we might want to know whether teachers believe they need more training in the use of manipulatives for teaching mathematics. For this particular research purpose, a researcher should ask teachers about their needs; it is not necessary to train or treat the teachers to obtain the research results. Thus, *nonexperimental* research is needed for this research purpose. The distinction between experimental and nonex-

---

[1] Examples of other approaches are (1) **deduction**, such as when we deduce a proof in mathematics based on certain assumptions and definitions, and (2) **reliance on authority**, such as relying on a dictator's pronouncements as a source of knowledge.

[2] The design of experiments is discussed in Part E of this book.

perimental research is explored in the next two topics of this book.

EXERCISE ON TOPIC 1

1. The empirical approach to knowledge is based on what?

2. Is the empirical approach used in everyday living?

3. What does the question of *why* establish?

4. How is the term *hypothesis* defined in this topic?

5. According to the topic, are samples often observed?

6. What do researchers do when they plan *how* to observe?

7. Are the results of all scientific studies expressed as numbers?

8. Are treatments given for the research purpose in experimental research *or* in nonexperimental research?

9. If you asked students for their opinions on switching from the semester system to the quarter system, would you be conducting experimental research *or* nonexperimental research?

Questions for Discussion

10. Briefly describe a time when you were misled by everyday observation (i.e., when you reached a conclusion based on everyday observation that you later decided was an incorrect conclusion).

11. You have probably encountered conflicting research reported in the mass media. For example, one study might indicate that X increases blood pressure while another study indicates that X does not increase it. Speculate on the reasons why various researchers might obtain different results when studying the same problem.

For Students Who Are Planning Research

12. Name a general problem area in which you might conduct research. At this point, your problem area may still be broad, such as "social phobia," *or* it may be narrow, such as "effectiveness of behavior modification in the treatment of social phobia." Note that you may want to name several problem areas for research and make a final selection at a later time.

13. Have you already made observations in your problem area(s)? If so, briefly describe them. (Keep in mind that observations may be direct, such as observing aggressive behavior on a playground, *or* indirect, such as asking adolescents for self-reports on their alcohol consumption.)

14. If you answered yes to Question 13, did you make informal observations *or* did you plan why, whom, how, and when to observe in advance of making the observations? Explain.

TOPIC 2 EXPERIMENTAL VS. NONEXPERIMENTAL STUDIES

In **experiments**, researchers give treatments and observe to see if they cause changes in behavior. A classic simple experiment is one in which we form two groups at random and give each group a different treatment. To form two groups at random, we can put the names of the available participants on slips of paper, mix them thoroughly, and pull some names for each group.[1] Notice that random assignment gives each participant an equal chance of being in either group.

Below are three examples of experiments.

EXAMPLE 1
Fifty students were divided into two groups at random. One group received math instruction via a correspondence course on the Internet. The other group was given instruction on the same math skills using a traditional textbook and workbook approach. The purpose was to see if instruction via the Internet was more effective than traditional instruction.

In Example 1, the group receiving the new type of instruction via the Internet is referred to as the **experimental group** while the group receiving traditional instruction is called the **control group**.

When the participants are divided at random (such as drawing names out of a hat to determine who will be in the experimental group and who will be in the control group), the experiment is called a **true experiment**. Not all experiments are true experiments,[2] as illustrated by Example 2.

EXAMPLE 2
A psychiatrist identified 100 clinically depressed clients who volunteered to take a new drug under her direction. She identified an additional 100 nonvolunteers with the same diagnosis and similar demographics (i.e., background characteristics such as age and gender) to serve as controls. The study was conducted to investigate the effectiveness of the new drug in treating depression.

In Example 2, the experiment was conducted by comparing the volunteers who were given the new drug with a group of nonvolunteers who were *not* given the new drug. This study is an experiment even though random assignment was not used. Note

that if a researcher administers treatments or arranges for their administration, the study is called an experiment whether or not groups of participants are formed at random.

Some experiments are conducted with only one group of participants, as illustrated in Example 3, in which the extra verbal praise is the treatment.

EXAMPLE 3
The students in one classroom were observed for an hour each day for a week in order to count the number of inappropriate out-of-seat behaviors. During the next week, the teacher provided extra verbal praise when students were in their seats at appropriate times. During the third week, the teacher stopped providing the extra verbal praise. The results showed less inappropriate out-of-seat behavior during the second week of the experiment.

In **nonexperimental studies**, researchers do not give treatments. Rather, they observe participants in order to describe them as they naturally exist without experimental intervention. One of the most common types of nonexperimental studies is a survey or poll in which participants are interviewed, questioned, or otherwise observed in order to determine their attitudes, beliefs, and behaviors as they exist without experimental intervention.

Nonexperimental studies come in many forms, which are explored in more detail in Topic 4. At this point, however, you should be able to distinguish between nonexperimental studies and experiments by determining whether treatments were administered for experimental purposes.

Note that you cannot distinguish between nonexperimental and experimental studies on the basis of the type of instrument (i.e., measuring tool) used. Instruments such as paper-and-pencil tests, interview schedules, and personality scales are used in both types of studies. The act of measurement is usually not considered to be a treatment. In fact, researchers try to measure in such a way that the act of measuring does not affect or change the participants. This is true in both experimental and nonexperimental studies.

By now, you may have inferred that the purpose of an experiment is to explore cause-and-effect relationships (i.e., treatments are given to see how they affect the participants). In the next topic, you will learn how nonexperimental studies are also sometimes used for this purpose.

---

[1] Other methods for drawing random samples are discussed in Part C of this book.

[2] Types of experiments are explored more fully in Part E, where you will learn the advantages of true experiments.

EXERCISE ON TOPIC 2

1. Are treatments given in nonexperimental studies?

2. In an experiment, Group A was given verbal praise for being on time for appointments while Group B was given no special treatment. Which group is the control group?

3. Is it necessary to have at least two groups of participants in order to conduct an experiment?

4. What is the purpose of a nonexperimental study?

5. Is a survey an experiment?

6. Does knowing that a multiple-choice test was used in a study help you determine whether the study was experimental *or* nonexperimental?

7. What is the major purpose of an experiment?

8. A social worker polled clients to determine their satisfaction with the services provided. Is this an "experimental study" *or* "nonexperimental study"?

9. A teacher tried three methods of teaching handwriting by using different methods with different students. Is this an "experimental study" *or* "nonexperimental study"?

Questions for Discussion

10. Suppose you read that an outbreak of intestinal disorders occurred in a town and the source was traced to contaminated chicken served in a popular restaurant. Is it likely the study that identified the source was "experimental" *or* "nonexperimental"? Why?

11. Have you ever conducted an informal experiment by giving a treatment to a person or a group and then observing the effects? If so, briefly describe it. Would you have obtained better information by including a control group? Explain.

12. Suppose you wanted to know whether reading to preschool children has a positive effect on subsequent reading achievement. Do you think it would be better to conduct an "experimental study" *or* "nonexperimental study"? Why?

For Students Who Are Planning Research

13. At this point, do you anticipate using an "experimental" *or* "nonexperimental" approach in your research? If it will be experimental, what treatments do you plan to administer?

14. If you plan to conduct experimental research, have you already conducted an informal experiment on your topic? If so, did you use a control group? Was it a true experiment? How will the experiment you are planning differ from the informal experiment you already conducted?

As you know from Topic 2, an **experiment** is a study in which treatments are given in order to observe their effects. When we conduct experiments, we ask, "Does the treatment (i.e., the input or stimulus) given by the researcher *cause* changes in participants' behavior (i.e., changes in the output or response)?"

When researchers want to investigate cause-and-effect relationships, they usually prefer experimental over nonexperimental studies. However, sometimes it is not possible to conduct an experiment for physical, ethical, legal, or financial reasons. An example is the effects of smoking on health. It would be unethical (because of potential harm to the participants) to treat some participants with smoke (such as requiring them to smoke a pack of cigarettes a day for 15 years) in order to observe the effects in comparison with a nonsmoking control group (which is forbidden to smoke for 15 years). Clearly, for this research problem, we cannot conduct an experiment. Notice that even if it were ethical to conduct such an experiment, it might not be practical because we probably would not want to wait 15 years to determine the answer to such an important question.

When it is impossible or impractical to conduct an experiment to answer a causal question, we must settle for information derived from nonexperimental studies. For example, we can identify both people who currently have lung cancer and a control group with similar **demographics** (i.e., background characteristics such as socioeconomic status) and describe the differences between the two groups in terms of previous lifestyle characteristics that might affect health such as diet, exercise, smoking, prescription drug use, illicit substance abuse, and so on.

A finding that smoking differentiates between the two groups that have similar demographics suggests that smoking is a possible cause of lung cancer. However, there are several dangers in this interpretation. First, smoking and cancer might have a common cause. For example, perhaps stress causes cancer and also causes people to smoke excessively. If this is the case, banning smoking will not prevent cancer, only reducing stress will. Another danger is that the researcher may have failed to identify control participants who were properly matched with those who have lung cancer. For instance, perhaps most of those with lung cancer reside in urban areas while most of those in the control group reside in rural areas. Because urban areas tend to have more smog than rural areas, smog might be the cause, and smoking might be coincidental. These types of problems would not arise in an experiment in which participants are divided at random to form two groups: one of which is made to smoke and the other forbidden to smoke. *They would not exist* because the random assignment would produce two groups that are equally likely to experience stress and equally likely to live in either rural or urban areas and, in fact, be about equal[1] in terms of all other potential causes of cancer.[2]

The example of smoking and lung cancer illustrates a specific type of nonexperimental study known as a **causal–comparative study** (sometimes called an **ex post facto study**).[3] The essential characteristics of this type of nonexperimental study are (1) we observe and describe some current condition (such as lung cancer) and (2) we look to the past to try to identify the possible cause(s) of the condition. Notice that researchers do *not* give treatments in causal–comparative studies. Instead, they only describe observations. Hence, they are conducting nonexperimental studies.

Although the causal–comparative method has more potential pitfalls than the experimental method, it is often the best researchers can do when attempting to explore causality. Note that when it is used properly, and the comparison groups are selected carefully, the causal–comparative method is a powerful scientific tool that provides data on many important issues in all the sciences.

---

[1] Because of the laws of probability, the larger the sample, the more likely that two groups formed at random will be equal in terms of their characteristics. Sample size is covered in Topics 23 and 24.

[2] The relationship between smoking and health has been examined in many hundreds of causal–comparative studies. On this basis, almost all experts agree that alternative interpretations are without merit. However, the results of some of the early studies on the effects of smoking on health were disputed because the studies were not true experiments (i.e., did not have random assignment to groups).

[3] Other types of nonexperimental studies are covered in the next topic.

EXERCISE ON TOPIC 3

1. According to the topic, do "experimental" *or* "causal–comparative" studies have more potential pitfalls when trying to identify cause-and-effect relationships?

2. We look to the past for a cause in which type of study?

3. Is causal–comparative research a type of experiment?

4. Are treatments given by researchers in causal–comparative studies?

5. Random assignment to treatments is used in which type of study?

6. How is the term *demographics* defined in this topic?

7. A researcher compared the health of adolescents who received free lunches during their elementary school years with the health of a comparable group of children who did not receive free lunches. The purpose was to determine the effects of free lunch on health. Did the researcher conduct an "experimental" *or* a "causal–comparative" study?

8. A researcher divided patients with diabetes who were being released from the hospital into two groups. Upon their release, the researcher provided normal counseling for individuals with diabetes to one group while providing the other group with extended counseling. The purpose was to determine the effects of the two types of counseling on patients' compliance with physicians' directions during the first month after hospitalization. Did the researcher conduct an "experimental" *or* a "causal–comparative" study?

9. What is another name for the term *causal–comparative study*?

Questions for Discussion

10. If you wanted to investigate the causes of child abuse, would you use the "experimental" *or* the "causal–comparative" method? Explain.

11. Suppose you read that a causal–comparative study indicates that those who take vitamins A and E tend to be less overweight than the general population. Are there any possible dangers in the interpretation that the vitamins *cause* people to maintain a healthy weight?

For Students Who Are Planning Research

12. If you will be conducting a nonexperimental study, will it be causal–comparative (i.e., looking to the past for the causes of some current condition)? If yes, briefly explain why you chose this method of research instead of the experimental method.

TOPIC 4   TYPES OF NONEXPERIMENTAL RESEARCH

As you know from Topics 2 and 3, researchers do not give treatments to participants in nonexperimental studies. Rather, they observe (i.e., measure) in order to describe the participants without trying to change them.

Nonexperimental studies take many forms because they serve many purposes. Some of the more common types of nonexperimental studies are briefly described here.

You learned in the previous topic about **causal–comparative research** in which researchers look to the past for the cause(s) of a current condition. It is used primarily when researchers are interested in causality, but it is *not* possible to conduct an **experiment**.

Another type of nonexperimental research is the **survey** or *poll*. The purpose of surveys is to describe the attitudes, beliefs, and behaviors of a population. We draw a sample of a population, study the sample, and then make inferences to the population from the sample data. For example, a researcher could survey a sample of people receiving food stamps to determine what types of food they purchase with the stamps. The results obtained from studying the sample can be generalized to the population (assuming that a good sample has been drawn).[1] Note that if we decide not to sample but, instead, interview everyone in the population (i.e., all people receiving food stamps), the study would be called a **census**. A census is a count (or study) of all members of a population.

While surveys usually include hundreds or thousands of participants, a **case study** usually involves only one. For example, some important theories in clinical psychology were developed based on intensive one-on-one case studies of individuals. In a case study, the emphasis is on obtaining thorough knowledge of an individual, sometimes obtained over a long period of time. Researchers do not confine themselves to asking a limited number of questions on a one-shot basis as they would do in a survey.

When researchers repeatedly measure traits of the participants over a period of time in order to trace developmental trends, we say we are conducting **longitudinal research**. For instance, a researcher could measure the visual acuity of a sample of infants each week for a year to trace their development.

In **correlational research**, researchers are interested in the degree of relationship among two or more quantitative **variables**. For instance, scores on a college admissions test and GPAs are quantitative and because people *vary* or differ on both of them, they are variables.[2] If a researcher conducts a study in which he or she is asking, "Did those with high admissions scores tend to earn high GPAs?" and "Did those with low admissions scores tend to earn low GPAs?" the researcher is asking a correlational question. To the extent that the answer to the question is true, we can say the test works (i.e., has validity for predicting GPAs).[3]

Experiments and all the types of research mentioned so far in this topic belong to the class of research called **quantitative**. A distinctive feature of quantitative research is that researchers gather data that are easy to quantify so that they can be analyzed with statistics. For instance, to measure attitudes toward Asian American immigrants, a quantitative researcher might use a questionnaire and count how many times respondents answer "yes" to statements about Asian Americans and then calculate the percentage who answered "yes" to each statement.

In contrast, **qualitative researchers** gather data (such as responses to open-ended interview questions on attitudes toward Asian Americans) that must be analyzed using informed judgment to identify major and minor themes expressed by participants. Most published qualitative research is collected using semi-structured interviews in which there is a core list of questions from which the interviewers may deviate as needed to obtain in-depth information.

Other differences between qualitative and quantitative research are explored in Topics 9 and 10. Part H of this book describes qualitative research methods in detail.

In **historical research**, information is examined in order to understand the past. Note that good his-

---

[1] Characteristics of good samples for quantitative research are explored in detail in Part C of this book. Considerations in sampling for qualitative research are described in Topics 60 and 61 in Part H of this book.

[2] Types of variables are described in Topics 5 and 6.
[3] Validity is explored in Part D of this book. Correlational studies employ a statistic called a *correlation coefficient*, which is described in Topic 49.

torical research is not just a matter of developing a chronological list of so-called facts and dates. Rather, it is an attempt to understand the dynamics of human history. As such, it is driven by theories and hypotheses. In other words, by reviewing historical evidence, researchers are able to develop theories that may explain historical events and patterns. These theories lead to hypotheses, which are evaluated in terms of additional historical data that are collected. Historical researchers may use qualitative methods (e.g., examining historical documents using insight and judgment to identify themes) or qualitative methods (e.g., counting certain types of statements made in historical documents). Historical research is typically taught in history departments and is not considered further in this book.

EXERCISE ON TOPIC 4

1. Suppose a researcher administered an intelligence test to young children each year for five years in order to study changes in intelligence over time. The researcher was conducting what type of study?

2. Is the study in Question 1 experimental?

3. If a researcher conducts a poll to estimate public support for free child care for mothers on welfare, the researcher is conducting what type of nonexperimental study?

4. An investigator determined the degree of relationship between vocabulary scores and reading comprehension scores. The researcher was conducting what type of nonexperimental study?

5. According to this topic, what is a distinctive feature of quantitative research?

6. Most published qualitative research is collected using what?

Questions for Discussion

7. Name a topic in your field of study that you might explore with a nonexperimental study. Which type of nonexperimental study would be most appropriate for your topic?

8. Think of a survey in which you were asked to serve as a participant. (You may have been sent a questionnaire in the mail, such as a consumer satisfaction survey, or you may have been contacted in person or by phone.) Did you cooperate and respond? Why? Why not?

9. Name two quantitative variables that might be studied using correlational research.

10. Suppose someone prepared a list of educational events and their dates of occurrence in the last 100 years. Would the list be an example of "good" historical research? Explain.

For Students Who Are Planning Research

11. If you will be conducting a nonexperimental study, which type will it be? Explain the basis for your choice.

A **variable** is a trait or characteristic with two or more categories. Participants *vary* in terms of the categories to which they belong. Example 1 has two variables.

EXAMPLE 1
A sample of registered voters was surveyed. Each voter was asked first to name his or her gender (male or female) and then to name the candidate for whom he or she planned to vote (Doe, Jones, or Smith). The purpose was to explore gender differences in voting preferences.

The two variables in Example 1 are (1) gender, with two categories and (2) the preferred candidate, with three categories (i.e., three possible candidates).

Be careful not to confuse a variable with its categories. For instance, "male" is one of the two categories of the variable called "gender." "Male" is not a variable. Here is how to visualize it:

One Variable ⇨	*GENDER*	
Two Categories ⇨	Male	Female

All variables have **mutually exclusive categories**. That is, each respondent to the survey will belong to one—and *only one*—category. For instance, the categories for "preferred candidate" are mutually exclusive because we ask, "For which *one* candidate do you plan to vote?" When conducting such a survey, we would not allow a participant to name two candidates (i.e., two categories) for the same political office.

We also try to define variables in such a way that the categories are **exhaustive**. To be exhaustive, a variable must have a category for each respondent. For instance, we would want to add a fourth choice of "undecided" for respondents who have not yet chosen among the three candidates. Note that "undecided" is also a mutually exclusive category because respondents would not be allowed to choose it as well as name one of the candidates.

Notice that both variables in Example 1 are "naming" variables (more properly called "categorical" variables).[1] Each participant "names" his

---

[1] *Naming data* are obtained from the *nominal scale of measurement*. Scales of measurement are discussed in Topic 41.

or her gender and "names" the preferred candidate. Other variables have quantitative categories that describe the amount of a characteristic. Consider Example 2.

EXAMPLE 2
The college admissions scores on the *Scholastic Aptitude Test* (*SAT*) were compared with students' freshman GPAs to determine how valid the *SAT* is for predicting GPAs.

Both the College Board's *SAT* scores (ranging from 200 to 800 per subtest) and GPAs (usually ranging from 0.00 to 4.00) are quantitative. In other words, each possible score is a category. A student who earns an *SAT* score of 550 belongs to the category called "550." Likewise, a student who has a GPA of 2.78 belongs to the category called "2.78."

Variables in nonexperimental studies are sometimes classified as being either **independent** or **dependent**. For example, when we conduct a causal–comparative study (see Topic 3 to review), the presumed cause (such as smoking) is called the *independent* variable, and the response or outcome (such as lung cancer) is called the *dependent* variable. Remember:

> The *independent* variable (stimulus or input)
> causes changes in the
> *dependent* variable (response or output).

Some researchers refer to any variable that comes first (whether or not it is presumed to be a cause) as "independent" and to the one that comes later as "dependent." For instance, *SAT* scores (the predictor variable) are usually determined before students earn their college GPAs. Thus, some researchers would call the *SAT* the independent variable and the GPA the dependent variable. It is also common to call the predictor variable the **predictor** and the outcome variable (such as GPA) the **criterion**. The term "criterion" means "standard." Hence, GPA is the standard by which the *SAT* is often judged. Ideally, high scores on the *SAT* should be associated with high GPAs while low *SAT* scores should be associated with low GPAs. To the extent that this is true, the *SAT* is judged to be adequate. To the extent that it is not true, the *SAT* is judged to be deficient. Procedures for determining the adequacy of a test are described in Part D of this book.

EXERCISE ON TOPIC 5

1. Adults who were taking a course to learn English as a second language were asked to name their country of birth and their number of years of formal education. In this example, how many variables were being studied?

2. In Question 1, which variable is a categorical variable?

3. In Question 1, which variable is quantitative?

4. A sample of adults was asked their level of agreement with the statement, "The President of the United States is doing a good job in foreign relations." They were permitted to respond either "strongly agree," "agree," "disagree," or "strongly disagree." How many variables were being studied?

5. What is meant by *mutually exclusive categories*?

6. A researcher looked for the causes of social unrest by examining economic variables such as poverty, income, and so on. Is social unrest an "independent" *or* "dependent" variable?

7. If we administer a basic math test to middle school children to see if the basic math test scores predict grades in high school algebra, what is the criterion variable?

8. Suppose you ask participants to identify their age group using these categories: "under 21," "21–39," "40–55," and "56+." Are these exhaustive categories?

9. In Question 8, how many variables are being studied?

10. What is the minimum number of categories that each variable must have?

Questions for Discussion

11. Suppose you want to measure income on a self-report questionnaire on which each participant will check off his or her income category. Name the categories you would use. Are they exhaustive and mutually exclusive? Explain.

12. Name a quantitative variable of interest to you and name its categories. Are the categories mutually exclusive and exhaustive? Explain.

For Students Who Are Planning Research

13. If you will be conducting a nonexperimental study, name the major variables you will be studying. For each, indicate whether the categories will be quantitative.

All experiments have at least one **independent variable** and one **dependent variable**. The purpose of experiments is to estimate the extent to which independent variables cause changes in dependent variables.

As you know from the previous section, an independent variable is a stimulus or input variable. Note that in experiments, researchers *physically manipulate* independent variables. By "physically manipulate," we mean the researcher does something physical to the participants. Examples of physical manipulation are (1) giving a new drug to some participants while giving a placebo to others, (2) providing some students with computers while denying computers to others, and (3) using group counseling with some clients while using individual counseling with others. Thus, to *physically manipulate* means to physically administer treatments.

Note that in *nonexperimental* studies, researchers do *not* physically manipulate independent variables. Instead, they observe independent variables as they occur (or have occurred) naturally. For example, we observe the health of people who have smoked cigarettes in nonexperimental studies—we do not provide participants with cigarettes, nor do we expose them to smoke. (See Topic 3 to review other differences between experimental and nonexperimental studies of causation.)

In a simple experiment, there is only one independent variable and only one dependent variable, as in Example 1.

EXAMPLE 1
On alternative weeks, a disruptive student is given extra praise for being in his seat when appropriate. The purpose of the study is to see if the extra praise will increase the amount of appropriate in-seat behavior.

In Example 1, the physical manipulation is giving or not giving extra praise, which is the independent variable (i.e., the stimulus or input variable). The dependent variable (i.e., response or outcome variable) is changes in the student's in-seat behavior.

Often, experiments have more than one dependent variable. For instance, in Example 1, we could observe to see not only if the treatment causes (1) more in-seat behavior, but also (2) improvement in the student's achievement and (3) improvement in

the student's attitude toward school during the weeks the extra praise is given. If we did this, we would have three dependent variables.

Many experiments also have more than one independent variable. Often, these are more interesting than those with only one independent variable because such experiments give us insights into the effects of combinations of variables on causality. Consider Example 2, which has two independent variables (i.e., child care and transportation money).

EXAMPLE 2
Voluntary, free job training was offered to all mothers on welfare in a small city. Four groups of the mothers were formed at random to explore the effects of these two independent variables: (1) providing or not providing free child care while in training and (2) providing or not providing transportation money to get to the job-training site. Each group was assigned at random to one of the four treatment conditions shown here:

GROUP 1 child care *and* transportation money	GROUP 3 *no* child care *and* transportation money
GROUP 2 child care *and* *no* transportation money	GROUP 4 *no* child care *and* *no* transportation money

It was predicted that those in Group 1 (the group that was given *both* child care and transportation money) would have the highest participation rates, those in Group 2 would have the next highest, those in Group 3 would have the next highest, and those in Group 4 would have the lowest.

Notice that in Example 2, we can determine (1) how effective child care is, (2) how effective transportation money is, and (3) the effectiveness of both child care *and* transportation money *in combination*. Thus, we get more information by looking at two independent variables in one study than by looking at each independent variable in a separate experiment (in which case, we could determine only points 1 and 2).

EXERCISE ON TOPIC 6

1. All experiments have at least how many dependent variables?

2. In an experiment, what is the name of a stimulus or input variable?

3. What does *physically manipulate* mean in an experimental context?

4. Are dependent variables physically manipulated?

5. Can an experiment have more than one independent variable?

6. Every other customer entering a shoe store was given a different coupon. One coupon offered a second pair of shoes for 50% off. The other coupon offered to reduce the total price by 25% if two pairs of shoes were purchased. The purpose was to determine which coupon was more effective in getting people to buy two pairs of shoes. In this experiment, what is the independent variable?

7. In Question 6, what is the dependent variable?

8. A teacher showed an educational film on daily nutritional needs to one group of students and gave a handout on the same material to another group. The purpose was to determine which was more effective in increasing students' knowledge of daily nutritional needs. In this experiment, what is the dependent variable?

9. In Question 8, what is the independent variable?

Questions for Discussion

10. Name a variable that would be easy for you to physically manipulate in an experiment. Then, name a variable that might be affected by your manipulation.

11. Name a variable that you would not be willing to physically manipulate for ethical or legal reasons.

For Students Who Are Planning Research

12. If you will be conducting an experiment, name the independent and dependent variables you will be studying.

A **research hypothesis** is a prediction of the outcome of a study. The prediction may be based on an educated guess or a formal theory. Example 1 is a hypothesis for a nonexperimental study.

EXAMPLE 1
It is hypothesized that first-grade girls will show better reading comprehension than first-grade boys.

In Example 1, the author is predicting that he or she will find higher comprehension among girls than boys. To test the prediction, a nonexperimental study would be appropriate because nothing in the hypothesis suggests that treatments will be given.

A simple research hypothesis predicts a relationship between two variables. From your study of Topics 5 and 6, it should be clear that the two variables in Example 1 are (1) gender and (2) reading comprehension. The hypothesis states that reading comprehension is related to gender.

Example 2 is a hypothesis for an experimental study.

EXAMPLE 2
It is hypothesized that children who are shown a video with mild violence will be more aggressive on the playground than those who are shown a similar video without violence.

In Example 2, the *independent variable* is violence (mild vs. no violence), and the *dependent variable* is aggressiveness on the playground.

The hypotheses in Examples 1 and 2 are examples of **directional hypotheses**. In a directional hypothesis, we predict which group will be higher or have more of some attribute.

Sometimes we have a **nondirectional hypothesis**. Consider Example 3.

EXAMPLE 3
It is hypothesized that the child-rearing practices of Tribe A are different from those of Tribe B.

The author of Example 3 is saying that there will be a difference but does not predict the direction of the difference. This is perfectly acceptable when there is no basis for making an educated guess as to the outcome of a study.

Instead of a nondirectional hypothesis, we might state a **research purpose**. Example 4 shows a research purpose that corresponds to the nondirectional hypothesis in Example 3.

EXAMPLE 4
The research purpose is to explore the differences in child-rearing practices between Tribe A and Tribe B.

A **research question** may also be substituted for a nondirectional hypothesis. Example 5 shows a research question that corresponds to the nondirectional hypothesis in Example 3 and the research purpose in Example 4.

EXAMPLE 5
The research question is, "How do the child-rearing practices in Tribe A and Tribe B differ?"

When using a research question as the basis for research, we usually should be careful *not* to state it as a question that can be answered with a simple "yes" or "no," as is done in Example 6.

EXAMPLE 6
The question is, "Do the child-rearing practices in Tribe A and Tribe B differ?"

Example 6 merely asks, "Do they differ?" This is not a very interesting research question because it implies that the results of the research will be only a simple "yes" or "no." Example 5 is superior because it asks, "*How* do they differ?"—a question that implies that the results will be complex and, thus, more interesting and informative.

The choice between a nondirectional hypothesis, a research purpose, and a research question is purely a matter of personal taste—all are acceptable in the scientific community. Of course, when we are willing and able to predict the outcome of a study, we should state a directional hypothesis—not a research purpose or question. In other words, a research purpose or question are suitable substitutes for a nondirectional hypothesis. It is inappropriate to use one as a substitute for a directional hypothesis.

If you have read research reports, you may have encountered references to another type of hypothesis: the **null hypothesis**. This is a *statistical hypothesis*, which needs to be considered when analyzing results obtained from samples in quantitative research studies. The null hypothesis need not be considered at this point. However, it will be explored in detail in Part F of this book.

Exercise on Topic 7

1. Which type of statement (hypothesis, purpose, or question) predicts the outcome of a study?

2. "It is hypothesized that college students who have firm career goals achieve higher GPAs than those who do not have firm career goals." Is this a "directional" *or* "nondirectional" hypothesis?

3. Would an "experimental" *or* "nonexperimental" study be better for testing the hypothesis in Question 2?

4. "It is hypothesized that children of immigrants and children of native-born citizens will differ in their attitudes toward school." Is this a "directional" *or* "nondirectional" hypothesis?

5. "The goal of this study is to examine college students' attitudes toward religion." Is this statement a "hypothesis" *or* "purpose"?

6. "Are children of alcoholics different from children of nonalcoholics in their social adjustment?" Is this research question stated appropriately? Why? Why not?

7. When we are willing to predict the outcome of a study, should we state a "directional" *or* "nondirectional" hypothesis?

8. What are the two alternatives to stating a nondirectional hypothesis?

Questions for Discussion

9. Restate this hypothesis as a research purpose: "It is hypothesized that there is a difference in job satisfaction between those who receive regular feedback on their job performance and those who receive irregular feedback."

10. Is the hypothesis in Question 9 "directional" *or* "nondirectional"? Explain.

11. Could an experiment be conducted to test the hypothesis in Question 9? Explain.

12. Restate this hypothesis as a research question: "It is hypothesized that those who exercise regularly and those who do not exercise regularly will differ in other behaviors that affect health."

For Students Who Are Planning Research

13. State a research hypothesis, purpose, or question for the research you are planning. (Note: You may have more than one of each.)

14. If you stated a hypothesis in response to Question 13, is it "directional" *or* "nondirectional"?

TOPIC 8 OPERATIONAL DEFINITIONS OF VARIABLES

Dictionaries provide us with **conceptual definitions** of variables. For example, in research on speech communication, we might be interested in students' ability to *recite*, which has a dictionary definition along these lines: "to repeat or speak aloud from or as from memory, especially in a formal way." This definition is perfectly adequate if we merely want to communicate the general topic of our research to other individuals.

Let us suppose, however, that we want to conduct an experiment on the effectiveness of two memory aids on the ability to recite. As we plan the research, we will soon realize that a conceptual definition is not adequate because it does not indicate the precise concrete or physical steps we will take in order to identify the variable. Redefining a variable in terms of physical steps is called *operationalizing* a variable. When we operationalize a variable, we are creating an **operational definition**. Example 1 shows the first attempt at creating an operational definition of students' ability to recite.

EXAMPLE 1
The ability to recite is defined as the number of words mispronounced, missing, or misplaced when students repeat Christian Abzab's poem *The Road Taken* aloud from memory in front of a panel of three teachers.

Notice that the definition in Example 1 is not fully operational because we might still have questions about the *physical arrangements* such as, "Will the students stand while reciting?" "In what type of room will the recitation take place (a classroom or auditorium)?" "Will the teachers be male or female?" and "Will the teachers already know the students?"

It is important to note that no attempt at operationalizing will result in a completely operational definition because there are an infinite number of physical characteristics that might be addressed in any definition (e.g., the humidity in the room, the level of lighting, the type of flooring, the color of the walls). Thus, instead of striving for completely operational definitions, we try to produce definitions that are adequate to permit a **replication** in all important respects by another researcher. A replication is an attempt to confirm the results of a study by conducting it again in the same way. Of course, there is much subjectivity in applying this criterion

of adequacy, and we may not all agree on when it has been met.[1]

Notice that a highly operational definition is not necessarily meaningful or relevant. For example, we could operationalize clients' self-esteem with the definition in Example 2.

EXAMPLE 2
Positive self-esteem is defined as answering "yes" when asked the question, "Do you feel good about yourself?"

The definition in Example 2 is reasonably operational because we know what specific question to ask and what response to listen for. However, it is quite narrow. For example, it does not tap self-esteem in the various dimensions of clients' lives, such as self-esteem in the workplace, in social settings, and so on. Thus, Example 2 illustrates that a definition can be operational without being adequate in other respects, such as being fully multidimensional.

Notice that if a researcher fails to provide operational definitions of variables, the definitions nevertheless exist because the researcher has to take physical steps to conduct the research. That is, the definitions exist but may be unstated. When they are unstated in a research report, the report is, at best, vague. In addition, it is difficult, if not impossible, to replicate the research.

Besides allowing for replication of research, operational definitions assist those who are trying to apply research in everyday settings. For instance, if research shows that a certain program is helpful in reducing spousal abuse, but the researcher fails to provide a highly operational definition, consumers of research will not know how to conduct the program in applied settings.

---

[1] We have the most confidence in results of research that have been replicated by independent researchers because a given researcher may have blind spots, unconscious biases, etc. Also, a given researcher may have been unlucky and have results that were influenced by large random errors. Independent replications by others reduce the odds that these factors are the cause of a particular finding.

EXERCISE ON TOPIC 8

1. Which type of definition indicates physical steps?

2. In practice, are operational definitions ever fully operationalized?

3. Which of the following definitions of *gregarious* is more operational?
   A. Talking on the phone with friends for at least two hours each week.
   B. Being open and friendly when in social gatherings with others.

4. Which of the following definitions of being *computer literate* is more operational?
   A. Taking at least two formal courses of instruction on the use of computers in an accredited school.
   B. Having knowledge of the origins and uses of computers in modern society and their implications.

5. To replicate the research of others, do we need "operational" *or* "conceptual" definitions?

6. Is it possible for an operational definition to be too narrow?

Questions for Discussion

7. Suppose you read a research report claiming that low socioeconomic status (SES) children have lower self-concepts than high SES children. In the report, the only definition of self-concept is "feeling good about oneself." How much credence would you give the results in light of the definition? What additional information, if any, would you want about the definition if you were planning to replicate the study?

8. In a research report, job satisfaction is defined as "the number of times each participant said 'yes' to questions such as 'Do you look forward to going to work most mornings?'" Is this definition completely operational? If not, what is missing from the definition?

9. Is the definition in Question 8 too narrow in terms of how we normally think about job satisfaction? Why? Why not?

10. Write a highly operational definition of "success in college."

11. Write a highly operational definition of "motivation to succeed on the job."

For Students Who Are Planning Research

12. Name the major variables you will be studying. Define each, trying to be as operational as possible. (Note: After you have read published research on your topic, you may want to come back here and redefine some of your variables in light of how other researchers have defined them.)

The results of **quantitative research** are presented as quantities or numbers (i.e., statistics). In **qualitative research**, the results are presented as discussions of trends and/or themes based on words, not statistics. In addition to the difference in how results are presented, there are a number of characteristics that distinguish the two types of research. To understand some of the major ones, consider this research problem: A metropolitan police force is demoralized, with signs such as high rates of absenteeism, failure to follow procedures, and so on. Furthermore, the press has raised questions about the effectiveness of the force and its leadership. In response, the police commission is planning to employ a researcher to identify possible causes and solutions.

If a researcher with a quantitative orientation is retained, he or she would probably begin with a review of the research literature on demoralized police departments. From the review, the researcher would attempt to develop hypotheses to be tested by research. This is a *deductive approach* to planning the research. That is, the researcher is deducing from the literature possible explanations (i.e., hypotheses) to be tested. In contrast, a qualitative researcher would tend to use an *inductive approach* to planning the research. He or she might, for example, begin to gather data on the specific police force in question by making preliminary observations and conducting informal interviews. The resulting preliminary findings might be used as a basis for planning what additional types of information to collect and how to collect them. Thus, rather than approaching the research task with preconceived notions based on published theory and research, a qualitative researcher would emphasize induction from the preliminary data that were collected.

Note that qualitative researchers (like quantitative researchers) typically examine previously published literature and include reviews of it in their research reports. However, quantitative researchers use literature as the basis for planning research while qualitative researchers do not.

When deciding what types of instruments (i.e., measuring tools) to use, quantitative researchers tend to emphasize those that produce data that can be easily reduced to numbers, such as structured questionnaires or interview schedules with objective formats, such as multiple-choice questions. In contrast, a qualitative researcher would tend to em-phasize instruments that yield words, such as unstructured interviews or direct, unstructured observations of police officers and their administrators.

When deciding which members of the police force to use as participants, quantitative researchers would tend to select large samples, which is made possible within a limited research budget by objective instruments such as an anonymous, objective questionnaire that takes little time to administer.[1] A qualitative researcher would tend to select a small sample for the reverse reason. When conducting the research, a quantitative researcher would tend to spend a small amount of time directly interacting with the participants (largely due to the nature of the instruments used). A qualitative researcher, on the other hand, might spend a considerable amount of time interviewing and observing various members of the force over an extended period.

While working with the participants,[2] qualitative researchers would be open to the possibility of making adjustments in the instrumentation, such as rewording questions or adding questions based on earlier responses by participants. A quantitative researcher would seldom make such adjustments during the course of a research project. Instead, quantitative researchers would plan their research in detail in advance and follow the plan closely throughout the study because mid-stream deviations might be viewed as introducing subjectivity into the study. It is important to note that while quantitative researchers emphasize "objectivity," qualitative researchers believe all observational processes are inherently subjective and open to interpretation. Because of this, qualitative researchers sometimes mention relevant details of their personal backgrounds (such as having a mother who was a police

---

[1] In addition, quantitative researchers usually attempt to select a *random sample* in which all participants have an equal chance of being selected. This can be done, for example, by drawing names out of a hat. The uses of random samples and their relationship to statistics are discussed in later topics. A qualitative researcher is more likely to select a *purposive sample* of people she believes are key informants in terms of social dynamics, leadership, etc.

[2] Note that the term "participants" implies that the individuals being studied have voluntarily agreed to participate in a given research project. When individuals are being observed without their consent, they are more likely to be called "subjects."

officer) in order to inform readers of their research on possible sources of bias in collecting and interpreting the data.

Also, quantitative researchers tend to summarize all responses with statistics and seldom report on the responses of individual participants. Qualitative researchers, on the other hand, tend to cite individuals' responses (such as quoting individual participants) in the Results section of a research report.

Finally, quantitative researchers tend to generalize the results to one or more populations, while qualitative researchers tend to limit their conclusions to only the individuals who were directly studied.

Should the police commission select a researcher with a "quantitative" or "qualitative" orientation? Criteria for making such a decision are described in the next topic.

EXERCISE ON TOPIC 9

1. Do "qualitative" *or* "quantitative" researchers tend to rely more on published research literature in planning research?

2. Which method of research relies on the inductive approach?

3. Which method of research is more likely to lead to a statistical report of results?

4. In which method of research would a researcher be more likely to make adjustments to the interview questions during the course of a research project?

5. In which method of research is the interaction between the researcher and the participants more intense and lengthy?

6. There are more likely to be quotations from participants in the Results sections of reports on which type of research?

7. In which type of research do researchers have little interest in generalizing the results to populations?

Questions for Discussion

8. In general, are you more likely to believe research results that are presented as themes and trends expressed in words *or* results described with statistics? Explain. (If you have not read academic research extensively, consider secondary reports of research such as those found in newspapers, magazines, and textbooks.)

9. Do you believe both qualitative and quantitative research have valuable roles in advancing knowledge in your field of study? Why? Why not?

For Students Who Are Planning Research

10. At this point, are you leaning toward conducting "qualitative" *or* "quantitative" research? Explain the basis for your choice. (Note that you will be learning more about qualitative research in the next topic.)

In the last topic, we finished with the question, "Should the police commission select a researcher with a 'quantitative' or 'qualitative' orientation?" Some of the criteria that should be considered when making such a decision are:

A. Some research questions inherently lend themselves more to the quantitative than the qualitative approach. For example, "What is the impact of terrorism on the U.S. economy?" is a question that lends itself to quantitative research because economic factors and indicators are usually described with numbers. On the other hand, "What is the emotional impact of terrorism on at-risk health care workers?" is a question that lends itself more to the qualitative approach than the first question because it focuses on emotional impact, which is more difficult to quantify. Note, however, that the second question could be examined with either qualitative or quantitative research.

B. When little is known about a topic, qualitative research should usually be initially favored. New topics are constantly emerging in all fields, such as new diseases like SARS, new criminal concerns such as domestic terrorism, and new educational techniques such as using the Internet for instructional purposes in classrooms. On new topics, there often is little, if any, previously published research. In its absence, quantitative researchers may find it difficult to employ the deductive approach (i.e., deduct hypotheses from previously published research). Also, quantitative researchers might find it difficult to write structured questions about a little-known topic. (How can you know exactly what to ask when you know little about a topic?) In contrast, qualitative researchers could start with broad questions and refine them during the course of the interviews as various themes and issues start to emerge. Based on the qualitative results, theories might be developed from which hypotheses could be deduced and subsequently tested by using quantitative research.

C. When the participants belong to a culture that is closed or secretive, qualitative research should usually be favored. A skilled qualitative researcher who is willing to spend considerable time breaking through the barriers that keep researchers out is more likely to be successful than a quantitative researcher who tends to spend much less time interacting with participants.

D. When potential participants are not available for extensive interactions or observation, the quantitative approach should be considered. For example, it might be difficult to schedule extensive interviews with chief executives of major corporations. However, the chief executives might be willing to respond to a brief objective-type questionnaire, which would provide data that can be analyzed with statistics.

E. When time and funds are very limited, quantitative research might be favored. Although this is an arguable criterion for selecting between the two types of research, it is suggested because quantitative research can be used to provide quick, inexpensive snapshots of narrow aspects of research problems. Qualitative methods do not lend themselves to the snapshot approach.

F. When audiences require "hard numbers" (such as legislators or funding agencies sometimes do), quantitative research should be favored or, at least, incorporated into a qualitative research project. When someone says, "Just the numbers, please," themes and trends illustrated with quotations are unlikely to impress them. For such an audience, one should, when possible, start by presenting statistics. This might open the door to consideration of more qualitative aspects of the findings. Notice that implicit in this criterion is the notion that both qualitative and quantitative approaches might be used in a given research project, with each approach contributing a different type of information.

Up to this point, we have been considering quantitative and qualitative research as though they are opposites. However, some researchers conduct research that is a blend of the two approaches. For example, a quantitative researcher who uses semi-structured interviews to collect data, reduces the data to statistics, but also reports quotations from participants to support the statistics, is conducting research that has some of the characteristics of both approaches.

As you can see, our hypothetical police commission needs to make a complex decision. How would you answer the question in the first paragraph of this topic? What is the basis for your answer? For more information on the characteristics of qualitative research, consult Part H of this book.

EXERCISE ON TOPIC 10

1. Which of the following lends itself more to quantitative research?
   A. How do the social relations of adolescents who use illicit drugs differ from those who do not use them?
   B. How do school attendance and grades earned in school differ between adolescents who use illicit drugs and those who do not use them?

2. Which of the following lends itself more to qualitative research?
   A. What are the differences between the social interactions of college students on commuter campuses and students on campuses where most students live on campus?
   B. To what extent does family income predict whether a student will choose to attend a commuter college or a college where most students live on campus?

3. Suppose you want to do research on members of a secretive fraternity. According to the information in this topic, which type of researcher is more likely to gain access to the participants?

4. If little is known about a new topic, which type of research is recommended for initial use?

5. For which type of research must participants usually be available for extensive interactions with researchers?

6. Which type of research is more suitable for getting a quick snapshot of a problem?

Questions for Discussion

7. How would you answer the two questions in the last paragraph of this topic?

8. Suppose a team of researchers wants to conduct research to identify the characteristics of professors whom students perceive as being excellent. Would you advise them to do qualitative *or* quantitative research? Why?

9. Name a problem in your field of study that would probably lend itself more to the quantitative than the qualitative approach.

For Students Who Are Planning Research

10. In light of the information in this topic, have you changed your mind about your answer to Question 10 in the Exercise on Topic 9? Explain.

TOPIC 11   PROGRAM EVALUATION

Consider a school that receives a foundation grant for a new program that emphasizes parental involvement and shared decision-making. In this program, decisions are made by an administrator with the advice and consent of both teachers and parents. The ultimate purpose is to help students improve in a variety of academic and social skills. In this case, as in most others, granting agencies almost always require a report on the implementation and effectiveness of the programs for which they provide funding. To prepare such a report, researchers conduct a **program evaluation** by engaging in *evaluation research*.

At first glance, it might appear that we should conduct *experimental research*, which, as you may recall from earlier topics, is a study in which we give treatment(s) (in this case, a program) in order to observe their effects. Indeed, while elements of evaluation research resemble experimental work, there are some major differences.

First, program evaluation is almost always *applied research* (i.e., research in which we wish to apply the findings directly to such practical decisions as whether to continue funding the program and whether to modify it). Experimental research, on the other hand, is often *basic research* in which researchers are attempting to understand underlying theories that explain behavior without necessarily looking for direct applications.

Second, new programs are, or should be, based on a *needs assessment*. A needs assessment is non-experimental research in which researchers attempt to determine the practical needs of those who will be served by the program. For a school-based program, we might ask questions such as, "What types of skills do the students need to acquire?" and "What types of program interventions to promote these skills will be most readily accepted by students, parents, and teachers?" Pure experimental research is seldom preceded by a formal needs assessment, which is associated with program evaluation because a major focus of evaluation is to estimate the extent to which a program has met the needs revealed in an earlier needs assessment.

Third, the programs, which are analogous to treatments in an experiment, are usually subject to change during the course of the evaluation. For example, perhaps a program is designed to give teachers a major role in decision-making, with only a minor role for parents. If, in midstream, it is found that the teachers' involvement is not as high as desired, adjustments may be made to give parents more of a voice in decision-making. Although it is almost unheard of for an experimental researcher to make changes in the nature of a treatment during the course of an experiment, skilled program evaluators are open to such modifications. In fact, program evaluators collect information during the course of a program that assists in the process of modifying the program while it is being implemented. Collecting this information is called **formative evaluation**.

Formative evaluation has two prongs. First, information is collected on the *process* of implementing a program. For example, when looking at the process, we might ask, "Were the parents notified of the program in a timely manner?" and "Were the proposed meetings of parents and teachers conducted?" These questions clearly ask about the process, not the ultimate goals of student improvement. The second prong of formative evaluation involves collecting information on the *progress toward the ultimate goals*. For example, periodic achievement tests might be administered to see if students are showing signs of improvement. If not, evaluators and program administrators might rethink the process they are implementing and make appropriate changes. By looking at *progress*, those responsible for the program can often prevent disappointment in the final results of a program evaluation.

When evaluators collect information about participants' attainment of the ultimate goals at the end of the program (such as at the end of a school year), the activity is called **summative evaluation**. A summative evaluation report contains information about the final or long-term benefits of the program for its ultimate clients (such as students). Summative evaluation often involves a comparison with a control group. For example, students in a program might be compared with similar students in other schools who are not in the program. Note that while experimental researchers typically strive to use random assignment (like pulling names out of a hat) to form experimental and control groups, program evaluators usually have to find an external group (such as students at another school) to serve as the control group.

As you can see, program evaluation is a complex, specialized form of applied research.

EXERCISE ON TOPIC 11

1. Is "program evaluation" *or* "experimental research" almost always *applied research*?

2. Is a needs assessment associated with "experimental research" *or* "program evaluation"?

3. Is it acceptable to modify the treatments (programs) during the course of a program evaluation?

4. Suppose, as part of a program evaluation, an evaluator asks, "How many children were reading at grade level by the end of the program?" Is this question relevant to "formative" *or* to "summative" evaluation?

5. Suppose that as part of a program evaluation, an evaluator asks, "Are the clients in the job-placement program writing better resumes?" Is this question relevant to "formative" *or* "summative" evaluation?

6. Suppose, as part of a program evaluation, an evaluator asks, "Were key program personnel hired on time?" Is this question relevant to "formative" *or* "summative" evaluation?

7. When we look at the process of implementing a program, are we conducting "formative" *or* "summative" evaluation?

8. Is examining program participants' *progress* toward attaining the ultimate goals of the program part of "formative" *or* "summative" evaluation?

9. Is the attainment of the final goals of a program by participants a topic for "formative" *or* "summative" evaluation?

Questions for Discussion

10. Suppose you were on the board of a foundation that was giving a grant for a program to a social welfare agency. Would you prefer to have the program evaluated by an employee of the program (such as the program director) *or* by an external, independent evaluator? Why?

11. Sometimes, government agencies and organizations fund certain programs despite prior negative summative evaluations. Speculate on some of the reasons for this. Are any of the reasons justifiable?

For Students Who Are Planning Research

12. Will you be evaluating a program in your research? If yes, name the program and indicate whether you will be conducting both "formative" *and* "summative" research.

When planning research, it is imperative to consider potential harm to participants that might result from their participation. Often, certain treatments that researchers might want to administer in experimental studies present hazards. For example, a research psychologist might expose an experimental group to an anxiety-provoking stimulus in a study designed to advance a theory of the sources and effects of anxiety. Clearly, some participants might suffer mental anguish as a result of being exposed to the treatment.

Participants also might be harmed in nonexperimental studies. For example, the process of exploring sensitive traits (e.g., relationships with abusive parents) might cause participants to focus on them again, leading to renewed anxiety, sleeplessness, and so on.

Because of such potential problems, the research community has developed a body of ethical values regarding the use of humans as participants. The primary value is that participants must be *protected from both physical and psychological harm*. Unfortunately, it is not always possible to anticipate all the potential for harm, especially when using new treatments or measuring tools. Because of this, most universities and large school districts have research committees that review research plans for potential harm to participants.

Another important value is that participants *have a right to privacy*. For example, most would probably agree that it would be a violation of parents' rights to privacy for researchers to question children about discord between their parents without parental consent, even if the results might be very useful to educators, sociologists, psychologists, and others.

A related value is that participants have a right to have the data collected about them as individuals kept *confidential*. Even if participants freely and knowingly provide information to researchers, the researchers have an obligation not to disclose the information to others *unless* the identities of the participants are disguised or hidden, which is often accomplished by using statistics such as group averages.

Also, almost all researchers agree that participants have a right to *knowledge of the purpose* of the research before they participate. Having this knowledge, they are in a better position to determine whether they want to participate. Unfortunately, complete honesty with participants about the purpose of a study sometimes makes it difficult or impossible to conduct research on important topics. For instance, suppose researchers want to study the influence of lobbyists on a group of state legislators. The researchers might get some legislators to allow the researchers to "shadow" them (i.e., follow them around unobtrusively) if the purpose is only vaguely described as "to understand the state's political process." However, how many legislators (especially those who allow themselves to be unduly influenced by lobbyists) would agree to being shadowed if researchers reveal the true purpose? Is it ethical to present only a vague general purpose that does not reveal specific goals? Do government employees have a right to privacy on the job? These types of questions illustrate the difficulties in balancing the need to protect participants with the need to collect information of benefit to society.[1]

A key to promoting these values is *informed consent*. To use informed consent, we inform the participants of (1) the general purpose of the research, (2) what will be done to them during the research, (3) what the potential benefit(s) to them and others might be, (4) what the potential for harm to them might be, and (5) the fact that they may withdraw at any time, even at midstream during the research, without penalty. This information should be provided in writing, and the participants (or their guardians) should sign the informed consent form to indicate that they understand it.

Another key to promoting the ethical values we are considering is to *debrief* participants after their participation in a study. Debriefing consists of reviewing the purpose(s) of the study and the procedure(s) used as well as offering to share the results with the participants when the results become available. The process of debriefing should also include reassurances that the data will remain confidential. In addition, participants should be allowed to ask for information about any aspect of the study in which they participated. During debriefing, researchers should try to identify participants who may need more help in overcoming unanticipated harm to them than a standard debriefing session provides.

---

[1] For more information on this topic, refer to *Ethical Principles in the Conduct of Research with Human Subjects*, published by the American Psychological Association. Visit www.apa.org for more information.

Exercise on Topic 12

1. Should researchers take steps to prevent psychological harm as well as physical harm to participants?

2. Should participants be told that they are free to withdraw from a study at any time without penalty?

3. Under the principle of informed consent, is it acceptable to hide the general purpose of a study from the participants?

4. Should informed consent be in writing?

5. Is debriefing done "before" *or* "after" a study is conducted?

6. What does debriefing cover?

7. Should information about participants be kept confidential even if the participants freely provided it to researchers?

Questions for Discussion

8. How would you answer these two rhetorical questions that are posed in the topic?
   • Is it ethical to present only a vague general purpose that does not reveal specific goals?
   • Do government employees have a right to privacy on the job?

9. Suppose a researcher wants to keep a class of third-grade students in from recess to administer an attitude-toward-school scale. The purpose is to help teachers understand their students' attitudes and how they might affect students' achievements. Is there potential for harm in this case? Would it be wise to seek informed consent from the parents? Why? Why not?

10. A researcher interviewed adolescents on their possible use of marijuana (with their informed consent). During the course of the interviews, some participants named other individuals who use marijuana but who have not provided informed consent to the researcher. Does this raise ethical concerns? What, if anything, can the researcher do to protect the other individuals?

11. Suppose one of your instructors asked you to be a participant in a research project but did not tell you the purpose of the research. Would you ask for information on these points before deciding whether to participate? Would you feel pressured to participate because the researcher was your instructor?

For Students Who Are Planning Research

12. Do you anticipate that the study you are planning has the potential to harm the participants? If yes, what measures will you take to mitigate the potential for harm?

13. Will you be obtaining informed consent? Will you have your consent form reviewed by your professor? By a university committee? By others? Explain.

A **theory** is a unified explanation for discrete observations that might otherwise be viewed as unrelated or contradictory. One of the most widely studied theories in learning is reinforcement theory. It defines positive reinforcement as anything that increases the frequency of a response from an animal or individual. For example, most of us have given praise as a reward to a dog for sitting. To the extent that the praise increases the sitting behavior, it constitutes positive reinforcement.

At first, reinforcement theory sounds obvious, and in a way, it is self-defining. So why has it been so carefully studied? Because it explains many apparently contradictory observations. For example, suppose at first we praise a dog regularly for sitting and after a while become lax and offer praise intermittently. Common sense might tell us to expect the sitting behavior to decrease with the decrease in praise. However, we might actually observe an increase in sitting because reinforcement theory indicates that intermittent reinforcement[1] is, under many circumstances, more effective than consistent reinforcement. Thus, reinforcement theory is a unified set of principles that help explain why certain behaviors increase in their frequency. Without it, we would observe behaviors that do not seem to be consistent or related to each other.

One of the major functions of research is to test hypotheses derived from an existing theory. To do this, we *deduce* hypotheses that are consistent with the theory. For example, an axiom of self-regulated learning theory states that the goals students adopt determine their level of cognitive engagement. From this, we might deduce that when students know they will be tested again on the same material, those who have lower goals (e.g., a goal of getting 70% right) should ask for less feedback about wrongly answered test items than those who have higher goals.[2] A study that confirms this hypothesis lends support to the underlying theory. Assuming the study is methodologically strong, failure to confirm a hypothesis calls the theory (or parts of it) into

question, causing theorists to consider reformulating it to account for the discrepancy.

Another major function of research is to provide the observations and conclusions on which we can *induce* theory. That is, we try to develop theories that explain events we have observed. Those who practice *qualitative research* often refer to this as **grounded theory** (i.e., theory that is grounded on observations).[3] Grounded theory is often thought of as evolutionary. That is, it usually is developed during the process of making observations, and it is regularly revised (i.e., evolves) as new observations warrant.

The desire by scientists to develop theories on all major aspects of human experience should not be surprising. Unified explanations of phenomena are clearly more useful than a collection of unrelated "facts" collected via nontheoretical research.

If you are looking for a research topic for a thesis or term project, you would be well advised to consider a theory of interest to you. Testing some aspect of it makes a potential contribution to our understanding of all aspects of behavior related to the theory. In addition, you will find it easier to defend your selection of a research topic and write the introduction to your research report if you can show that your study has implications for validating and refining an important theory.

When thinking about theory as a basis for research, keep in mind that no theory of human behavior is universal (i.e., there almost always are exceptions to the rule). This is why we usually examine *trends across groups* in order to test or develop theories. However, do not overlook the possibility of designing a study specifically to examine those individuals who do not perform as predicted by a theory. Understanding how the dynamics of their behavior differ from those who act in the way predicted by theory may help in refining a theory to take account of exceptions.

---

[1] In this discussion, the technical terms for various schedules of reinforcement are not discussed.

[2] For more information on this theory and to see an example of research based on the theory, see Azevedo, R., & Cromley, J. G. (2004). Does training on self-regulated learning facilitate students' learning with hypermedia? *Journal of Educational Psychology, 96,* 523–535.

[3] For more information on the use of the grounded theory approach to research, see Topic 65 in Part H of this book. For an example of a study that employs grounded theory, see Noonan et al. (2004). Challenge and success: A qualitative study of the career development of highly achieving women with physical and sensory disabilities. *Journal of Counseling Psychology, 51,* 68–80.

EXERCISE ON TOPIC 13

1. How is a *theory* defined in this topic?

2. Do we use "induction" *or* "deduction" to derive a hypothesis from a theory?

3. What are the two major functions of research mentioned in this topic?

4. If a hypothesis derived from a theory is not confirmed, what implications does this have for the theory?

5. Is grounded theory based on "induction" *or* "deduction"?

6. Is the use of grounded theory more likely to be associated with "qualitative" *or* "quantitative" research?

Question for Discussion

7. Examine the discussion of a theory in a textbook in your field. Does the author of the textbook cite research that supports it? Does he or she suggest unresolved issues relating to the theory that might be explored in future research? Explain.

For Students Who Are Planning Research

8. Is the purpose of your research to test a hypothesis deduced from a theory? (This is typically done by quantitative researchers. See Topics 9 and 10 for a brief explanation of the differences between qualitative and quantitative research.) Explain.

9. Is the purpose of your research to make observations on which a theory may be built? (This is typically done by qualitative researchers. See Topics 9 and 10 for a brief explanation of the differences between qualitative and quantitative research.) Explain.

10. Will you be conducting research without reference to theory? (Note that it is possible to plan and conduct research on practical matters without explicit reference to theory. For instance, suppose your local schools went on double shifts because of overcrowding, and you want to investigate the effects of the double shifts on students' attitudes and achievements. While there may be several theories that relate to this situation, you might conduct your research *as a practical, nontheoretical matter* in order to better inform decision-makers and taxpayers on this matter.) If you will not be referencing theory, will the results of your research still have important practical implications? Explain.

PART B

REVIEWING LITERATURE

Reviewing the research conducted by others is often the first step in planning a new research project. In this part, we will first explore the reasons for reviewing literature and how it will help you identify a suitable idea for research as well as help you select appropriate research tools and methods. Second, we will examine how to locate literature electronically. Because it is assumed that you already know how to locate books and articles in mass-circulation periodicals and newspapers, the emphasis here is on how computerized databases can make your search of academic journals more efficient and precise. Finally, we will consider some basic principles for writing literature reviews, including how to cite references.

NOTES

TOPIC 14 REASONS FOR REVIEWING LITERATURE

If you are planning your first research project for a class assignment or a thesis, start by identifying a broad problem area. This could be a practical problem such as "the education of bilingual children" or "dependence on welfare," or it could be a more theoretical one such as "How valid is attribution theory in informal learning situations?" The second step is to review literature on the topic. Examining both the theoretical and research literature on a topic will usually help you identify a testable hypothesis of limited scope (limited so that it can be tested within a reasonable amount of time and with the resources you have available).[1]

If you are having difficulty identifying a research hypothesis, you might consider *replicating* a study that has already been published.[2] In a *strict replication*, researchers try to mimic the original study in all important respects because the purpose is to see if the same types of results will emerge. Of course, a strict replication should be undertaken only on studies with potentially important implications. Note that the findings of a study that others are not able to replicate are usually dismissed by the academic community as invalid.

Another possibility is to locate an important study and conduct a *modified replication* (i.e., a replication with some major modification(s) such as examining a new population or using an improved measurement technique). Notice, though, that if the study fails to replicate, you will not know whether it is because the original study was in error or because your modifications changed the nature of the study.

Because there are many topics on which the results of published research are conflicting, a third possibility is to plan a study designed to resolve a conflict. Published reviews of research often point out such conflicts and offer possible explanations of them.

After reviewing research, you may arrive at a creative idea that is *not* a direct extension of existing research. While there are important cases of this in the history of science, they are rare. It is extremely unlikely that a novice researcher will have such an insight at the beginning of his or her professional career.

In addition to helping you identify testable hypotheses, reviewing published research provides other benefits. First, you may identify measuring tools (called *instruments*) that were used successfully by other researchers and also avoid those found to be seriously flawed. Second, you may be able to avoid dead ends (i.e., one of your ideas for research may have already been thoroughly investigated and shown to be not fruitful). Third, you can learn how to write research reports by paying careful attention to the style and organization used by authors of published research. To do this, do not read just for content but also notice how research reports are written. The importance of reading large numbers of original research reports before attempting to write one's first research report cannot be overstated. Students who ignore this advice are likely to struggle with both the organization and wording of their reports and, despite their best efforts, produce a sophomoric report.

When you write a research report, you will be expected to cite relevant research. When writing a research report for publication in a journal, it is typical to integrate the literature into your introduction. In theses and dissertations, you probably will be required to present your literature review in a separate chapter immediately following the chapter that contains the introduction. Note that a well-crafted review of research shows your readers the context within which you were working. It can also help to justify your study if you use it to establish the importance of your topic and to show how your research flows from important research conducted by established researchers.

Finally, your review of research allows you to demonstrate to your instructors, thesis committee members, and others that you were able to locate research relevant to your hypothesis, evaluate the literature, use it in planning your research, and cite it appropriately in your review of literature.

In the next topic, we will explore how to search for literature electronically, and in Topic 16, we will consider how to organize it. Topic 17 will provide some important suggestions for effective writing, and Topic 18 will show you the basics of citing references.

---

[1] See Topic 7 to review hypotheses as well as purposes and questions, which are alternatives to hypotheses, as the heart of research. A testable hypothesis is one that can be tested through direct observation.

[2] Check with your professor to see if this is acceptable in light of the objectives for the course.

Exercise on Topic 14

1. When planning research, should you first identify a broad problem area *or* develop a testable hypothesis?

2. Suppose you conducted a replication of a study but used a sample from a population different from the one used in the first study. What type of replication did you conduct?

3. Should you be surprised if you find conflicting results in the research literature on a given topic?

4. "According to this topic, students would be wise to try to find a creative, new research idea to explore in their first research project." Is this statement true *or* false?

5. In journal articles, the literature review is usually integrated into which part of the article?

6. How can you use a review of literature to help justify a study you have undertaken?

Question for Discussion

7. The three possibilities for identifying a research project described in this topic are to conduct a strict replication, to conduct a modified replication, and to conduct a study designed to resolve a conflict in the results of published research. Are any likely to be of greater benefit to science than any of the others? Explain.

For Students Who Are Planning Research

8. Have you begun reading the literature on your problem area? If yes, are you planning a strict replication of a previous study? A modified replication? A study that might resolve a conflict in the literature? Explain.

9. Was your research purpose or hypothesis explicitly suggested in the literature you have read?

In this topic, we will consider how to use electronic databases (i.e., databases accessible via computers) to locate articles in academic journals. Note that journal articles are the major source of original reports of empirical research as well as the primary source of information on established and emerging theories.

Three of the major databases in the social and behavioral sciences are (1) *Sociological Abstracts*, which contains *Sociological Abstracts* and *Social Planning/Policy & Development Abstracts*, covering journal articles published in more than 1,600 journals; (2) *PsycINFO*, which contains *Psychological Abstracts*, with abstracts of journal articles worldwide since 1974; and (3) *ERIC*, which contains abstracts of articles in education found in more than 600 journals dating from 1966 to the present.[1] While the following examples illustrate the use of the *ERIC* database, the principles for searching all three databases are quite similar, except where noted below.

The best access point for the *ERIC* database is at www.eric.ed.gov. Unlike most other databases, access is free of charge to any user, and you can access it from any computer connected to the Internet without restrictions such as passwords. (Other electronic databases are usually free of charge to students through their college libraries, which pay license fees that permit students and professors to use them without additional charge.)

The first step in searching a database is to examine its thesaurus. At www.eric.ed.gov, click on "Search *ERIC* Database" and then click on "*ERIC* Thesaurus." Click on the "Browse" button if you want to scan all the "keywords" in the database. You can also enter any term to find out if it is used by *ERIC* in classifying journal articles in the database.

The Thesaurus can help you refine your topic. For example, if you enter "Drinking" in a search of the Thesaurus, the results will give you a brief definition called a "scope note" that indicates that the term "drinking" is defined as "consumption of alcoholic beverages." It also indicates that a "nar-

rower term" is "alcohol abuse." If you look up "alcohol abuse," you will learn that it is defined as "excessive or otherwise inappropriate ingestion of alcoholic beverages." In addition, you will learn that "alcoholism" is a "narrower term" than "alcohol abuse," while a "broader term" is "substance abuse." Related terms such as "alcohol education," "driving while intoxicated," and "fetal alcohol syndrome" are also given. With this information from the Thesaurus, you can determine which of the *ERIC* terms will be most appropriate for your literature search.

The terms found in the *ERIC* Thesaurus are known as "keywords" (formerly known as "descriptors"). In an *ERIC* search for articles with the keyword *Alcohol Abuse* (with the box to limit the results to journal articles checked), references for 957 articles will be located (as of the time of this writing).

Frequently, researchers want to narrow their database searches in order to make them more precise. An important instruction for doing this is *AND*. For example, if we use the instruction to locate articles with "*alcohol abuse AND treatment*," *ERIC* will identify only 122 articles that deal with *both* alcohol abuse *and* its treatment.

We can also make our search more precise by using *NOT*. Using the instruction "*alcohol abuse NOT college*" will identify all articles relating to alcohol abuse but exclude any that relate to alcohol abuse at the college level.

You can conduct a search for all articles containing either (or both) of two keywords by using *OR*. For example, the instruction to find "*dyslexia OR learning disabilities*" will locate all articles with either one of these descriptors. Thus, using *OR* broadens a search.[2]

A unique feature of *AskEric* is that it permits users to submit written questions, and employees of *ERIC* will search the literature for you (at no charge). This can be very helpful if you are having difficulty locating literature on your specific research topic.

Unlike *ERIC*, *PsycINFO* allows you to search by author. This is especially useful if you know the name of an important researcher (or theorist) in your research area and want to identify additional

---

[1] The emphasis in this topic is on journal articles. Note that *PsycINFO* also abstracts books, *Sociofile* also abstracts dissertations, and *ERIC* also abstracts unpublished documents, such as convention papers, which are available on microfiche.

[2] The terms *AND*, *NOT*, and *OR* are known as "logical operators."

publications by him or her. In addition, *PsycINFO* permits a search of keywords in only the titles of publications. For instance, a search for "alcohol abuse" in any field yields an unmanageable 4,798 publications (at the time of this writing). Restricting the search to articles containing the term in their titles yields only 173 articles. These are the 173 of the 4,798 that are most likely to deal directly with alcohol abuse (as opposed to publications in which it is dealt with as a side issue) because the authors mentioned alcohol abuse in the titles of their articles.

Other important electronic databases for locating journal articles and other types of literature are de-scribed in Appendix C. Whichever databases you use, you will save time in the long run and conduct more fruitful searches if you first read carefully the instructions for using the particular database that you are accessing. (Instructions can usually be accessed from the home page of a database.) While all databases permit searches for publications that deal with particular keywords, many have special features (such as a search of titles only in *PsycINFO*) to assist users.

For more information on accessing these three databases plus the ones described in Appendix C, consult the reference librarian at your college or university library.

EXERCISE ON TOPIC 15

1. Which database is free of charge to any user?

2. What is the first step in searching a database?

3. In *ERIC*, what is a "scope note"?

4. The terms found in the *ERIC Thesaurus* are known as what?

5. Which of the following will yield a larger number of references?
   A. A search using "alcohol abuse *AND* treatment."
   B. A search using "alcohol abuse *OR* treatment."

6. If you wanted to search for journal articles on Term A but wanted to exclude articles that also include Term B, which logical operator should you use?

7. If we search for "discipline *AND* rewards," will we retrieve more references than if we searched using each term separately?

Question for Discussion

8. If you have searched for journal articles electronically in the past, briefly describe your experience(s). Was it easy to do? What suggestions do you have for others who will be doing it for the first time?

For Students Who Are Planning Research

9. Name some keywords you might use in an electronic search of the literature. Have you checked in a thesaurus to see if they are valid for use in the database you plan to access? Have you (or will you) use the logical operators described in this topic? Explain.

TOPIC 16   ORGANIZING A LITERATURE REVIEW

When writing a literature review, first describe your broad problem area and provide conceptual definitions of major terms if you believe your audience may not know their meanings.[1]

The second step is to establish the importance of your topic. One way to do this is to show that your topic was deemed important enough to be investigated by others, as illustrated in Example 1, which consists of the first two paragraphs in the introduction to a research report. (Notice that the second sentence is a definition.)

EXAMPLE 1
This study assesses the relationship between physical function and psychological well-being among individuals living with rheumatoid arthritis (RA). RA is a chronic disease involving inflammation and stiffening of the joints, which can result in pain, fatigue, and joint deformity (Schumacher, 1993). As a result, individuals with RA can experience considerable functional impairment, which can disrupt their work and social life (Devins et al., 1993; Felts & Yelin, 1989; Katz, 1995; Yelin, Feshbach, Meenan, & Epstein, 1979).

An association between physical impairment and depression or depressive symptoms among individuals with RA has been established in the literature (Katz & Yelin, 1993, 1994, 1995; Peck, Smith, Ward, & Milano, 1989; Wolfe & Hawley, 1993). Furthermore, there is longitudinal evidence that.... (p. 253)[2]

You may also establish the importance of a topic by citing statistics that indicate how many people are affected by a particular problem (e.g., how many individuals were the victims of armed assault last year) or how many people are in the population of interest (e.g., how many children enrolled in special classes for the gifted). Some of the major sources for statistics are described in Appendix D.

The next step is to write a *topic-by-topic* description of relevant research and provide major and minor subheadings to guide readers through a long literature review. For example, some of the **major headings** and *minor subheadings* used by Reis, Collins, and Berscheid (2000) in their review of research on the influence of social relationships on human development are: **Conceptualization of Relationships** (*The Concept of Relationships, Types of Relationships, Cultural Variations in Relationships*) and **The Role of Relationships in Human Survival and Well Being** (*Innate Social Response Systems, Face Perception, Attachment*).[3]

Group references together when they have something in common. In Example 2, the authors cite three references for the findings they report in the first sentence.

EXAMPLE 2
Researchers studying tobacco use and emotional distress in adolescents have proposed that psychological risk factors, such as difficult family situations or a tendency toward risk taking, underlie both phenomena (Covey & Tam, 1990; Escobedo et al., 1998; Kaplan, Landa, Weinhold, & Shenker, 1984). A longitudinal study of adult twins points to the existence of a genetic predisposition to both depressive symptomatology and a propensity to use tobacco (Kendler et al., 1993). In addition, Breslau et al. (1998) suggested that a personality disorder such as neuroticism may be driving both tobacco use and emotional distress. (p. 959)[4]

Also, note that you should indicate the *results* of the research you are citing—as was done in Example 2—and not just describe the research methodology.

Sometimes, it is appropriate to trace the history of a topic by describing the first important article on it and tracing how theories on it evolved as more evidence became available. A search of the *Social Sciences Citation Index* will help greatly if you want to do this (see the last entry in Appendix C).

At the end of a long review of literature, it is appropriate to summarize the review, with attention to how the review relates to your study. For example, you might point out that there are contradictions in

---

[1] See Topic 8 for a discussion of the differences between conceptual and operational definitions. Conceptual definitions may also be integrated throughout a literature review as new terms are introduced. Operational definitions are usually provided in the Methods section of research reports.

[2] Source: Neugebauer, A., Katz, P. P., & Pasch, L. A. (2003). Effect of valued activity disability, social comparisons, and satisfaction with ability on depressive symptoms in rheumatoid arthritis. *Health Psychology, 22*, 253–262.

[3] Source: Reis, H. T., Collins, W. A., & Berscheid, E. (2000). The relationship context of human behavior and development. *Psychological Bulletin, 126*, 844–872.

[4] Source: Orlando, M., Ellickson, P. L., & Jinnett, K. (2001). *Journal of Consulting and Clinical Psychology, 69*, 959–970.

the research, which your research might help resolve. You might also point out gaps in the literature that your study might help fill.

Exercise on Topic 16

1. According to the topic, what is the first thing one should do in a literature review?

2. Should you organize a literature review around topics *or* should you summarize each reference separately regardless of the topics?

3. What two ways are suggested for showing the importance of your topic?

4. Should references that have something in common be grouped together *or* discussed separately in a literature review?

5. Is it appropriate to indicate the results of the research being cited?

6. According to the topic, is it ever appropriate to cite older references in a literature review? Why?

Questions for Discussion

7. Novice researchers sometimes write a summary of each publication they are citing and then string the summaries together, one after the other. They consider their string of summaries as an effective literature review. What are the weaknesses of this approach?

8. Students are usually expected to cite more references in master's theses than they would be expected to cite when writing a journal article, even in an article for a major, prestigious journal. Speculate on the reason(s) for this.

For Students Who Are Planning Research

9. Name some of the headings and subheadings you anticipate you might use to organize your literature review. (Note that these might change after you have read the literature on your topic.)

TOPIC 17   WRITING A LITERATURE REVIEW

A literature review should be a *critical* assessment of the literature on a topic. Before beginning to write, you should already have assessed the quality of the works you will be discussing, and these assessments should "show through" in your writing. Like a movie critic, you should provide general information on the content of the works you are citing and comment on what you think are the strong and weak points of individual works. When you present a finding or statement from the literature without critical comment, your readers are likely to assume that you believe the underlying methodology or logic is reasonably sound.

Examples 1 through 3 illustrate three approaches that might be used when presenting your critical assessments. The first one briefly identifies weaknesses, the second identifies strengths, and the third is neutral, which suggests that the writer thinks the underlying methodology is strong enough that weaknesses do not need to be discussed.

EXAMPLE 1 (WEAKNESSES CITED)
"In a preliminary pilot study, X was found to be stronger than Y (Doe and Smith, 2004)."

"Based on the performance of only 15 registered nurses, Jones (2003) reported that...."

EXAMPLE 2 (STRENGTHS CITED)
"The three large-scale national surveys indicate that a large majority is opposed to this new policy (Baxter, 2003; Galvan & Baxter, 2004; Barnes, 2004)."

"In the only experiment using random assignment to treatments, the authors found that....(Brown, 2002)."

EXAMPLE 3 (NEUTRAL)
"Treatment X has been found to be superior to Treatment Y in a number of experiments (e.g., Black & Solis, 2002; Noble & Heath, 2003)."

These are additional suggestions for writing effective literature reviews:

1. Each paragraph in a literature review should be organized around a topic. In order to promote clarity of communication, authors of scientific writing typically make the first sentence of each paragraph the topic sentence (although other arrangements are acceptable if they facilitate communication).

2. When a number of authors have made the same point, they should usually be grouped together in a single reference citation.

3. When a large number of authors have reported a common finding, consider using "e.g." followed by just a sample of the authors.

4. One or more paragraphs (or even whole sections) might be devoted to describing a particular individual's written work when the work is both important and central to one or more points being made in the literature review.

5. Consider providing explicit definitions of all important technical terms.

6. When presenting a previously published definition of a concept, consider quoting it because some of its meaning may be lost in paraphrase. This is especially important when citing an expert's definition.

7. Because direct quotations break the flow of a presentation, they should be used sparingly. Quotations normally should be used only for (1) presenting definitions (see Suggestion 6 above), (2) presenting important points made by notable individuals, and (3) clarifying differences of opinion in the literature when seeing the differences in wording (such as the wording of theories) might help readers understand the issues involved.

8. Use transitional terms and phrases (e.g., "however," "as a consequence," and "indeed") within a paragraph to help readers understand the organization of the paragraph.

9. When a number of parallel points (i.e., separate points on the same topic) are to be discussed, consider using "First," "Second," "Last," and so on, to assist readers in following the list.[1]

10. When presenting a list of brief items, consider giving each one a letter such as "(a)" for the first item, "(b)" for the second one, and so on.

11. Discuss in detail the research methods that were used when differences in research methodology might help explain differences in findings.

---

[1] Avoid the common pitfall of using incorrect adverbs such as "Secondly" and "Lastly" when presenting a list.

12. Follow a particular style manual for citing references carefully and consistently. (Note that all the excerpts that you will read for the following exercise illustrate the Harvard method, which is also known as American Psychological Association [APA] style.) Pay attention to details such as punctuation, order of information in a reference citation, and so on.

EXERCISE ON TOPIC 17

1. If you do not discuss the research methodology used in references you are citing in a literature review, what are your readers likely to assume?

2. Should a literature review be "critical"?

3. When a large number of authors have reported a common finding, what should you consider using?

4. When is it appropriate to devote one or more paragraphs to describing a particular individual's written work?

5. Is it appropriate to indicate the results of the research being cited?

6. When should you discuss in detail the research methods that were used?

7. Why should you use transitional terms and phrases in a paragraph?

Questions for Discussion

Directions: For each of the numbered suggestions (1 through 12) in this topic, consider whether they were applied in the six literature review excerpts in Appendix B. Write your findings below.

8. In your opinion, was suggestion number 1 applied in any of the excerpts? Explain.

9. In your opinion, was suggestion number 2 applied in any of the excerpts? Explain.

10. In your opinion, was suggestion number 3 applied in any of the excerpts? Explain.

11. In your opinion, was suggestion number 4 applied in any of the excerpts? Explain.

12. In your opinion, was suggestion number 5 applied in any of the excerpts? Explain.

13. In your opinion, was suggestion number 6 applied in any of the excerpts? Explain.

14. In your opinion, was suggestion number 7 applied in any of the excerpts? Explain.

15. In your opinion, was suggestion number 8 applied in any of the excerpts? Explain.

16. In your opinion, was suggestion number 9 applied in any of the excerpts? Explain.

17. In your opinion, was suggestion number 10 applied in any of the excerpts? Explain.

18. In your opinion, was suggestion number 11 applied in any of the excerpts? Explain.

19. In your opinion, was suggestion number 12 applied in any of the excerpts? Explain.

For Students Who Are Planning Research

20. Have you started writing a literature review on your topic? If yes, what types of changes will you make in it based on what you learned in this topic?

21. In your opinion, are any of the suggestions (1 through 12) hard to follow? Are any of them especially easy to follow? Explain.

NOTES

TOPIC 18   CITING REFERENCES

While there are a number of methods (or *styles*) for citing references, the Harvard method is the most widely used one in the social and behavioral sciences. This method is also known as the author-date referencing system.

The American Psychological Association (APA) has adopted and modified the Harvard method, and the *Publication Manual of the American Psychological Association* describes in detail how to use this method.[1] In this topic, we will consider some of the basics for citing sources and preparing a reference list using the Harvard method.

In the text, the last name(s) for a reference can be made the subject of the sentence, as in Example 1, or referred to parenthetically, as in Example 2. The form shown in Example 1 obviously emphasizes the authorship, while the form shown in Example 2 emphasizes the content of the statement (in this case, by making "managerial sociology" the subject of the sentence).

EXAMPLE 1
Doe (2004) has pointed out that despite being a relatively new field of inquiry, managerial sociology has made important contributions to our understanding of this issue. Specifically....

EXAMPLE 2
Despite being a relatively new field of inquiry, managerial sociology has made important contributions to our understanding of this issue (Doe, 2004). Specifically....

Making the authors' surnames the subjects of sentences is helpful when you want to compare and contrast the findings (or thoughts) of two or more authors, as shown in Example 3.

EXAMPLE 3
While Lopez (2003) reported that X increased as a function of Y, Jones (2004) reported no increase. The reason for this discrepancy is difficult to determine. However, Jones used a larger sample and better....

As you know from the previous topic, it is often a good idea to group authors together when they make a common point. However, except for school assignments where you might be required to show all references, long strings of references for a single point should usually be avoided. To do this, use the abbreviation "e.g.," meaning "for example," which is done in Example 4. Note that the author points out there are more studies but is citing only some of the most important ones.

EXAMPLE 4
The superiority of X over Y in the treatment of Z has been widely reported in the literature. The strongest evidence to date has been obtained by numerous researchers who have used large, national samples (e.g., Solis, 2001; Wong, 2002; Smith & West, 2003; Brett, 2004). These studies tend to confirm the principle that....

The reference list at the end of a research report should include references for only those citations that were cited in the body of the report. Do not include all relevant references, as you might in a bibliography or suggested reading list.

The items in a reference list should be listed alphabetically by authors' surnames, as shown in Example 5. Note that the first two references in Example 5 are for journal articles, the third one is for a book, and the last one is for material found on a Web site.

EXAMPLE 5
Adams, J. G. (2003). The effects of anything on everything. *Journal of Behavior Therapy and Analysis, 23,* 55–72.
Brennan, K. P., & Strang, T. S. (2002). The reliability of popular measures of depression. *Personality and Social Disorders in Education, 44,* 145–157.
Chin, W. D. (2002). *The art of being kind.* New York: Brooks Publishing.
Lopez, F. L. (2003). "Cognitive structure of intelligence." Retrieved February 23, 2003, from www.apa.org/info/st1445

If you are following APA style when writing for a journal or class project, it is important to note details such as the following:

For a journal article: The title of the article is in lowercase except for the first word (or first word following a colon), and the title of the journal is in upper and lowercase and is italicized. It is followed by the volume number, which is also italicized.

---

[1] Copies of the manual can be found in psychology departments' required textbook sections of most colleges and universities. Go to www.apa.org if you want to purchase a copy directly from APA.

For a book: The title of the book is in lowercase except for the first word (or first word following a colon) and is italicized.

For material found on the Web: Provide the date on which the material was accessed because the content of a Web site might vary from day to day.

For all sources: Follow the punctuation used in the examples carefully. For instance, when writing in English, a comma is not necessary between two elements in a list. However, in APA style, a comma is used between the names of two authors (e.g., Brennan, K. P., & Strang, T. S.).

Regardless of the particular style you are following, apply it accurately and consistently. Failure to do so will raise questions about the care you have taken with other aspects of your research project.

All the excerpts in Appendix B follow APA style. You can use these as models when you cite sources and prepare a reference list.

EXERCISE ON TOPIC 18

1. The American Psychological Association adopted and modified which method for citing references?

2. When you put the authors' surnames in parentheses, what are you emphasizing?

3. In addition to emphasizing authorship, what is the other reason why you might want to make the authors' surnames the subjects of sentences in your literature review?

4. Instead of citing all references relevant to a particular topic, you can use what abbreviation to begin the list of some sample references?

5. In APA style, should the reference list include references for additional readings *or* should it contain only references for citations made in the body of the research report?

6. In the citation for a journal article, should the title of the article be put in italics?

7. In the reference for a book, should the title of the book be put in italics?

Question for Discussion

8. Is the Harvard method widely used in your area of study? Is it used at all? If no, what is the name of the most dominant style? (Examining journal articles in your field will help you determine the answer to this question. Also, some journals include instructions to authors near the beginning or end of each issue of the journal.)

For Students Who Are Planning Research

9. Have you used the Harvard method before? Will you be using it when you write the report of your research? Explain.

Part C

Sampling

When it is impractical to study an entire population, we draw a sample, study it, and infer that what is true of the sample is probably true of the population. Because inferences to a population are only as good as the method used to draw the sample, we will explore in detail the advantages and disadvantages of various methods of sampling. The issue of sample size is also discussed in this part of the book.

NOTES

We frequently draw a **sample** from a **population**, which is the group in which we are ultimately interested. A population may be large, such as all social workers in the United States, or small, such as all social workers employed by a specific hospital. If we study every member of a population, we are conducting a **census**. For large populations, however, it is more efficient to study a sample instead of conducting a census. After drawing a sample, we study it and then make inferences to the population. That is, we infer that the characteristics of the sample probably are the characteristics of the population.[1]

Obviously, the quality of our samples affects the quality of our inferences; a poor sample is likely to lead to incorrect inferences. The two questions we ask when evaluating a sample are: "Is the size adequate?" (a question that is discussed in Topics 23 and 24) and "Is the sample biased?"

We obtain an **unbiased** sample by giving every member of a population an equal chance of being included in the sample. One way to do this is to put the names of those in the population on slips of paper, mix them up, and draw as many as we need for the sample. The result is a **simple random sample**.[2]

Note that we cannot give every member of a population an equal chance of being included unless we can identify all members of the population. Failure to identify all members of a population is a major source of bias in sampling. For example, if our population of interest consists of all homeless individuals in a city, but we can identify only those who seek public assistance and those who seek food and clothing at charitable institutions, we can sample only from these select members of the population. This creates a bias against the less-visible homeless who may be less resourceful, more destitute (or less destitute), and so on. To the extent that a sample is biased against the less-visible homeless, our inferences about all homeless individuals will be incorrect to an unknown extent (i.e., it is not possible to estimate how much error a bias of this type has caused because we do not have information on less-visible homeless individuals).

We also obtain biased samples when we use **samples of convenience** (also known as *accidental samples*). For instance, if a psychology professor wants to study a principle of learning theory as it applies to all college sophomores but only uses those students who happen to be enrolled in his or her introductory psychology class, the sample is biased against all other college sophomores. This introduces many possibilities for error. For example, the professor may have a reputation for being easy and thus attracts to his or her classes students with learning styles that are different from those of the general population of college sophomores. Also, of course, different colleges attract different types of students, and this professor has sampled only from those where he teaches.

A third major source of bias is **volunteerism**. Volunteerism takes two forms. First, sometimes we simply issue a call for volunteers. This is often done in medical research in which researchers advertise for potential participants, such as those with chronic heart conditions, in order to test new methods of treatment. What is wrong with this? The possibilities are almost endless. For instance, some people may volunteer because they are becoming desperate as their condition worsens, whereas those who are doing better may be less inclined to expose themselves to experimental treatment, *or* those who volunteer may be more persistent and resourceful (and thus in better health) than the general population of those with heart conditions. These two opposing possibilities illustrate why we strive to eliminate bias—because we often cannot even speculate accurately on the direction in which a given bias affects the results of a study.

Second, volunteerism may bias a sample even if we begin by identifying a random sample from an entire population. For instance, we might draw a random sample of all freshmen at a college and contact them to take part in a study of attitudes toward the use of technology in higher education. For a variety of reasons, many of those in the random sample we have selected may refuse to participate. Those who do participate, in effect, are volunteers and may be fundamentally different from nonvolunteers—such as by being more interested in technology and more concerned about their education.

---

[1] The process of *inferring* from a sample to a population is also called *generalizing*.

[2] Another method for drawing a simple random sample is described in the next topic.

EXERCISE ON TOPIC 19

1. In the topic, how is *population* defined?

2. If we study every member of a population, what type of study are we conducting?

3. How can we draw an unbiased sample?

4. Suppose we draw a random sample from a population of college students but some of those selected refuse to take part in our study. Are those who participated in our study a "biased" *or* an "unbiased" sample of the population?

5. If you mail questionnaires to all clients of a social worker and 50% of them are completed and returned, is your sample "biased" *or* "unbiased"?

6. Suppose a psychologist has his or her clients participate in an experiment he or she is conducting because they are readily accessible. What type of sample is being used?

7. Briefly describe one way we can draw a simple random sample.

Questions for Discussion

8. People who receive questionnaires in the mail often fail to return them, creating a bias because those who do return them are volunteers. Speculate on some things a researcher can do to get more people to respond. (Consider mailed questionnaires you have received in the past and your reasons for responding or not responding while considering this question.)

9. Are you convinced by the text that researchers should go to great lengths to avoid bias in their samples? Why? Why not?

10. Suppose you drew a random sample of all licensed clinical psychologists in your community to interview by phone. On the days you made the phone calls, some of them were not available to be interviewed, so you drew replacements for them at random from the population of licensed clinical psychologists. Speculate on whether the sample is biased *or* unbiased in light of the fact that replacements were drawn at random.

For Students Who Are Planning Research

11. Do you anticipate you will be drawing a sample for your study *or* will you be conducting a census?

12. If you will be sampling, do you anticipate that you will be using a biased sample? If yes, what do you anticipate will be the source of the bias? Is there anything you can do to reduce the bias? Explain.

TOPIC 20   SIMPLE RANDOM AND SYSTEMATIC SAMPLING

As you know from the previous section, **a simple random sample** is one in which every member of a population is given an equal chance of being included in a sample.

Putting names on slips of paper and drawing them from a hat is one way to obtain a random sample. Another way is to use a table of random numbers, a portion of which is reproduced in Table 1 near the end of this book. It consists of numbers that are unrelated to each other or to anything else. To use such a table, you must give each member of a population a *number name*, and each name must contain the same number of digits. For example, if there are 70 members of a population, name an individual 00 (it does not matter who the first person is because we are just renaming individuals with "number names" at this point—not selecting individuals). Name a second individual 01, name a third individual 02, and so on.[1] After giving each individual a unique number name, flip to any page in a book of random numbers (we have only one page of such a book in Table 1) and, without looking, point to a number—this is the number of the first person selected. Let us assume that the first number you pointed to was the first digit in the first row in Table 1, which is the number 2. The digit to the right of it is 1; together, they constitute the number 21. Thus, person number 21 has been selected. Now, move two digits to the right. The next two digits (ignoring the space between them, which is there only to help guide your eye) are 0 and 4. Thus, person number 04 has been selected. The next two digits are 9 and 8. Because there are only 70 people in the population, no one is named 98. This selection does not help us, so we continue to the right in the first row (Row #1) in the table. The next two digits are 0 and 8, which selects person number 08. We continue in this manner until we have the number of participants we need for the sample.[2]

It is important to note that random samples are subject to error. For example, quite by chance a random sample might contain a disproportionately large number of males, high achievers, and so on. Error created by random sampling is simply called **sampling error** by statisticians. Fortunately, if we use a sample of adequate size (a topic discussed in Topics 23 and 24), sampling error is minimized. In addition, we can evaluate the effects of sampling errors by using inferential statistics, which are discussed in detail in Part F of this book.

Notice that bias also creates errors when sampling (see Topic 19). However, errors due to bias are nonchance errors, which are not reduced by increasing sample size. For instance, if you sample for a political survey and your method is biased against Republicans, increasing the sample size while using the same sampling method only gives you a larger sample of voters who tend not to be Republicans. The larger sample is no less biased than the smaller one. It is important to note that whenever random sampling is not used, scientists presume that whatever other method used is biased.

Another method of sampling that many researchers regard as being essentially equivalent to simple random sampling is **systematic sampling**. In this type of sampling, every *n*th person is selected. The number "*n*" can be any number such as two, in which case we select every second person.[3] However, there is a potential problem with this method. Suppose someone has arranged the population in such a way that every second person is somehow different from the others. Perhaps the population has been arranged in this order: man next to woman, next to man, next to woman, and so on. If we draw every other person, we will obtain a sample of all males or all females. Because we cannot be sure that no one has ordered a list of the population in a way that might affect the sample, an alphabetical list (as opposed to any other kind, such as a class roster) is preferred when using systematic sampling. In addition, we use a random starting point. For instance, if we are going to draw every third person, we select from the first three people on the list using simple random sampling. Finally, we need to go completely through the alphabetical list—through the letter *z*—because different national origin groups tend to concentrate at different points in the alphabet. Following this procedure yields a good sample, but note that it is a systematic sample; it should *not* be referred to as a random sample because the two procedures are different.

---

[1] Notice that because the population size (70) contains two digits, every member of the population must be given a two-digit number name.
[2] Computer programs may also be used to select random samples.

[3] Divide the population size by the desired sample size to determine the value of *n*.

Exercise on Topic 20

1. Is there a sequence or pattern to the numbers in a table of random numbers?

2. In this topic, you learned how to use a table of random numbers to draw what type of sample?

3. What is the name for errors created by random sampling?

4. How can we minimize sampling errors?

5. Can we minimize the effects of a bias in sampling by increasing the sample size?

6. Suppose you want to sample from a population of 99 clients and your random starting point in Table 1 is the first digit in the second row. What are the numbers of the first two clients selected?

7. Suppose you want to sample from a population of 500 clients and your random starting point in Table 1 is the first digit in the fifth row. What are the numbers of the first two clients selected?

8. If you draw every other person from a list of the population, you are using what type of sampling?

9. What is the potential problem with systematic sampling?

10. How can we get around the problem you named in the answer to Question 9?

Questions for Discussion

11. Suppose a friend was planning to use simple random sampling in a research project from which she wants to generalize to all students on a campus. Would you recommend drawing names from a hat *or* using a table of random numbers? Why?

12. Suppose a friend predicts that candidate Smith will win a local election, and the prediction is based on the opinions expressed by his or her friends and neighbors. What would you say to help your friend understand that this method of sampling is unsound?

For Students Who Are Planning Research

13. Will you use sampling to obtain participants for your research? If yes, do you plan to use random sampling, stratified sampling, or some other method of sampling? Explain.

14. Do you think your planned method of sampling might create a bias? Explain.

Topic 21 Stratified Random Sampling

As you know from the previous two topics, simple random sampling gives each member of a population an equal chance of being included in a sample. The resulting sample is, by definition, *unbiased*, yet may contain *sampling errors*, which are errors created by chance (i.e., at random). The technical term we use when discussing the magnitude of sampling errors is **precision**. Our results are more precise when we reduce sampling errors. The two major ways to reduce sampling errors are to increase sample size, which is discussed in Topics 23 and 24, and to use stratification in conjunction with random sampling, which is called **stratified random sampling.**

To obtain a stratified random sample, first divide a population into strata. For example, we usually can easily divide a population into men and women because gender is easily identifiable. If we draw separately at random from each stratum (i.e., separately from men and from women), we will obtain a stratified random sample.

Note that we usually draw the same percentage of participants, *not* the same number of participants, from each stratum.[1] Thus, if there are 600 women and 400 men in a population and if we want a sample size of 100, we would draw 10% of the women (i.e., $600 \times .10 = 60$) and 10% of the men (i.e., $400 \times .10 = 40$). Thus, our sample consisting of 60 women and 40 men is representative in terms of gender (i.e., it accurately represents the gender composition of the population). Note that while the resulting sample will be accurate in terms of its gender composition, the sample from each gender might not be representative of their respective groups. For instance, the sample of 60 women drawn at random might be unrepresentative of the 600 women in the population due to errors created by random sampling. Nevertheless, for studies in which there might be differences associated with gender, it is better to assure that men and women are represented in the correct proportions by using stratified random sampling than to take a chance on gender representation by using simple random sampling.

At first, some students think that men and women should have equal representation in the sample. To illustrate why this is wrong, suppose you were trying to predict the outcome of a local election on a proposition requiring equal pricing of services such as dry cleaning for men and women. Because women are traditionally charged more than men, women might be more likely to vote in favor of the proposition than men. Thus, because there are more women voters in the population (600 women vs. 400 men), there should be more women voters in our sample (60 vs. 40). Notice, however, that if men and women do not differ in their opinions on this particular issue, stratification will not increase the precision of our result. In other words, if men and women are the same in their opinions (perhaps 80% approve and 20% disapprove), it does not matter if we have a sample consisting of all men, all women, or something in between because in any of these combinations, about 80% will say they approve. In other words, the stratification variable of gender is irrelevant if those in the various strata are the same in terms of what we are studying. Thus, stratification will help us only if we stratify on a variable that is relevant to the issue being studied.

We can further increase our precision (remember, this means reducing sampling errors) by using multiple strata in selecting a given sample. We might, for example, stratify on the basis of gender and age by drawing separate random samples from each of the four subgroups shown here:

Women Ages 18–39	Men Ages 18–39
Women Ages 40+	Men Ages 40+

Of course, we are not confined to using just two variables for stratification: Having a larger number is better as long as they are relevant and *independent* of each other. To see what is meant by independence, suppose we stratified on both age and number of years employed. Since older people have had more years in which to be employed, the two are probably highly correlated. Thus, stratifying on age has probably already accounted to a great extent for years of employment.

Keep in mind the primary purpose of stratification, which is to ensure that different subgroups are represented in the correct proportions. Our goal in stratification is *not* to make comparisons across

---

[1] If equal numbers are drawn, the responses from each stratum can be statistically weighted to make the statistical result reflect the population proportions.

subgroups but to obtain a single sample that is representative in terms of the stratification variables.

EXERCISE ON TOPIC 21

1. Our results are more *precise* when we reduce what?

2. Is it possible for a random sample to contain sampling errors?

3. What is the first step in stratified random sampling?

4. Do we usually draw the same number *or* the same percentage from each stratum?

5. If the population of freshmen and the population of sophomores on your campus are the same in their opinion on a particular issue on which you will be conducting a survey, will it be to your advantage to stratify by drawing samples separately from each group?

6. What does stratification do to precision?

7. Is it possible to stratify on more than one variable?

8. Is the primary purpose of stratifying to be able to compare subgroups (such as comparing freshmen and sophomores in Question 5)?

Questions for Discussion

9. Think of an issue on which you would want to conduct a survey using the students at your college or university as the population. Name the issue and two variables you think would be relevant for stratification purposes when drawing a stratified random sample.

10. Students were given a test on a research article they read for class. One question asked, "What type of sampling was used in the research?" Students who answered using only the term "random sampling" lost a point for the question. The instructor's comment was that the answer was ambiguous. Do you think the instructor was right in taking off the point? Why? Why not?

For Students Who Are Planning Research

11. If you planned to use simple random sampling (see Topic 20), do you now think your study would be improved if you used stratified random sampling instead? If yes, on what basis do you plan to stratify?

TOPIC 22 OTHER METHODS OF SAMPLING

In the previous three topics, you learned about simple random sampling, systematic sampling, and stratified random sampling. In this topic, we will consider several other methods.

In **cluster sampling**, we draw groups (or clusters) of participants instead of individuals. For example, suppose we want to survey a sample of members of United Methodist churches throughout the United States. If we obtain a membership list with addresses, we might draw a simple or stratified random sample of individuals and mail questionnaires to them. However, mailed questionnaires are notorious for their low response rates. We might get a better response rate if we draw a sample of clusters—in this case, congregations—and contact the ministers of the congregations to request that they personally distribute the questionnaires to their church members, collect the completed questionnaires, and mail them back to us. If the ministers are convinced that our survey is appropriate and important, they might use their influence to help us obtain responses from the members of their congregations (i.e., clusters). Of course, for cluster sampling to be unbiased, we must draw the clusters *at random*. This could be done by assigning a number to each congregation and using a table of random numbers to select a sample of the congregations. (See Topic 20 for a description of how to use a table of random numbers.)

A major drawback to cluster sampling results from the fact that each cluster tends to be more homogeneous in a variety of ways than the population as a whole. Suppose, for example, that church members in the South tend to be more conservative than members in the North. Then, members of any one cluster in the South are unlikely to reflect accurately the attitudes of all members nationally. If we draw five clusters (i.e., congregations) at random, we might obtain a large number of participants, especially if one or two congregations have very large memberships. However, by drawing only five clusters, we could easily obtain a sample in which most of the churches are in the South or most are in the North, potentially creating much sampling error. To avoid this problem, we need to draw a large number of clusters.[1] To help increase precision, we could

also stratify on geography and draw a random sample of clusters from each stratum, which would assure, for example, that the North and South are represented in the correct proportions.

Another method is **purposive sampling**. When we use this method, we purposively select individuals whom we believe will give us the best information. For example, we might observe over a long period that several members of the academic senate at a university consistently vote on the winning side on controversial issues. We might decide that rather than interviewing a random sample drawn from the whole membership of the senate, we will interview only these consistent winners to predict the outcome on a new issue. While this method is interesting and may be useful at times, it is dangerous—in this case because professors may change their orientations or a new issue may raise different kinds of concerns than those raised by earlier issues. Qualitative researchers frequently use purposive sampling. For more information on sampling in qualitative research, see Topics 60 and 61 in Part H of this book.

Snowball sampling can be useful when attempting to locate participants who are hard to find. For example, suppose you want to study heroin addicts who have never had institutional contacts (e.g., never sought treatment or had been arrested). How will you find them? With the snowball technique, you initially need to find *only one*. If you can convince this one individual that you have a legitimate research concern and that the data will remain confidential, he or she may put you in contact with several others. Each of these may help you contact several more. This technique is based on trust. If the initial participants trust you, they may identify and convince others to trust you also. Of course, snowball samples should be presumed to be biased because individuals are not drawn at random, but without using snowball sampling, there are many special populations that we would be unable to study, such as successful criminals (i.e., criminals who have never been caught), homeless individuals with no institutional contacts, and others who are hard to identify and locate. Both quantitative and qualitative researchers use snowball sampling.

---

[1] Sample size for quantitative research is discussed in Topic 23. Note that statisticians consider each cluster to be a single participant. Thus, if five clusters are drawn,

the sample size is 5. A comparison of sample sizes in both qualitative and quantitative research is discussed in Topic 61.

EXERCISE ON TOPIC 22

1. To conduct a survey on a campus, a researcher drew a random sample of 25 class sections and contacted the instructors who administered the questionnaires in class. This researcher used what type of sampling?

2. Which type of sampling is based on trust between participants and a researcher?

3. What is a major drawback to cluster sampling?

4. Which type of sampling is especially useful when attempting to locate participants who are hard to find?

5. Briefly define purposive sampling.

6. What must we do in cluster sampling to obtain an unbiased sample of clusters?

7. Suppose you identified a person who has engaged in an illegal activity to be a participant in your research, and then you identify others who have engaged in the same activity through the first person's contacts. You are using what type of sampling?

Questions for Discussion

8. To study a sample of all nurses employed by hospitals in a state, a researcher drew two hospitals (clusters) at random, both of which happened, by chance, to be large public hospitals, each with hundreds of nurses, yielding a large sample. Are you impressed with the sample size? Why? Why not?

9. Name a population (other than those mentioned in the topic) for which snowball sampling might be better than other types of sampling. Explain the reason(s) for your answer.

For Students Who Are Planning Research

10. In light of Topics 19, 20, 21, and this topic, what type of sample do you plan to draw? If you will be using a less-than-satisfactory sample, explain why it was necessary to draw such a sample.

In Topics 19 through 22, you learned about various methods of drawing samples.[1] You should have surmised from the topics that the most important criterion when judging the adequacy of a sample is whether there is bias. **Sample size** is an important but secondary consideration. Let us see why with an example. Suppose you are conducting a survey on whether the main cafeteria on campus should remain open during evening hours. Being a commuter with only day classes, you go to the cafeteria at lunchtime and ask every tenth student who enters to participate in the survey.[2] Of the 100 participants in your survey, 80% have no opinion and 20% want evening hours. After considering your results, you decide that you should have used a larger sample, so you obtain another 100 participants in the same way. This time, you get 85% with no opinion and 15% who want evening hours. Being very cautious, you sample again, and this time you get a 75%–25% split. Combining results from your three surveys, you get the total results shown in the bottom row of this table:

	No Opinion	Want Evening Hours
Sample 1	80%	20%
Sample 2	85%	15%
Sample 3	75%	25%
Total	**80%**	**20%**

Notice that for all practical purposes the three results are the same. That is, only a small minority wants evening hours. With a total sample size of 300, you might feel rather comfortable that you have pinned down an answer close to the truth. However, there is a serious problem in your method of sampling resulting from the fact that each time you sampled, you sampled only from those eating lunch in the cafeteria. Thus, the sample is biased against those who are not on campus during lunch hours. Specifically, it is biased against evening students who are the members of the population most likely to want evening cafeteria hours. If you con-

tinue to increase your sample size by sampling only at lunchtime, obtaining the responses of many more hundreds of students, the increase in sample size will be of no benefit in correcting the bias. Instead, you would get much more accurate results by using an unbiased sample—even if you study only a small, unbiased sample. As a rule, then, small, unbiased samples tend to yield more accurate results than biased samples, even if the sizes of the biased samples are large and the sizes of the unbiased samples are small.

Increasing sample size is of benefit in research because it increases **precision**. When we say we have highly precise results, we are saying that the results will vary by only a small amount from sample to sample, which is what will happen if each sample is large. Notice that in our cafeteria example, the results of the three samples were reasonably close, so we could correctly say that we have a reasonable degree of precision. However, because of the bias in the method of sampling, it would be more accurate to say that our results are *precisely wrong* to the extent that the bias has consistently thrown us off in the same direction each time we sampled. Thus, as you can see, we should strive first to obtain an unbiased sample and then seek a reasonably large number of participants.

If increasing the size of a sample increases precision, which is desirable, especially when we are using unbiased (random) sampling, then the larger the sample, the better—right? Yes, this is true, but we obtain *diminishing returns* for each unit of increase in sample size. To understand this principle, consider the following two cases in which the sample size was increased by 50 participants.

	Original Sample Size	Increase	New Sample Size
Researcher A	50	+50	100
Researcher B	3,000	+50	3,050

Considering the data in the box immediately above, we can see that Researcher A gets a much bigger payoff for increasing her sample size by 50 because she has doubled her sample size, which gives her a big boost in precision. Researcher B, on the other hand, gets a very little increase in precision because the addition of 50 to his original sam-

---

[1] The topics on sampling in this part of the book emphasize sampling in quantitative research. For sampling in qualitative research, see Topics 60 and 61.
[2] Selecting every *n*th person is an example of *systematic sampling* (see Topic 20).

ple of 3,000 can have little influence on the results since the responses of the 50 additional participants will be overwhelmed by the responses of the first 3,000. Thus, at some point, the returns (in terms of an increase in precision) diminish to the point that further increases in sample size (such as adding 50 participants) are of very little benefit. Because of this principle, even the most important and prestigious national surveys are often conducted with only about 1,500 respondents.

EXERCISE ON TOPIC 23

1. Is sample size the primary criterion when judging the adequacy of a sample?

2. Does increasing sample size reduce bias?

3. Does increasing sample size increase precision?

4. Researcher A increased his sample size from 200 to 250, and Researcher B increased her sample size from 1,000 to 1,050. Which researcher will get a bigger payoff in increased precision by adding 50 participants?

5. If a researcher uses a very large sample, is it still possible for the results to be wrong?

6. Does each additional participant you add to a sample make an equal contribution to increasing precision?

7. According to the topic, prestigious national surveys are often conducted using about how many respondents?

Questions for Discussion

8. A magazine editor conducted a poll by printing a questionnaire in an issue of the magazine for readers to mail back. Several thousand readers returned completed questionnaires. Suppose a friend reads the results of this poll and is convinced that it reflects the views of all adults in the United States. What would you say to convince him that he might be wrong?

9. Consider the statement, "The larger the sample, the better." Explain why this statement might be misleading to a novice researcher.

For Students Who Are Planning Research

10. What is the anticipated sample size for your study? On what basis did you make your decision on sample size? (Note that you will be learning more about sample size in the next topic.)

One of the first questions students ask when planning their theses or classroom research projects is, "How many participants do I need?" Students often ask this question even before a discussion of the purposes of the research and the procedures that will be used. Without this information, however, it is impossible to make informed decisions on the appropriateness of various sample sizes.

The following are the major factors that influence our decisions on how large samples should be.[1]

First, researchers frequently conduct **pilot studies**, which are studies designed to obtain preliminary information on how new procedures and instruments work. For example, when studying a new drug, we might conduct a pilot study to determine the route of administration and the maximum tolerable dose. We might also try out a new questionnaire to determine if there are ambiguous questions, questions that participants refuse to answer, and so on. Pilot studies are usually conducted on small samples, such as 10 to 100. Based on the results, procedures and instruments can be modified for use in more definitive future studies with larger samples.

Second, some research procedures are so expensive and time-consuming that researchers must limit the sizes of their samples. For instance, when conducting qualitative research, we might plan to spend considerable time interacting with each participant and thus we might have to be content with a small sample.

Third, we might want to document the incidence of something rare, such as the incidence of heart attacks among men ages 18 to 30. If we draw a small sample, such as 25 participants, and wait a year, we probably would not observe any heart attacks, but we would be wrong to conclude that there are no heart attacks in this population. For this type of work, if we cannot afford to use very large samples, we should let someone else with adequate resources do it because small samples are not useful for observing the incidence of rare events.

Fourth, we need to consider the variability in our population. If there is very little variability (i.e., the population is homogeneous), we can obtain accurate results from a small sample. For example, the population of small bags of Frito chips is homogeneous with respect to their weight because the manufacturer strives to be consistent in this respect. Studying a random sample of only 50 would give us about the same information as studying a random sample of 1,000. However, if a population is very heterogeneous, we need a large sample. Suppose, for example, we want to study the rate of reading literacy among adults in a large metropolitan area. There undoubtedly is great variability, ranging from the totally illiterate to the exceptionally literate. If we draw a sample of only 50 individuals from such a diverse group, we might get major errors such as not having a single illiterate person in our sample. Using a larger sample, however, we would be more likely to capture the diversity of the entire population.

Fifth, if we are looking for small differences, we need to use large samples. For instance, suppose the population of female voters is just slightly more in favor of a ballot proposition than the population of male voters. In small random samples of these voters, the random sampling errors could overwhelm the small difference and might even produce a result in which it appears that the males are slightly more in favor of the proposition. Using large samples in this case is necessary if we want to identify the correct direction and size of this small difference.

So what is large and what is small? The answer is relative to what is being studied and the traditional sample sizes used in various types of research. A national public opinion poll with a few hundred respondents, for example, would be considered to have a small sample because survey researchers have learned over the years that it takes about 1,500 respondents to get highly precise results at the national level. On the other hand, an experiment in which clients are given a new form of psychotherapy for several years might be considered to have a very large sample if the sample size were a few hundred because it is traditional in this type of research to use small numbers of participants. Thus, it is important to read many examples of the type of research you are planning to conduct to learn about the various research traditions—including traditional sample sizes—researchers use.

When a small population is of interest, Table 2 near the end of this book is helpful for estimating a

---

[1] The topics on sampling in this part of the book emphasize sampling in quantitative research. For sampling in qualitative research, see Topics 60 and 61.

sample size for survey work in which we want to estimate the percentage of individuals who have some trait such as holding a particular belief. Using the sample size (*n*) recommended in the table that corresponds to the population size (*N*) will usually hold our error down to about 5%. That is, the true percentage in the whole population should fall within 5% of the percentage we obtain from the sample. For example, the table indicates that for a population of 200, we need a sample size of 132 (more than half of the population), but for a population of 400, we need a sample size of only 196 (less than half of the population), illustrating a practical application of the principle of diminishing returns discussed in the previous topic.

EXERCISE ON TOPIC 24

1. What are pilot studies?

2. Do we usually use "small" *or* "large" samples in pilot studies?

3. If we suspect that a trait is rare in a population, should we use "small" *or* "large" samples to identify the incidence of the trait?

4. In what type of research might we spend considerable amounts of time interacting with participants, and what effect might this have on sample size?

5. Suppose we suspect that there is only a very small difference in the math abilities of boys and girls at the sixth-grade level. Should we use a "small" *or* "large" sample to measure this difference?

6. If the members of a population are very homogeneous in their attitudes toward smoking cigarettes, would it be acceptable to use a small sample to identify the percentage who are opposed to smoking?

7. According to Table 2, if there is a population of 1,900 students in a school, what is the recommended sample size?

8. According to Table 2, if there are 130 nurses in a hospital, what is the recommended sample size?

9. What is the symbol for population size in Table 2?

Questions for Discussion

10. Some research articles based on small samples in academic journals are characterized by their authors as being pilot studies. Do you think the publication of pilot studies is justifiable? Why? Why not?

11. Examine Table 2 carefully. Does it make sense that for small populations, we need to use a larger percentage (e.g., for a population of 10, we need to use all 10, which is 100% of the population) than for a larger population (e.g., for a population of 20,000, we need to use 377, which is 1.9% of the population)? Explain.

For Students Who Are Planning Research

12. In light of the information in this topic and in Topic 23, what is your anticipated sample size? Explain the basis for your decision. (Note that your decision may hinge, in part, on practical matters such as the availability of participants and your financial resources.)

PART D

MEASUREMENT

In this part, we will examine some essentials of measurement, with an emphasis on how to assess the validity of tests and measures. Reliability, which is closely linked to validity, is also explored in detail. In addition, we will consider how norm groups help us interpret scores in norm-referenced measurement, as well as criterion-referenced measurement, which is an important alternative to norm referencing. Finally, the distinguishing features of measures of optimum performance and measures of typical performance will be explored.

This part of the book emphasizes measurement in quantitative research. For information on measurement in qualitative research, see Topics 62 and 63 in Part H of this book.

NOTES

The generic term for any type of measurement device (e.g., test, questionnaire, interview schedule, or personality scale) is **instrument**. Thus, for example, one might ask the question: "What type of *instrument* did the researcher use to collect the data?" In formal research reports, you will usually find the heading **instrumentation**, which is the name of the section of the report where the measurement devices used in the research are described. An important issue that is often addressed in this section is the question of **validity**.

We say an instrument is **valid** to the extent that it measures what it is designed to measure and accurately performs the function(s) it is purported to perform. For instance, consider an achievement test that emphasizes knowledge of facts on the westward movement in the United States. It will be only *modestly valid* when administered to students whose instruction emphasized critical appraisal of historical evidence on that period in history. Likewise, a typing test used by an employer is likely to be only *partially valid* if it is administered to applicants who are applying for a job that includes filing in addition to typing.

It is important to note that validity is *relative* to the purpose of testing. If the purpose is to measure achievement of students exposed to instruction on critical thinking, a test that measures only factual knowledge will be largely lacking in validity. For the purpose of measuring the achievement of students exposed to instruction in which the acquisition of factual knowledge was emphasized, the same test will be much more valid. Thus, before we can have an informed discussion of the validity of a particular instrument, the purpose for testing must be clearly stated.

Also, note that validity is a *matter of degree*. Therefore, it is appropriate to discuss *how valid* a test is—not *whether* it is valid. Given the imperfect state of measurement practice, it is safe to say that no test is perfectly valid.

Let us briefly explore some reasons why perfect validity eludes us. First, almost all tests tap only a *sample* of the behavior underlying the constructs we are trying to measure. Consider the construct of aptitude for college (i.e., having the abilities to succeed in college). College aptitude tests emphasize verbal and mathematical skills and leave untapped other skills that relate to success in college, such as ability to use a personal computer to do homework,

knowledge of how to use an academic library, command of effective study skills, and having the maturity to persist in the face of difficulty in a course of instruction. Even within the domains that are tapped by a college aptitude test, only a small sample of verbal and mathematical problems can be presented within a test of reasonable length. Just as when we sample participants from a population (see Part C of this book), some samples are better than others, and all samples are subject to error.

Another reason why perfect validity eludes us is that some traits we want to measure are inherently elusive. Consider cheerfulness. We have all known people whose cheerfulness is contagious. However, even though we know it when we see it, how can we measure this trait in a systematic way in order to study it? We could, for example, ask a series of questions on how participants interact with others in various types of contexts, how they view adversity, etc. On the other hand, we might observe participants and rate them on the cheerfulness they exhibit in their interactions with others (e.g., Do they smile? Is the tone of their voice upbeat? and so on). While these procedures probably tap certain aspects of cheerfulness, they fail to capture the *full essence* of the trait. This illustrates the old principle that often the whole is greater than the sum of its parts. To compound the problem, we often examine only some of the parts when we measure a given trait (e.g., we look at only certain behaviors that indicate cheerfulness, and we do this in only certain public settings).

The problem of elusiveness, at first glance, seems to plague those with a quantitative orientation more than those with a qualitative orientation because quantitative researchers seek to reduce elusive constructs, such as cheerfulness, to numerical scores. Qualitative researchers, on the other hand, tend to measure in ways (such as unstructured interviews) that yield words to describe the extent to which traits are present. Yet unless qualitative researchers refer to specific behaviors and events in their reports, they will fail to describe results in enough detail so readers can picture the meanings that have been attached to a construct such as cheerfulness. Thus, listing events, quoting participants, and describing specific interactions, while less artificial than numerical scores, can also miss the essence of a trait, such as the feeling you get when you are with a genuinely cheerful person.

In the next three topics, you will learn about some of the major methods used to assess the extent to which instruments are valid.

EXERCISE ON TOPIC 25

1. What is the generic term for any type of measurement device?

2. An instrument is said to be valid to the extent that it does what?

3. Suppose we purchase a commercial reading test that is highly valid for students who receive reading instruction that emphasizes phonics. Is it possible that the test is of limited validity for students who are taught with a method that does not emphasize phonics?

4. According to this topic, is it safe to say that no test is perfectly valid?

5. Tapping only a sample of the behaviors underlying the constructs we wish to measure has what effect on validity?

6. If a trait is elusive, is it "easy" *or* "difficult" to measure it with a high degree of validity?

Questions for Discussion

7. Have you ever taken an achievement test in school that was seriously flawed in its validity? If so, describe the test and state why you believe it was seriously flawed. In your discussion, mention the purpose for testing.

8. Name a trait you think is *elusive* and thus may be difficult to measure with great validity. Be prepared to defend your answer.

For Students Who Are Planning Research

9. What types of instruments (e.g., tests, questionnaires, interview schedules, or personality scales) do you plan to use in your research?

10. Will the instruments and measurement procedures you named in response to Question 9 measure a *sample* of the behavior underlying the construct? Have you considered how to draw the sample? Explain.

11. Measuring the ability to add one-digit numbers is *not* very elusive. Are the traits you plan to measure inherently more *elusive* than measuring this mathematics skill? Explain.

To determine the **content validity** of an instrument, we make judgments on the appropriateness of its contents. For achievement tests, this type of validity is essential.

Suppose for a moment you were the instructor of your research methods class and want to build an achievement test on the material in this book through Topic 25. What steps could you take to maximize the content validity of the test? First, you would need to consider the amount of testing time and the types of items. For example, you could ask many more multiple-choice items than essay items in a given amount of testing time. Let us assume you decided to write 35 multiple-choice items to be administered in a 50-minute period. You could write one item on each of the 25 topics, assuring that a broad sample of the material was covered. Then, you could allocate the remaining 10 items to those topics you deemed to be most important. (To be fair, you should have indicated to students during instruction which ones were more important than others.) Then, you would need to determine which skill level(s) to measure. Would you test primarily for facts and definitions (e.g., "Which of the following is the definition of validity?") or for higher-level skills (e.g., "Which one of the following statements from a test manual tells us something about the content validity of a test?")?

Although the above example has been simplified, it illustrates three principles for writing achievement tests with high content validity. First, a broad sample of content is usually better than a narrow one. Second, important material should be emphasized. Third, questions should be written to measure the appropriate skills, such as knowledge of facts and definitions, application of definitions to new situations, drawing inferences, making critical appraisals, and so on. Of course, the skills should be those covered in instruction. Keeping these principles in mind, you can make *judgments* of the content validity of achievement tests written by yourself and those written by others.

Although content validity is most closely associated with achievement testing, it may sometimes be applied when evaluating other types of instruments. For example, if you want to measure the broad construct called *self-concept* with a series of questions, you could consider sampling from each of the narrower constructs that constitute it, such as physical self-concept, academic self-concept, social self-concept, and so on, assuring that a broad sample has been covered. If you believe one type of self-concept is more important than others for your research purpose (e.g., academic self-concept for a study in a school setting), you might emphasize one type over the others by asking more questions about it. Finally, you will need to write the questions in such a way that they elicit common, shared meanings from the examinees. To do this, you should consider the examinees' educational levels and the meanings they are likely to attach to particular words in your questions. Will they find some words too difficult to understand? Are some terms ambiguous in their meaning? Careful consideration of these points regarding the contents of instruments helps improve their validity.

We also make judgments when we consider **face validity**. In this approach to validity, we judge whether an instrument appears to be valid *on the face of it*. In other words, on superficial inspection, does it appear to measure what it purports to measure? For instance, one might use a spatial relations test for selecting people for pilot training. A test that uses drawings of geometric shapes moving in space would have less face validity than one that uses drawings of miniature airplanes moving in space. That is, the second one has more face validity on the surface, even though both tests might be equally valid for measuring the underlying ability to visualize objects moving in space. Thus, face validity is primarily a public relations concern. Note that we usually prefer to use tests that *look like* they are related to their purpose because this promotes public acceptance of testing and motivates examinees to do their best.

It is possible for a test to have high face validity for a certain purpose while having low content validity. An extreme example makes the point clear: A test consisting of items such as a drawing of one airplane followed by a plus sign and two more airplanes might have some face validity for pilot selection (because of the drawings of airplanes) but would have essentially no content validity because the skill being tested (adding one-digit numbers) is not appropriate for selecting adults who are likely to be successful in pilot training.

Occasionally, we deliberately use instruments with *low face validity*. For example, in a recent survey on the drug Viagra (a drug for the treatment of sexual dysfunction in males, which is obviously a sensitive topic), the pollsters asked about a variety of drugs even though they were concerned only with attitudes toward Viagra. The face validity of the survey questions was deliberately diluted with questions about other drugs in the hope of reducing the potential sensitivity of the questions on the drug of interest. In general, low face validity is desirable when we want to disguise the true purpose of the research from the respondents. This can, of course, raise ethical issues (see Topic 12).

EXERCISE ON TOPIC 26

1. For which type of instrument is content validity essential?

2. Should we consider the types of skills required by achievement test items when judging content validity?

3. "To improve content validity, it is usually desirable to cover only a narrow sample of content from the broad content area to be covered by an achievement test." Is this statement "true" *or* "false"?

4. Is content validity relevant only to achievement tests?

5. Which type of validity is based on superficial inspection?

6. Which two types of validity rely on judgments?

7. Is it possible for a test to have high face validity but low content validity?

8. When might a researcher deliberately use an instrument with low face validity?

Questions for Discussion

9. Suppose an instructor fails to tell students the types of items (e.g., multiple-choice or essay) that will be on a midterm examination. Could this affect the validity of the results? Explain.

10. Have you ever taken an achievement test in which the content emphasized was different from the content you concentrated on while studying for the test? If so, describe the discrepancy, and speculate on what caused it (e.g., Was there a miscommunication between you and the instructor?).

For Students Who Are Planning Research

11. Will you be evaluating the content validity of any instruments you will be using in your research? Explain.

12. Will your instrument(s) have high face validity? Explain.

TOPIC 27   EMPIRICAL VALIDITY

In the empirical[1] approach to validity, we make planned comparisons to see if a measure yields scores that relate to a **criterion**. To see what this means, consider Example 1.

EXAMPLE 1
Nine applicants for the position of clerk–typist were administered a new employee test, yielding scores from 15 to 35. Because there was a labor shortage, all nine were hired even though some had low test scores. After six months on the job, the employees were rated on their job performance by their supervisors on a scale from 10 (excellent performance) to 1 (poor performance). Here are their scores and ratings:

Employee	Test Score	Supervisors' Ratings	
Jose	35	9	Top third on test.
Jane	32	10	
Bob	29	8	
Fernando	27	8	Middle third on test.
Sue	25	7	
Debbie	22	8	
Milly	21	6	Bottom third on test.
Ling	18	4	
John	15	5	

Comparing the test scores with the supervisors' ratings provides information about the validity of the new employee test. The set of ratings is called the *criterion*, which is the standard by which the test is being judged. Because the purpose of an employee test is to *predict* success on the job, the most appropriate test of its validity is **predictive validity**, which poses this question: To what extent does the test predict what it is supposed to predict?

So how valid is the employee test in Example 1? We can begin to answer the question by examining the table. First, notice that those in the bottom third on the test are also in the bottom third in terms of ratings, suggesting that the test is highly valid for identifying those who will get low ratings on the job. Next, notice that the results for the top and middle thirds are more mixed. For example, Bob, who is in the top third on the test with a score of 29, has a rating of 8, which is the same as the ratings of Fernando and Debbie, who are in the middle third.

Thus, while the test has some validity at these high levels, it is less than perfectly valid.

We can obtain more information on the test's predictive validity if we look at the rank order of individuals on the test in comparison to their rank order on the ratings. In Example 1, the individuals are already ordered from high to low in terms of test scores. Notice that their order on ratings is to some extent similar but not the same. For instance, Jose has the highest test score, but only the second highest rating. Sue is higher than Debbie on the test, but Debbie is higher than Sue on the ratings. Despite exceptions such as these, the overall ordering of individuals by the test is similar to their ordering in terms of ratings.

A third way to look at a test's predictive validity is to compute its **validity coefficient**. A validity coefficient is a *correlation coefficient* used to express validity. Correlation coefficients are described in detail in Topic 49. At this point, we will consider only some basic properties of validity coefficients. In practice, they range from 0.00 to 1.00.[2] At the upper limit, a 1.00 indicates perfect validity. For practical purposes, this can be thought of as indicating that the ranks on the test are identical to the ranks on the criterion. At the lower limit, 0.00 indicates that there is no relationship between the ranks on the test and the ranks on the criterion, which indicates that knowing the test scores is of no benefit when predicting the criterion. For the data[3] in Example 1, the value of the validity coefficient is .88, indicating a high degree of validity—higher than is usually found in validity studies of this type. For example, researchers found a correlation of only .19 for the prediction of job performance using short-term memory tests.[4]

So how high should predictive validity coefficients be? Of course, higher is better. But how high are they in practice? For an employee test validated against supervisors' ratings, we would be surprised to obtain a coefficient greater than about .60, and we would not be at all surprised to get one as low as

---

[1] The definition of *empirical* that applies to this discussion is "relying or based on observation rather than theory."

[2] It also is possible to obtain negative coefficients, but they are very rare in validity studies. Negative correlation coefficients are discussed in Topic 49.

[3] The data were created for instructional purposes to illustrate what a strong relationship looks like.

[4] Source: Verive, J. M., & McDaniel, M. A. (1996). Short-term memory tests in personnel selection: Low adverse impact and high validity. *Intelligence, 23,* 15–32.

.20 or less, indicating poor validity. Why are employee tests only modestly to poorly valid? For two reasons: First, success on the job is a complex construct involving many traits such as interpersonal skills (e.g., getting along with coworkers), psychomotor skills (e.g., typing), work habits (e.g., being punctual), and so on. It is not reasonable to expect a single test (especially a paper-and-pencil test) to predict all these traits successfully. Second, coefficients are not higher because criteria such as supervisors' ratings are themselves less than perfectly reliable and valid. Thus, even if a test, in truth, were perfectly valid, the coefficient would be less than 1.00 if the supervisors failed to put the employees in the correct order. (Note that human judgments are subject to biases and other sources of errors.)

Sometimes, we determine the empirical validity of a test that is *not* designed to predict future behavior. For example, a new, self-administered version of the Addiction Severity Index (ASI) was validated by correlating scores on it with scores obtained using the expensive and time-consuming original version, which involves a lengthy, structured clinical interview. The original version, which had been widely accepted as being highly valid, was the *criterion* (or "gold standard") by which the new version was judged. In this study, the Drug Domain subscale on the self-administered version of the ASI had a *validity coefficient* of .62, which is moderately high, indicating that to a reasonable extent the less expensive version of the ASI provided information similar to the more expensive, original version.[5]

Another approach is to correlate scores on a test that is being validated with scores on a *different test* of the same trait. For example, scores on the *Beck Depression Inventory* were correlated with scores on the *Revised Hamilton Psychiatric Rating Scale for Depression*, which resulted in a validity coefficient of .71. This relatively strong correlation indicates that to the extent that one of the measures is valid, the other one has a similar degree of validity.[6]

A validity coefficient that is obtained by administering the test and collecting the criterion data at about the same time is called a **concurrent validity coefficient** (as opposed to a **predictive validity coefficient**). The general term for both types of validity examined in this topic is **criterion-related validity**. Notice that in both predictive and concurrent validity, we validate by comparing scores with a criterion. The following table shows the relevant features of both.

Types of Criterion-Related Validity[1]	What is the **criterion**?	When is the **criterion** measured?
1. **Predictive Validity**	A measure of what the test is designed to predict.	After examinees have had a chance to exhibit the predicted behavior.
2. **Concurrent Validity**	An independent measure of the same trait that the test is designed to measure.	At about the same time that the test is administered.

[1]Both types of criterion-related validity employ the empirical approach. That is, they are based on data that have been collected (planned empirical data collection)—not subjective judgments or theory.

[5] Source: Butler, S. F. et al. (2001). Initial validation of a computer-administered Addiction Severity Index: The ASI-MV. *Psychology of Addictive Behaviors, 15,* 4–12.
[6] Source: Beck, A. T., Steer, R. A., & Brown, G. K. (1996). *Manual for the Beck Depression Inventory–Second Edition.* San Antonio: The Psychological Corporation.

EXERCISE ON TOPIC 27

1. What is the term for the "standard" by which a test is judged?

2. How is *empirical* defined in this topic?

3. What question does predictive validity answer?

4. If a test is perfectly valid, what value will its validity coefficient have?

5. In light of this topic, would you be surprised to get a validity coefficient of .95 for a paper-and-pencil employee test when validated against supervisors' job-performance ratings?

6. If a test has no validity whatsoever, what value will its validity coefficient have?

7. If we collect the criterion data at about the same time the test is being administered, we are examining what type of empirical validity?

Questions for Discussion

8. Suppose a researcher validated a new multiple-choice reading test by correlating the test scores with teachers' ratings of students' reading abilities (i.e., the scores on the test were correlated with the ratings made by teachers). What is your opinion on using teachers' ratings for this purpose? Could teachers' ratings themselves be less than perfectly valid? Explain.

9. Suppose you wanted to validate a new measure of self-esteem. Name a criterion you might use in a criterion-related validity study. Be prepared to justify its use.

10. The validity of an achievement test might be validated using either content validity (see Topic 26) or concurrent validity (such as correlating the scores with teachers' judgments of students' achievements). Which approach to validity is, in your opinion, more useful for achievement tests? Should both be used? Explain.

For Students Who Are Planning Research

11. Will you be evaluating the empirical validity of the instruments you will be using in your research? Explain. (Note that if you use a published instrument, information on empirical validity may already be available in the manual for the instrument.)

NOTES

TOPIC 28 JUDGMENTAL–EMPIRICAL VALIDITY

The type of validity that relies on subjective judgments *and* empirical data (i.e., data based on observations) is **construct validity**.

A **construct** stands for a collection of related behaviors that are associated in a meaningful way. For example, "depression" is a construct that stands for a personality trait manifested by behaviors such as lethargy, flat affect when speaking, loss of appetite, loss of sexual drive, preoccupation with suicidal thoughts, difficulty in concentrating on tasks, and so on. Notice that each of these is an *indicator* of depression—the construct itself does not have a physical being outside of its indicators. That is, we infer its existence by observing the *collection* of related indicators. The emphasis on *collection* is important to notice because any one indicator may be associated with several constructs. For example, although loss of appetite is an indicator of depression, it may also be an indicator of anxiety, fear, physical illness, and so on. Thus, loss of appetite is indicative of depression only when it is found in association with a number of other indicators of depression.

To determine the construct validity of an instrument, we begin by hypothesizing about how the construct the instrument is designed to measure should affect or relate to other variables. For example, we might hypothesize that students who are depressed will earn lower grades and be more likely to drop out of college than students who are not depressed. Note that this is a *hypothesis* (see Topic 7) because it *predicts* a relationship between depression and grades earned in college. Also, note that we arrived at the hypothesis by making a subjective judgment regarding the likely effects of the indicators of depression on grades. If we test the hypothesis using empirical methods, we are conducting a construct validity study.

Consider how this works for a new, 50-question paper-and-pencil depression *scale*.[1] To determine its construct validity, we could test the hypothesis stated above using a sample of college students as participants. First, suppose we find *no* relationship between the scores obtained on the depression scale and success in college. What does this mean? Either (1) the scale lacks validity for measuring depression

(i.e., it measures something else that is not related to grades earned in college) or (2) the hypothesis is wrong. If we hold firmly to our belief in the hypothesis, we will have to conclude that the empirical evidence argues against the validity of the scale.

Next, suppose we find a relationship between scores obtained on the new depression scale and success in college. What does this mean? Either (1) the depression scale is, to some degree, valid for measuring depression or (2) the depression scale measures a variable other than depression that is also related to grades earned in college. This "other variable" could be many things. For example, maybe the scale is heavily loaded with signs of depression that are also signs of anxiety so that it is more a measure of anxiety than depression. Because debilitating anxiety may lead to poor grades earned in college, the scores on the scale may relate to success in college because it measures anxiety, not depression.

At this point, you should be able to see that determining construct validity is a complex matter that involves both judgment and empirical data. Also, you should see that it offers only *indirect* evidence regarding the validity of a measure. Notice that direct evidence on the validity of a depression scale could be obtained by determining *criterion-related validity* (see Topic 27). For example, this could be done by correlating scores obtained with the depression scale with clinical psychologists' judgments on how depressed each participant is. This is direct evidence because we are comparing scores from a depression scale with some other established measure of depression, not with an entirely different variable such as grades earned in college.

Consider another example: the construct called *dependence on others*. We might hypothesize that younger children are, on the average, more dependent on adults than are older children. If we test the hypothesis and find that the scores on a dependence scale fail to relate to age among children, this result would argue against the validity of the dependence scale. On the other hand, if we find the predicted relationship between the dependence scores and age, this empirical evidence would suggest that the scale might be valid.[2]

---

[1] Instruments that measure personality traits are often called *scales* to distinguish them from *tests* of cognitive skills, which have right and wrong answers.

---

[2] As you know, validity is a matter of degree.

Because the evidence generated by construct validity studies is indirect, we should be very cautious about declaring a measure to be valid based on a single study. Instead, we would hope to see a series of construct validity studies for a given measure—testing various hypotheses derived by considering how the construct should be related to other variables—before reaching firm conclusions.

From one perspective, the indirect nature of the evidence obtained in construct validity studies may be regarded as a weakness. However, when there are a series of construct validity studies on a given instrument, we gain insights into how meaningful the scores are in various contexts. This gives richness to our understanding of how well an instrument works, which is a strength of this approach to validity.

Historically, construct validity has been most closely associated with personality scales. However, its proper application can yield useful information about all types of instruments.

It is often desirable to examine a given instrument in several different types of validity studies. The types of validity considered in Topics 26, 27, and this topic are summarized in Table 1.

Note that it is becoming increasingly common to think of all types of validity as subcategories of construct validity because judgments about constructs must be made in all types of validity studies *and* some type of data must also be collected. For instance, when determining the content validity of an algebra achievement test (see Topic 26), we might count the number of test items that measure each type of material, which yields data (i.e., the counts). Then, we must make judgments about the appropriateness of these counts in terms of the construct of "algebra achievement." In classical test theory, however, content, criterion-related, and construct validity are considered separate classes of validity.

Table 1

A Comparison of Major Approaches to Validity

Approaches to Validity	Types	How Determined
Judgmental	Content	Make expert judgments of the appropriateness of the contents.
	Face	Make judgments based on superficial appearance.
Empirical	Predictive	Correlate test scores with criterion scores obtained after examinees have had a chance to perform what is predicted by the test.
	Concurrent	Correlate test scores with criterion scores obtained at about the same time.
Judgmental–Empirical	Construct	Hypothesize a relationship between the test scores and scores on another variable. Then, test the hypothesis.

EXERCISE ON TOPIC 28

1. How is the term *construct* defined in this topic?

2. Is "fear" a construct?

3. To determine construct validity, we begin by hypothesizing what?

4. Does confirming a hypothesis in a construct validity study offer "direct" *or* "indirect" evidence on the validity of a test?

5. Is the process of determining construct validity purely judgmental?

6. Which two types of validity are classified as "empirical" in Table 1?

7. Which two types of validity are classified as "judgmental" in Table 1?

8. It is becoming increasingly common to think of all types of validity as subcategories of what type of validity?

Questions for Discussion

9. In your opinion, what are some of the physical indicators of (or behaviors associated with) the construct called "industriousness"?

10. To determine the construct validity of a paper-and-pencil industriousness scale, a researcher hypothesized that scores earned on it should be correlated with the number of promotions employees receive on the job. Do you think this is a good hypothesis for a construct validity study? Explain.

11. Consider the physical signs of *shyness*. Propose a hypothesis that might be tested in a construct validity study on an instrument designed to measure this construct.

For Students Who Are Planning Research

12. Will you be considering the construct validity of any instruments you will be using in your research? Explain.

NOTES

A test is said to be **reliable** if it yields *consistent* results. It is easy to see what this means by considering an extreme example. Suppose your professor writes a midterm exam on research methods that contains only four multiple-choice items. The items are on four different important concepts that were emphasized during instruction. Thus, the exam is valid in the sense that it covers appropriate content. Even students who have thoroughly mastered the course content, however, should be concerned about taking such a test because it would be very easy to misinterpret a question or to miss a key term in it and get it wrong, yielding a score of 3 out of 4 right, or 75% correct. On the other hand, students who have moved through the semester in a fog—not understanding even basic concepts—should be pleased at the prospect of taking this exam. With only four items, the odds of getting a few right by guessing and thus passing the test, are reasonably high.

Now suppose some students complain about their scores on the midterm, so your professor writes four new multiple-choice items, and again, they are all on appropriate content. After administering the test at the next class meeting (without announcing there would be a second test, so students are not motivated to study again), should your professor expect to obtain the same scores as he did the first time? In all likelihood, no. Some students who were lucky in guessing the first time will have their luck wash out. Other students who misinterpreted a key term in a question will not do so on the new set of items. Examining the scores from the two tests provides your professor with information on the *consistency of results* or *reliability*. In this case, he or she would probably find that the scores are rather inconsistent from one test to the other.

What can your professor do to increase the reliability of his or her midterm? Obviously, your professor can increase the length of the test. This reduces the effects of the occasional ambiguous item and the effects of guessing. After realizing this principle, your professor instructs a graduate assistant to prepare a 100-item test overnight. The assistant, being pressed for time, takes the easy route and pulls a standardized test off the shelf. Although it has 100 items, they are on educational psychology, which includes some research concepts but also much material not covered in the research methods class. Administering this test should give

highly reliable results. If we administer it twice, for example, those who do not know the name of the "father of educational psychology" the first time the test is administered will not know his name the second time.[1] Likewise, those who have a good command of educational psychology should do well on both tests. Also, those who do not know the material will have little chance of getting a good grade by guessing on such a large number of items. However, the professor has created a new problem: The test lacks **validity** because it covers the wrong content (see Topics 25 through 28). This example illustrates an important principle: *A test with high reliability may have low validity.*

Here is another example of this principle: An employer wants to reward the best employees with end-of-year bonuses. The employer decides that to be perfectly fair, a completely objective method for determining who should get the bonuses should be used. To do this, the employer examines the employees' time cards, and selects those who were never late for work during the previous year to receive bonuses. Notice that this method of measurement is highly reliable: Another person could independently perform the same procedure and, if careful, would identify exactly the same employees for bonuses, yielding consistent (reliable) results. But is the procedure valid? Probably only minimally so because the employer's measurement technique is limited to only one characteristic. Those who are outstanding in a number of other ways (such as identifying more effective ways to advertise products) but who were late to work even once are excluded from getting bonuses. Thus, the procedure is reliable, but it is of questionable validity.

This brings us to the next principle: When evaluating instruments, *validity is more important than reliability*. This should be clear from considering the example of the employer basing bonuses on employees' time cards. A complex measure involving subjective judgments of employees' performances that taps a variety of important types of behavior and achievement on the job would be much more valid (even if it turned out to be only modestly

---

[1] Edward Thorndike of Teachers College (Columbia University) is widely cited as the father of educational psychology primarily because of his influence in promoting the use of empirical methods for studying education.

reliable) than a highly reliable measure that considers only punctuality.

Finally, there is a third principle: *To be useful, an instrument must be both reasonably valid and reasonably reliable.*

To understand the complex relationship between reliability and validity, consider Figures 1 through 4 below.

In Figure 1, the gun is aimed in a valid direction (toward the target), and all the shots are consistently directed, indicating that they are reliable.

Figure 1. Reliable and valid.

In Figure 2, the gun is also aimed in the direction of the target, but the shots are widely scattered, indicating low consistency or reliability. The poor reliability makes it unlikely we will hit the target. Thus, poor reliability undermines an attempt to achieve validity.

Figure 2. Unreliable, which undermines the valid aim of the gun. Not useful.

In Figure 3, the gun is not pointed at the target, making it invalid, but there is great consistency in the shots, indicating that it is reliable. (In a sense, it is very reliably invalid.)

Figure 3. Reliable but invalid. Not useful.

In Figure 4, the gun is not pointed at the target, making it invalid, and the lack of consistency in the direction of the shots indicates its poor reliability.

Figure 4. Unreliable and invalid. Not useful.

Of course, Figure 1 represents the ideal in measurement. For most measures in the social and behavioral sciences, however, we should expect the direction of the gun to be off at least a small amount, indicating less-than-perfect validity. We should also expect some scatter in the shots, indicating less-than-perfect reliability.[2] Clearly, our first priority should be to point the gun in the correct *general direction*, which promotes validity. Then, we should work on increasing reliability.

---

[2] Examination of the technical manuals for published tests indicates that professional test makers tend to be more successful in achieving high reliability than in achieving high validity. This is because it is relatively easy to increase reliability by increasing the number of objective-type test items, while the tasks that need to be undertaken to increase validity vary greatly from construct to construct and may not be obvious.

EXERCISE ON TOPIC 29

1. A test is said to be reliable if it yields what?

2. Should you expect a very short multiple-choice test to be highly reliable?

3. Is it possible for a test with high reliability to have low validity?

4. Overall, is "validity" *or* "reliability" more important when evaluating an instrument?

5. If a test is highly reliable but highly invalid, is it useful?

6. In light of this topic, should you expect most tests to be both perfectly reliable and perfectly valid?

7. "Professional test makers tend to be more successful in achieving high reliability than in achieving high validity." Is this statement "true" *or* "false"?

Questions for Discussion

8. Consider the example of the employer who was trying to identify the "best" employees using a measure of punctuality because it was reliable even though it was not especially valid. Name one or two other traits that might be examined in evaluating employees. Comment on whether you think each of your suggestions can be measured reliably. Also, comment on whether you think each is more valid than punctuality for determining which employees should receive bonuses.

9. Suppose you were offered a choice between two midterm examinations for your research methods class. The first one contains eight short essay questions, and the second contains 38 multiple-choice questions. Both are on appropriate content. Which would you prefer to take? Why? In your opinion, which one is likely to be more reliable?

For Students Who Are Planning Research

10. Will you be evaluating the reliability of any instruments you will be using in your research? Explain. (Note that reliability will be considered in more detail in the next topic.)

NOTES

How can we determine reliability? The classic model is to measure twice and then check to see if the two sets of measurements are consistent with each other.

First, consider **interobserver reliability**. Suppose we want to test the hypothesis that tall people are waited on more quickly in retail stores than short people. To do this, we could observe unobtrusively[1] to (1) classify each customer as tall, medium, or short, and (2) count the number of seconds from the time each customer enters the store to the time a salesperson speaks to him or her.

Because judgments of height made from a distance might not be reliable, we could check their reliability by having two observers independently observe. We could then determine the *percentage* of participants that were put in the same height category (tall, medium, or short) *by both observers*. How high should the percentage be? Although there is no standard answer to this question, it is clear that if the percentage gets too low (say less than 60% agreement), we have a serious problem: Either one or both of the observers are not a good judge of height. Such a lack of consistency in their judgments would make the study meaningless.

Measurements of the number of seconds also might be unreliable if, for example, the observers are distracted by other events, are inattentive to the measurement task, and so on. To check on this possibility, we could compare the measurements reported by the two observers. When there are two quantitative scores per participant (such as the number of seconds for each customer, as indicated by each of the two observers), we can check on the degree of relationship by computing a correlation coefficient.[2] As you may recall from our discussion of empirical validity (see Topic 27), a correlation coefficient may vary in value from 0.00 to 1.00.[3] A 1.00 indicates perfect reliability. That is, the rank order of the customers based on the observations by

one observer is the same as the rank order based on the observations made by the other observer. When we use *correlation coefficients* to describe reliability, we call them **reliability coefficients**. When we use reliability coefficients to describe the agreement between observers, they are usually called **interobserver reliability coefficients**.

Notice that when studying interobserver reliability, we usually obtain the two measurements *at the same time* (i.e., the two observers observe the same participants at the same time). In contrast, in **test–retest reliability**, we measure at *two different points in time*. For example, suppose we want to know the reliability of a new test designed to assess the ability to learn college-level math. We might administer the test one week and then readminister it two weeks later. Because the ability to learn college-level math should not change very much from week to week, we would expect the scores from the two administrations to be consistent. Once again, for two sets of scores, we would compute a correlation coefficient, which would indicate the *test–retest reliability* of the test.

Some published tests come in two parallel (or equivalent) forms that are designed to be interchangeable with each other; they have different items that cover the same content. When they are available, **parallel-forms reliability** should be determined. This is usually done by administering one form of the test to examinees and about a week or two later, administering the other form to the same examinees, thus yielding two scores per examinee. When the sets of scores are correlated, the result indicates the *parallel-forms reliability* of the test.

How high should a reliability coefficient be? Most published tests have reliability coefficients of .80 or higher, so we should strive to select or build instruments that have coefficients at least this high, especially if we plan to interpret the scores for *individuals*. For *group averages* based on groups of participants of about 25 or more, instruments with reliability coefficients as low as .50 can be serviceable. To understand why we can tolerate rather low reliability coefficients in research in which we are examining averages, first keep in mind that reliability coefficients indicate the reliability of *individuals' scores*. Theory tells us that averages are more reliable than the scores that underlie them because when computing an average, the negative errors tend to cancel out the positive errors. For instance,

---

[1] We attempt to measure *unobtrusively* to avoid changing participants' behavior. For example, if salespeople know that we are observing them, they might modify their normal behavior toward customers.

[2] See Topic 49 of this book for a detailed discussion of correlation.

[3] Correlation coefficients may also be negative, as discussed in Topic 49. In the unlikely event that you get a negative when studying reliability, think of it as representing no reliability.

suppose we want to compare the average age of parents who read extensively with their sixth-grade children with the average age of parents who do not. Asking children their parents' ages is likely to be unreliable. However, we might expect about half the children to overestimate the ages and half to underestimate them. To the extent that this is true, the averages may be reasonably accurate because the underestimates will cancel the overestimates.

At this point, you might examine Appendix E, which contains a discussion of other methods of determining reliability.

EXERCISE ON TOPIC 30

1. We need to use at least how many observers to determine interobserver reliability?

2. When there are two quantitative scores per participant, we can compute what statistic to describe reliability?

3. Do we usually measure at two different points in time to estimate interobserver reliability?

4. Do we usually measure at two different points in time to estimate test–retest reliability?

5. According to this topic, most published tests have reliability coefficients that are about how high?

6. According to this topic, serviceable reliability coefficients may be how low if we are measuring in order to examine group averages?

Questions for Discussion

7. In your opinion, which of the following variables mentioned in this topic would probably be easier to measure reliably: (1) height of customers based on observations made from a distance *or* (2) number of seconds from the time each customer enters a store until a salesperson greets him or her, also based on observations from a distance? Explain your choice.

8. For which of the following would test–retest reliability (with the instruments administered two weeks apart) probably be more appropriate: (1) a questionnaire on voters' opinions on the honesty of two presidential candidates *or* (2) a questionnaire on prejudice against minority groups? Explain your choice.

For Students Who Are Planning Research

9. Will you be considering the reliability of any instruments you will be using in your research? If so, which method(s) for examining reliability will you use? Explain.

TOPIC 31 NORM- AND CRITERION-REFERENCED TESTS

Tests designed to facilitate a comparison of an individual's performance with that of a norm group are called **norm-referenced tests (NRTs).**[1] For example, if you take a test and are told that your *percentile rank* is 64, you know that you scored higher[2] than 64% of those in the norm group. Often, the norm group is a national sample of examinees, but it also may be either an entire local population (such as all seniors in a school district) or a sample of a local population (such as a random sample of all seniors in a state).

Tests designed to measure the extent to which individual examinees have met performance standards are called **criterion-referenced tests (CRTs).**[3] For example, suppose we want to test student nurses on their ability to give an injection. We might draw up a list of 10 behaviors that must be performed correctly for a student to pass the test, such as measuring the correct amount of medication, using a sterile needle, and so on. In this case, performing all the behaviors correctly is the criterion (i.e., performance standard).[4] Notice that the interpretation of an examinee's test score is independent of how other students perform. For example, you might be the best in a group with nine items right, but you along with everyone else have failed. Being higher or lower than others who take the same criterion-referenced test is irrelevant to the interpretation.

Those who build norm-referenced tests approach the task differently from those who build criterion-referenced tests. NRTs are intentionally built to be of medium difficulty. Specifically, items that are answered correctly by about 50% of the examinees in tryouts during test development are favored in the selection of items for the final versions of the tests. It is essential that an NRT be somewhat difficult (but not too difficult) because this level of difficulty facilitates the comparison of an individual with a group. This can be seen most easily at the extremes. For example, if we foolishly built an NRT that was so easy that all participants in the norm group got every item right, we could not interpret scores in terms of who has a higher or lower score than other examinees because everyone has the same score. The same problem would occur if we built an NRT that was so difficult that all the examinees got all the items wrong.

In contrast, when building CRTs, item difficulty is of little concern. Expert judgment is used to determine the desired level of performance and how to test for it. These judgments are influenced very little by how "difficult" a task is. Certainly, this approach is often appropriate. For example, would you want the professors at a nursing school to drop the item on measuring the correct amount of medication before injecting it simply because it is too difficult for their students? Of course, we would want them to include the item regardless of its difficulty level.

The need to have items of modest difficulty in NRTs is the basis of a major criticism of this type of test. Specifically, the criticism is that building NRTs is primarily driven by statistical considerations (i.e., item difficulty) and not by content considerations. Of course, those who build NRTs do consider carefully the content that a test should cover, but essential content may be deleted if the items that measure it are very easy or very difficult in try-outs of the items.

Which type of test should be favored in research? The answer depends on the research purpose. Here are two general rules:

1. If your purpose is to describe specifically what examinees know and can do, criterion-referenced tests should be used.

---

[1] Some individuals use the terms *norm-referenced tests* and *standardized tests* interchangeably. However, it is better to reserve the term *standardized* to describe tests that come with standard directions for administration and interpretation. Both *norm-referenced tests* and *criterion-referenced tests* may be standardized.

[2] Strictly speaking, a percentile rank indicates the percentage of those in a norm group that an examinee scored *as high as or higher than.*

[3] You may recall that the term criterion-related validity was used in Topic 27. Note that the word *criterion* is being used in both contexts to mean a *standard*. In Topic 27, we discussed using a standard for validating tests. Here, we are discussing using a standard to interpret the scores of individuals. These are, of course, separate matters, even though we use the same adjective.

[4] Performance standards are established by expert judgments and may be less than 100% correct, depending on the trait being measured. For example, on a typing test, we might require only 95% accuracy. Of course, performance standards are not always expressed as a percentage. We can use descriptive labels such as "expert," "novice," and so on.

Example: To what extent voters can understand a ballot proposition.

Example: Have students mastered the essentials of simple addition?

2. If we want to examine how a local group differs from a larger norm group, norm-referenced tests should be used.[5]

Example: How well are students in New York doing in reading in comparison with the national average?

EXERCISE ON TOPIC 31

1. A norm-referenced test is designed to facilitate a comparison of an individual's performance with what?

2. Are norm groups always national samples?

3. What is the definition of a criterion-referenced test?

4. In which type of test are items answered correctly by about 50% of the participants favored in item selection?

5. In which type of test are items selected based on the content they cover without regard to item difficulty?

6. Which type of test should be used in research where the purpose is to describe specifically what examinees can and cannot do?

Questions for Discussion

7. Assume you are a parent and your child's second-grade teacher offers to provide you with *either* scores on a "norm-referenced test" *or* a "criterion-referenced test" of your child's basic math ability. Which would you choose? Why?

8. If you were conducting research on the percentage of students whose swimming skills are good enough for them to save themselves if they jump into the deep end of a pool, would you choose a "norm-referenced test" *or* a "criterion-referenced test"? Why?

For Students Who Are Planning Research

9. Will you be using norm-referenced tests in your research? Criterion-referenced tests? Explain.

---

[5] To make predictions, we need tests that differentiate among participants. For example, if all examinees earn the same score on a college admissions test, the scores cannot be used to predict who will and who will not succeed in college. Because norm-referenced tests are specifically built to make differentiations by being of medium difficulty, they are also useful in prediction studies.

When we measure achievement, aptitude, and intelligence, we want examinees to show us their best—to perform at their optimum.

An **achievement test** measures *knowledge and skills individuals have acquired*. When we conduct research on the effectiveness of direct, planned instruction, we should use achievement tests designed to measure the objectives of that instruction. To the extent that the tests do that, they are *valid* (i.e., they measure what they should).

Multiple-choice tests of achievement are popular with researchers because of the ease with which they can be administered and scored. Indeed, they are often appropriate when we want a quick snapshot of participants' achievements. We can also measure achievement by having participants write answers to open-ended questions (e.g., essay questions), by evaluating participants' overt performances (e.g., a musical performance), or by assessing products (e.g., a portfolio of watercolor paintings). Scoring of the latter types is more time-consuming than scoring multiple-choice tests and may be *unreliable* unless we make sure that the scorers know specifically what characteristics of the essays, performances, or products they are to consider and how much weight to give to each characteristic in arriving at the scores. For example, to evaluate the ability of a student nurse to give an injection, we could develop a list of desirable characteristics, such as "measures the appropriate amount of medication," "checks the patient's armband," etc. These can be the basis for a *checklist* (a list of desirable characteristics of a product or performance, each of which is awarded a point) or a *rating scale* (e.g., "excellent," "above average," "average," "below average," "poor," which are applied in evaluating each characteristic).

An **aptitude test** is designed to *predict some specific type of achievement*. An example is the College Board's *Scholastic Aptitude Test* (*SAT*), which is designed to predict success in college. The validity of an aptitude test is determined by correlating the scores participants earn (such as *SAT* scores determined while participants are in high school) with a measure of achievement obtained at a later date (such as freshman GPA in college). Other widely used aptitude tests are reading readiness tests (designed to predict reading achievement in the first grade by measuring whether examinees can discriminate among shapes, have basic concepts

such as color names, etc.) and algebra prognosis tests (designed to predict achievement in algebra by measuring basic math skills that are used in algebra). Most widely used aptitude tests are developed by commercial test publishers. Typically, they have low to modest validity (with validity coefficients of about .20 to .60). The modest predictive validity of aptitude tests is understandable because they measure only some of the skills needed for achievement in a particular area. For instance, many other skills such as persistence in the face of difficulty, study habits, as well as physical characteristics such as being chronically ill can affect achievement, but are not measured by aptitude tests. Published aptitude tests, however, usually have high reliability (with reliability coefficients of .80 or higher).

An **intelligence test** is designed to *predict achievement in general*, not any one specific type. The most popular intelligence tests (1) are culturally loaded and (2) measure knowledge and skills that can be acquired with instruction (with questions such as, "How far is it from New York to Los Angeles?"). The arguable assumption underlying them is that all people are exposed to such information and more intelligent people are more likely to retain the information. Almost all contemporary experts on measurement, however, reject the notion that such tests measure innate (inborn) intelligence. At best, they represent one type of intelligence that has been acquired in some specific cultural milieu. Commercially available intelligence tests of this type have very low to modest validity for predicting achievement in school—a degree of validity that can be achieved with less controversial aptitude tests.

Extensive efforts have been made to develop culture-free intelligence tests. Typical efforts in this area have concentrated on nonverbal tasks because of the high cultural load of language usage. These tests are usually less predictive of subsequent achievement than the more traditional intelligence tests, possibly because achievement is accomplished in a cultural context.

Research on intelligence can be controversial when, for example, researchers assume that intelligence tests measure innate ability or that they measure all important aspects of intelligence. Issues such as racial and ethnic differences in innate intelligence, if worthy of study at all, cannot be satisfactorily investigated with the instruments available at this time. Even if such instruments were available for use in research, there would not be legitimate educational or social purposes for conducting research on possible racial or ethnic differences in intelligence.

Because of increasing awareness of widespread misinterpretations of intelligence test scores and the structural limitations of intelligence tests (e.g., arguable assumptions underlying them), intelligence tests are used in research much less frequently now than they were several decades ago.

EXERCISE ON TOPIC 32

1. Which type of test is designed to predict achievement *in general*?

2. An algebra prognosis test is an example of what type of test?

3. A test designed to measure how much students learn in a particular course in school is what type of test?

4. A test designed to predict success in learning a new set of skills is what type of test?

5. A list of desirable characteristics of a product or performance is known as what?

6. How can we increase the reliability of scoring essays, products, and performances?

7. According to this topic, are intelligence tests good measures of innate ability?

8. According to this topic, how valid are commercially published aptitude tests?

Questions for Discussion

9. Did you ever take an achievement test on which you did not perform up to your optimum? If yes, briefly describe why. Was the test maker or test administrator responsible for your less-than-optimum performance? Were you responsible? Explain.

10. Name a specific type of achievement for which you think scores obtained by using a checklist or rating scale applied in the measurement of overt behaviors would be more valid than scores obtained by using a multiple-choice test.

For Students Who Are Planning Research

11. Will you be using an achievement test in your research? Have you selected it yet? Explain.

12. Will you be using an aptitude test? What will it be designed to predict? Explain.

13. Will you be using an intelligence test? Will it be one designed to be "culture-free"? If yes, do you believe it is fully "culture-free"? Explain.

TOPIC 33 MEASURES OF TYPICAL PERFORMANCE

As you know from the previous topic, when we measure achievement, aptitude, and intelligence, we encourage examinees to show us their best. When we measure personality traits such as attitudes, interests, dispositions, as well as deep-seated personality traits, we want to determine participants' *typical* level of performance. For instance, when selecting employees to work as salespeople, we might want to know how assertive each applicant typically is, not just how assertive they claim to be during an interview or in their responses to an assertiveness scale (a series of questions that are scored to get an overall assertiveness score). Our concern here is that the applicants might indicate what is *socially desirable* rather than indicate their true level of assertiveness in order to increase their chances of employment.

People are often hesitant to reveal they have *socially undesirable* traits even when they have nothing directly to gain by being deceitful. Thus, the responses of participants in research projects may frequently be influenced by social desirability. To the extent that we can reduce the influence of social desirability, we increase the validity of personality measures.

There are three basic approaches to reducing social desirability in participants' responses in order to measure without the influence of social desirability. First, by administering personality measures anonymously, we may reduce this tendency. Another approach is to observe behavior unobtrusively (without the participants' awareness—to the extent this is ethically possible) and rate selected characteristics such as aggressiveness.

A third approach is to use *projective techniques*. These provide loosely structured or ambiguous stimuli such as ink blots. As participants respond to these stimuli, such as by telling what they see, they are presumed to be projecting their feelings and beliefs and revealing them in their responses. For example, we might infer that participants whose responses to ink blots contain numerous references to aggressiveness are themselves aggressive. To the extent that participants are unaware of the specific traits an investigator is looking for, the tendency to give socially desirable responses is reduced. The literature on popular projective techniques is quite mixed in the assessments of their validity and reliability, with some studies showing that they are remarkably deficient in these respects. Thus, they are

best used only by those who have had formal training in their administration and scoring. Furthermore, they are seldom used in personality research because (1) they are time-consuming to administer and score, (2) they do not naturally lend themselves to numerical results; instead, the interpretations are usually in terms of words, and (3) their validity is highly suspect. Instead, researchers usually use objective-type personality measures in which participants respond to statements or questions with restricted choices such as true–false, Strongly agree to Strongly disagree, and checklists in which respondents check off the characteristics they believe are true of themselves.

Scales that have choices from "Strongly agree" to "Strongly disagree" are known as **Likert-type scales**.[1] Each statement in a Likert-type scale should present a clear statement on a single topic. For example, to measure attitudes toward school, we might use statements such as, "In the mornings, I look forward to going to school" and "I get along well with my teacher." To reduce response bias (such as marking "Strongly agree" to all items without considering the individual items), it is a good idea to provide some positive and some negative statements and score them according to whether the associated statements are positive or negative. For instance, if we award five points for Strongly agreeing to a positive statement toward school, we would award five points for Strongly disagreeing with a negative statement toward school. This is called **reverse scoring** by researchers.

Of course, the statements in a Likert-type scale should be derived from an analysis of the possible components of the attitude. For attitude toward school, we might have several statements concerning attitudes in each of these areas: (1) learning in academic areas, (2) relationships with classmates, (3) relationships with teachers and staff, (4) participation in extracurricular activities, and so on. Such an analysis helps to assure that the contents of the attitude scale are comprehensive, which will contribute to its content validity (see Topic 26).

In short, when we measure personality traits, we want respondents to tell us what they are typically like, not how well they can make themselves look. This is quite different from measurement of cogni-

---

[1] Named for Rensis Likert, who popularized the format.

tive skills with achievement, aptitude, and intelligence tests on which we want respondents to do their best.

EXERCISE ON TOPIC 33

1. Do we usually want participants to show us their best when we measure personality traits?

2. In this topic, what is the main reason for administering personality measures anonymously?

3. What do we reduce by observing behavior unobtrusively?

4. Loosely structured stimuli are used in which type of personality measure?

5. According to this topic, which type of personality measure is seldom used in personality research?

6. What are the choices in a Likert-type scale?

7. Is content validity a relevant concern when assessing the validity of a Likert-type scale for measuring attitudes?

Questions for Discussion

8. Have you ever given a socially desirable response when it was not true of you when being interviewed or answering a questionnaire? If yes, briefly describe why. Is there anything the interviewer or questionnaire writer could have done to increase the odds that you would be more forthright?

9. Write three statements that could be used with a Likert-type scale to measure attitudes toward your research methods class. Each should be on a different aspect of the class, such as the textbook, the instructor, and so on. Two should be positive statements and one should be negative. Explain how they would be scored.

For Students Who Are Planning Research

10. Will you be using a measure of typical performance in your research? If so, to what extent might it be subject to the influence of social desirability? Explain.

11. Will you be measuring attitudes? If yes, will you use a Likert-type scale? Explain.

PART E

EXPERIMENTAL DESIGN

As you know from Part A, researchers give treatments in experiments in order to observe their effects on participants' behavior. In this part, we will examine various designs for experiments. Specifically, we will consider designs for true experiments, pre-experiments, and quasi-experiments. We will also consider the external validity of experiments (which answers the question, "Can we generalize beyond the experimental setting?") as well as their internal validity (which answers the question, "Did the treatments, in fact, cause the observed differences?").[1]

---

[1] This part highlights some of the main ideas in Campbell, D. T., & Stanley, J. C. (1963). *Experimental and quasi-experimental designs for research*. Chicago: Rand McNally.

NOTES

As you know from earlier topics, the purpose of an experiment is to explore cause-and-effect relationships. In this discussion, we will use terminology and symbols first suggested by Campbell and Stanley.[1]

First, let us examine a classic design for exploring cause-and-effect relationships:

Design 1:

Assign participants at random to groups.	Group A: (Experimental Group)	Pretest	Experimental Treatment	Posttest
	Group B: (Control Group)	Pretest	Control Condition	Posttest

Design 1 is the **pretest-posttest randomized control group design**. By assigning participants at random to groups, we are assured that there are no biases in the assignment.[2] That is, the two groups of participants are equal except for random differences.

If the experimental group makes greater gains from pretest to posttest than the control group in Design 1 *and* if we have treated the two groups the same in all respects except for the experimental treatment, we can attribute the difference to only one of two causes: (1) the treatment or (2) random errors. As you will see in Part F of this book, we can use inferential statistics to assess the role of random errors in creating any differences we observe. Thus, we can tolerate random errors because we can interpret the results in light of their possible effects. There are no generalizable statistical techniques for assessing the influence of bias. Hence, we strive to avoid bias in the assignment to the two conditions (i.e., experimental and control conditions).

We can simplify the representation of Design 1 by using symbols suggested by Campbell and Stanley: R (which stands for random assignment to groups), O (which stands for observation or measurement, whether pretest or posttest), and X (which stands for experimental treatment). There is no

symbol for "control condition," so it is represented by a blank. Note that a control condition may include some type of treatment (in education, it might be a traditional form of instruction; in medicine, it might be a placebo—a sugar pill). Thus, the control condition is the standard by which we will judge the effectiveness of the experimental treatment. Using symbols, Design 1 looks like this:

$$R \quad O \quad X \quad O$$
$$R \quad O \quad \quad \ O$$

The advantage of using a pretest is that it permits us to determine how much each group has *gained*, not just whether they are different at the end of the experiment. However, sometimes having a pretest causes a problem because it can sensitize participants to the experimental treatment and in effect become part of the treatment. For instance, by taking a pretest at the beginning of an experimental course of instruction, participants can gain an overview of what will be covered, in how much depth the material will be covered, and so on. Thus, changes we observe in the experimental group may be the result of a *combination of the pretest and the treatment*. This problem is called **pretest sensitization** (also called the **reactive effect of testing**). It can be overcome by conducting an experiment without a pretest, as is shown in Design 2, which is the **posttest-only randomized control group design**.

Design 2:

$$R \quad X \quad O$$
$$R \quad \quad \ O$$

At first, the lack of a pretest may seem to be a flaw, but remember that the comparability of the two groups in Design 1 was achieved by assigning participants at random to the two groups. This initial comparability is also achieved in Design 2 by this process. In other words, it is not the pretest that makes the two groups comparable. Rather, it is the random assignment that does this.

We can have the best of both designs by using the **Solomon randomized four-group design**, which is a combination of Designs 1 and 2. Solomon's design is shown in Design 3. Because it has four rows of symbols, it has four groups. The first two rows are the same as Design 1, while the bottom two rows are the same as Design 2. In effect,

[1] Campbell, D. T., & Stanley, J. C. (1963). *Experimental and quasi-experimental designs for research*. Chicago: Rand McNally.
[2] See Topic 20 for a discussion of how to select participants at random. If we select half of them at random to be the experimental group and make the rest the control group, we have used random assignment to groups.

the Solomon design is two experiments conducted at the same time.

Design 3:

```
R   O   X   O
R   O       O
R       X   O
R           O
```

The advantage of Design 3 is that we can compare the first two groups to determine how much gain is made, and we can also compare the last two groups to determine whether the treatment is more effective than the control condition in the absence of a pretest (without pretest sensitization). The only potential drawback to Design 3 is that a researcher must begin with a reasonably large pool of participants so that when they are divided into four groups, each of the groups will have a sufficient number to yield reliable results. How many is enough? The answer is complex, but generally speaking, it probably would be unwise to use the four-group design instead of a two-group design if you have a total pool of fewer than 48 participants.

All three of the above designs are called **true experimental designs**. True experimental designs are easy to spot because they all are characterized by random assignment to treatments.

Note that sometimes it is not possible to assign participants at random. For instance, for ethical and legal reasons, we might not be able to withhold a particular treatment from individuals. In such a case, we might treat an entire group with a treatment mandated by law and use another group that is not required to have the treatment as the control group. Because the participants were *not* assigned at random to treatments, such experiments are *not* true experiments.

EXERCISE ON TOPIC 34

1. What is the purpose of an experiment?

2. How can we ensure that there are no biases in the assignment of participants to groups in an experiment?

3. In a diagram for an experimental design, the symbol "O" stands for what?

4. In a diagram for an experimental design, the symbol "X" stands for what?

5. What is the name of the potential problem caused by the pretest in the pretest-posttest randomized control group design?

6. What is the name of the true experimental design that has no pretests?

7. What is a potential drawback to the Solomon randomized four-group design?

8. True experimental designs are easy to spot because they all are characterized by what?

Question for Discussion

9. Briefly describe an experimental problem for which you probably would not be able to assign participants at random to conditions.

For Students Who Are Planning Research

10. Will you be conducting an experiment? If so, will you be using a true experimental design? Explain.

Suppose we observe significant changes in participants' behavior in an experiment. Can we attribute these changes to the effects of the treatment(s)? Depending on the design of the experiment, there may be explanations for the changes other than the treatment. These alternative explanations are called **threats to internal validity**. It is easiest to understand them in the context of a poor experiment with no control group (specifically, one in which we pretest, treat, and then posttest one group of participants). Using the symbols described in the previous topic, the design looks like this:

$$O \quad X \quad O$$

Suppose the treatment (X) was designed to improve participants' self-concept, and we observe an average gain of 9 points in self-concept from pretest (the first O) to posttest (the second O). Of course, the treatment could be responsible for the increase. Another possibility is the internal threat called **history** (i.e., other environmental influences on the participants between the pretest and posttest). For example, perhaps some of the participants read a new self-help book that improved their self-concepts during the same period of time that the treatment was being administered. Thus, the gain could have resulted from reading the book and not from the treatment.

Another threat in this design is **maturation**. Perhaps the participants matured during the period between the pretest and posttest, and the increase is due to maturation and not the treatment.

Instrumentation is another threat. This refers to possible changes in the instrument (measurement procedure) from the time it was used as a pretest to the time it was used as a posttest. For instance, the particular observers who made the pretest observations may have been less astute at noticing signs of good self-concept than the observers who made the posttest observations.

Another threat is **testing**, which is defined as the effects of the pretest on the performance exhibited on the posttest. For example, while taking the pretest self-concept scale, students may have learned how to interpret the questions. Their posttest performance might be affected by this learning experience.

Statistical regression is another threat that occurs only if participants are selected on the basis of their extreme scores. For example, perhaps a large group of students was administered a self-concept scale, and those in the lowest 20% were selected for treatment in the experiment. A fundamental principle of measurement is that those who are extremely low on a screening test will, on the average, probably have a higher score when tested again, purely because of the nature of random errors created by the less-than-perfect reliability of the measures we use—whether or not the treatment is effective.[1]

The next threat to internal validity can occur when we have two comparison groups that are *not* formed at random. Suppose for example we use the students in one school as the experimental group and those in another as the control group. Because students are not assigned to schools at random, we are using **intact groups** (i.e., previously existing symbols for the groups). We diagram this by putting a dashed line between the symbols for the groups, which indicates that the groups were intact, as shown here:

$$\begin{array}{ccc} O & X & O \\ \hline O & & O \end{array}$$

Notice that when we do not assign participants to the two groups at random, there is a very strong possibility that the two groups are not initially the same in all important respects, which is the threat called **selection**. Selection can *interact* with all the other threats to internal validity. For example, consider **selection–history interaction**. Because the selection of participants for the two groups was not at random, they may be systematically subjected to different life experiences. For example, it may be that the teachers in the school with the experimental group took a self-concept workshop, which was not part of the treatment, and applied what they learned to their students. Thus, the improvement in self-concepts may be the result of the teachers' efforts and not of the treatment. Another example is **selection–maturation interaction**. Perhaps the two groups, on the average, were at somewhat different developmental stages at the time of the pretest, which would have led to different rates of matura-

---

[1] Statistical regression is hard to grasp unless you have a good background in measurement theory. However, you may recall from your study of other sciences the principle of "regression toward the mean." Those who are very low will, on the average, tend to be higher on retesting (closer to the mean—an average), and those who are very high will tend to be lower on retesting.

tion in the two groups, which could affect self-concept.

Selection can also interact with a threat called **mortality** (i.e., differential loss of participants from the groups to be compared). For example, those in an experimental school may have a higher dropout rate than those in a control school. If those who drop out have lower self-concepts, the posttest mean for the experimental group will be higher than the pretest mean, resulting in a statistical change in the average that is not the result of the treatment. At the same time, the control group will not have as much of a change because it has a lower dropout rate.

All threats to internal validity can be overcome by using a **true experimental design** (see Topic 34), in which participants are assigned at random to experimental and control conditions. Because random assignment has no bias (or favorites), both groups are equally likely to experience the same environmental events (have the same history), mature at the same rates, drop out at the same rates, and so on.

EXERCISE ON TOPIC 35

1. What is the name of the threat that says taking a pretest may affect performance on a posttest?

2. Suppose that an experimental group is being taught letters of the alphabet as a treatment. At about the same time, the students are watching an educational program on television, from which they learn the names of the letters. What is the name of the threat that this problem illustrates?

3. If observers are more tired and less astute when making posttest observations than when making pretest observations, what threat is operating?

4. What is the name of the threat posed by nonrandom assignment of participants to experimental and control groups?

5. If infants naturally improve in visual acuity and thus perform better at the end of an experiment than at the beginning, what threat is operating?

6. Under what circumstance will statistical regression operate?

7. How can we overcome all the threats to internal validity?

Question for Discussion

8. Suppose a researcher gave a series of wellness workshops over a six-month period and then determined that five of the employees had quit smoking during the six-month period. His or her interpretation was that the workshops caused the decrease in smoking. Is this interpretation flawed? Explain.

For Students Who Are Planning Research

9. If you will be conducting an experiment, which threats, if any, will it be subject to? Explain.

Consider this example: You drew a sample from a population and divided it into an experimental group and a control group. To conduct the experiment, you administered the experimental treatment and control condition in a laboratory on a college campus. Suppose the results of your experiment showed that the experimental group improved significantly more than the control group. Can you accurately **generalize** from the sample to the population (i.e., is it accurate to assume that the treatment administered to the experimental group will work as well in the population as it did in the sample)? Also, will the treatment be as effective in the population's natural setting as it was in the artificial laboratory setting? The answers depend on the extent to which the experiment is subject to what researchers call **threats to external validity**.

The first threat is **selection bias** and its interaction with the experimental (independent) variable. You probably recall from Part C of this book that if a sample is biased, our ability to generalize to a population is greatly limited. In a very strict, scientific sense, no generalizations should be made when this is the case. This threat reminds us that if a biased sample of participants is used in an experiment (such as using the students who happen to be in one professor's class), we will not know whether the effects of the treatment (observed in that class) can be expected if the treatment is administered to the entire population. Of course, the way to control this threat is to select the participants for an experiment at random from a population because a random sample is, by definition, unbiased.

Another threat is the **reactive effects of experimental arrangements**. This threat reminds us that if the experimental setting is different from the natural setting in which the population usually operates, the effects we observe in the experimental setting may not generalize to the natural setting. For example, if a treatment is administered in a laboratory to fifth-graders, the responsiveness of the students may be different from the responsiveness of the population of fifth-graders when the treatment is used in public school classroom settings. In other words, it can be risky to generalize from an experimental setting to a natural setting. The way to control this threat is to conduct experiments under natural conditions, when possible.

The possible **reactive effect of testing** (also called **pretest sensitization**) is another threat. This means that the pretest might influence how the participants respond to the experimental treatment. For example, if we give a pretest on racial prejudice and then administer a treatment designed to lessen prejudice, how participants respond to the treatment may be affected by the experience of taking the pretest. That is, having to think about prejudice (while taking the pretest) might change participants' sensitivity to the treatment. This is a problem if we want to generalize about how well the treatment will work in the population *if* the population will not be given a pretest. This threat was discussed in Topic 34, where you learned that we can conduct true experiments without pretests, thereby eliminating this threat.

Multiple-treatment interference is a threat that occurs when a group of participants is given more than one treatment. For example, at first we might give participants no praise for correct answers, then start giving them moderate amounts of praise, and finally give them large amounts of praise. Suppose we find that large amounts of praise work best. Will it work in the same way in the population? Our generalization will be risky if those in the population will *not* first be given the no-praise condition, then the moderate-praise condition, and finally, large amounts of praise. In other words, the fact that these participants first received small and then moderate amounts of praise might make their responses to large amounts of praise different from the responses of a population that will receive *only* large amounts of praise.

Take care to distinguish between **internal validity** (see Topic 35) and **external validity**. As you know from this topic, the external validity of an experiment is concerned with, "To whom and under what circumstances can the results be generalized?" Internal validity is concerned with the question, "Is the treatment, *in this particular case*, responsible for the observed change(s)?" Thus, threats to internal validity are potential explanations for the observed changes. That is, they are possible explanations that become **confounded**[1] with the treatment as an explanation for any observed changes. Threats to internal validity are controlled by using *true experimental designs* (see Topic 34).

---

[1] *To confound* has many meanings. In this context, it means *to throw into confusion*.

Note that internal and external validity are separate considerations. Even if an experiment has excellent internal validity, it may not be appropriate to generalize the results to other populations because of the threats to external validity discussed in this topic. Likewise, a study with high external validity might have poor internal validity because the threats to internal validity have confounded our understanding of what caused the observed changes. Thus, each one of these two types of threats should be considered and evaluated independently.

EXERCISE ON TOPIC 36

1. Which type of validity deals with the question of whether we can generalize with confidence to a larger population in a natural setting?

2. Which type of validity deals with whether the treatment is responsible for the changes observed in the experimental setting?

3. What is the name of the threat that warns us to be careful in generalizing the results to a population when an experiment is conducted on a nonrandom sample?

4. Suppose a random sample of workers in a factory is exposed to five different reward systems, with each system being used for one month. What is the name of the threat that reminds us that the results may not generalize to the population of workers if the population is to be exposed to only the last reward system tried in the experiment?

5. Suppose an experimental classroom has research observers present at all times. What is the name of the threat that reminds us that the results may not generalize to other classrooms without observers?

6. If a pretest causes a change in participants' sensitivity to a treatment, what threat is operating?

Question for Discussion

7. Briefly describe a hypothetical experiment that has high internal validity but low external validity.

For Students Who Are Planning Research

8. If you will be conducting an experiment, which threats to external validity, if any, will it be subject to? Explain.

TOPIC 37   PRE-EXPERIMENTAL DESIGNS

The three designs we will examine in this topic are of very limited value for investigating cause-and-effect relationships because of their poor internal validity. Thus, they are called **pre-experimental designs**. We have already seen one of them in Topic 35: the **one-group pretest–posttest design**. Its diagram is shown here as Design 4.[1]

Design 4:

O   X   O

You may recall from Topic 35 that changes from pretest to posttest in Design 4 may be attributable to *history, maturation, instrumentation, testing,* and, if the participants were selected on the basis of extreme scores, *statistical regression*[2] (see Topic 35 for a discussion of these threats to internal validity). These threats are possible explanations for any changes observed from the pretest to the posttest. Of course, what we want to determine is what changes, if any, the treatment (X) caused. Thus, the interpretation of pretest to posttest change is *confounded* by multiple explanations.

Design 5 is called the **one-shot case study**. In it, one group is given a treatment (X) followed by a test (O). This is its diagram:

Design 5:

X   O

If a teacher provides instruction on a unit of material and follows it with an achievement test, he or she is using Design 5. For instructional purposes, there is nothing wrong with this design. For instance, the posttest will help the teacher determine what grades to assign for students' achievements on the unit of instruction. However, if we want to know whether the instruction *caused* whatever achievement we see on the test, the design is useless because it fails to make comparisons. We cannot determine whether the students achieved anything

as a result of the instruction without a pretest (or a randomly selected control group). In other words, for all we know, the achievement they display on the posttest is at the same level they might have displayed on a pretest, if there had been one.[3]

Design 6, the **static-group comparison design**, has two groups, but participants are not assigned to the groups at random. The dashed line between the two groups indicates they are **intact groups** (i.e., previously existing groups that were not formed at random).

Design 6:

$$X \quad O$$
$$\text{-----------}$$
$$O$$

The obvious problem with Design 6 is the threat to internal validity called *selection* (the selection of the two groups was not made in such a way that we can have confidence that they are initially the same in all important respects).[4] Furthermore, without a pretest, we do not have a basis for knowing whether the two groups were similar at the beginning of the experiment. For instance, the treatment might have been totally ineffective, but the experimental group might have been superior to the control group at the beginning of the experiment and retained the same amount of superiority throughout the experiment. This initial superiority would produce a difference in favor of the experimental group in the posttest results, which could trick us into assuming that the treatment caused the difference.[5]

Because of their weaknesses, the three pre-experimental designs are of very limited value in exploring cause-and-effect relationships. However, they are sometimes useful in *preliminary pilot studies* in which our goal is to try out potential treatments and measuring tools to learn more about their

---

[1] Each of the designs in this part is given a number for reference in class discussions. The numbering system is not a universal one. Thus, in discussions outside of class, refer to the names of the designs given in boldfaced type, not to the design numbers.

[2] Campbell and Stanley (1963) note that this design is also subject to the *interaction of selection with history, maturation,* etc. See Campbell, D. T., & Stanley, J. C. (1963). *Experimental and quasi-experimental designs for research.* Chicago: Rand McNally.

[3] Campbell and Stanley (1963) note that this design is subject to the internal threats of history, maturation, selection, and mortality.

[4] Campbell and Stanley (1963) note that this design is also subject to the internal threats of mortality and the interaction of selection with history, maturation, etc.

[5] You may recall from Topic 34 that a pretest is not essential in a two-group design *if* the participants are assigned at random to the groups because the random assignment assures that the two groups are initially the same *except for random differences,* which can be assessed with inferential statistics. See the discussion of Design 2 in Topic 34.

acceptability and accuracy, not to ferret out causal relationships. For example, we might administer a new drug to a small group of participants in order to observe for side effects, to determine the maximum tolerable dosage, to explore different routes of administration, and so on. The results can be used in planning a subsequent true experiment on the effects of the drug, using a design that has a randomized control group (see Topic 34).

EXERCISE ON TOPIC 37

1. Are pre-experimental designs useful for identifying cause-and-effect relationships?

2. Suppose we gave a new program to all students in a school. At the end of the school year, we administered a standardized test to the students in the school as well as to students in another school who were serving as a control group. Is the comparison of the average scores for the two groups of students useful for determining the effects of the program?

3. What is the name of the pre-experimental design used in Question 2?

4. If a researcher gives a pretest on knowledge of child abuse to a group of social workers, then gives them a series of seminars on child abuse followed by a posttest, what is the name of the pre-experimental design he or she used?

5. Is the design used in Question 4 useful for determining cause-and-effect relationships?

Questions for Discussion

6. Suppose we selected participants at random from a population and then used the one-group pretest–posttest design. Would random selection make this design good for exploring cause-and-effect relationships?

7. Have you ever used a pre-experimental design in any of your professional or everyday activities (e.g., try doing something in a new way and observing for its effects without a control group)? If so, briefly describe it. Discuss whether you shed light on a cause-and-effect relationship.

For Students Who Are Planning Research

8. If you will be conducting an experiment, will you be using a pre-experimental design? If yes, explain why you will be using such a design given that it has serious weaknesses.

TOPIC 38 QUASI-EXPERIMENTAL DESIGNS

As you know from Topic 34, true experimental designs, which involve random assignment to treatment conditions, are excellent for exploring cause-and-effect relationships. Often, however, it is not possible to assign participants at random. When this is the case, pre-experimental designs (see Topic 37) should be avoided. Instead, **quasi-experimental designs**, which are of intermediate value for exploring cause-and-effect, should be used.[1]

Design 7, which is diagrammed again immediately below, was first discussed in Topic 35, where we considered threats to internal validity. It is a widely used quasi-experimental design that has two intact groups (not assigned at random as indicated by the dashed line). This is the **nonequivalent control group design**, which we will call Design 7.

Design 7:

$$O \quad X \quad O$$
$$\overline{}$$
$$O \qquad O$$

You may recall from Topic 35 that this design is subject to the threats of *mortality*, *selection*, and *interaction of selection* with other threats such as *history*. Thus, it is far from ideal but superior to the pre-experimental designs, which are not directly interpretable in terms of causal effects. When random assignment to groups is not possible, Design 7 may provide useful results.

Even though participants are not assigned at random to the two groups in Design 7, researchers often use some form of matching to increase the internal validity of the results. For example, in studying the effects of patients' satisfaction with their experiences in hospitals, the patients in one hospital that is undergoing organizational change might be designated as the "experimental group" while the patients in another hospital that is not undergoing organizational change might be designated as the "control group." To form matched groups, we might select a sample from the first hospital and determine their status on these demographics: medical condition, age, gender, and socioeconomic status. Then, we could handpick participants from the other hospital who are similar in terms of the

same demographics. Although this is better than using unmatched samples from both hospitals, there is still the danger that the two groups may not have been matched on all relevant variables. For instance, in this example, we have not taken into account whether the patients have insurance or not. Those with insurance and those without insurance may be fundamentally different in their views of patient satisfaction. Obviously, assigning participants at random to the two conditions (using a true experimental design) would be vastly superior because the random assignment would assure us that the two groups were initially the same on *all variables* except for random differences, whose effects can be assessed with inferential statistics, a topic that is considered in detail in Part F of this book.

Design 8, which is known as the **equivalent time-samples design**, has only one group (or possibly only one participant). Treatment conditions are alternated (preferably on a random basis), as indicated in the diagram by alternating X_1 (an experimental treatment) with X_o (a control condition or comparison treatment).

Design 8:

$$X_oO \quad X_1O \quad X_oO \quad X_1O$$

The participants in Design 8 are, in effect, serving as both the control participants (when they are receiving X_o) and the experimental participants (when they are receiving X_1). This is a major advantage because we know the experimental participants and control participants (who are actually the same individuals) are identical in their genetic characteristics, income level, attitudes, beliefs—in fact, in all ways—at the beginning of the experiment. A major disadvantage of this design is the strong possibility of *multiple-treatment interference*. In this case, the second time the participants receive X_1, they have already been exposed to and possibly changed by the earlier exposure to X_1O.

Notice that giving the treatments repeatedly strengthens internal validity because it is unlikely that these threats to internal validity are operating only at the times when X_1 is given but not when X_o is given. For example, it is unlikely that participants mature only at X_1 and not at X_o. Similarly, it is unlikely that *history* confounds the interpretation by causing changes only when X_1 is given.

In psychology, a single-group design in which treatments are alternated is often called an ABAB

---

[1] Only the two most widely used quasi-experimental designs are presented in this topic. For a discussion of others, see Campbell, D. T., & Stanley, J. C. (1963). *Experimental and quasi-experimental designs for research.* Chicago: Rand McNally.

design, where A and B indicate alternating treatments. Typically, when this design is used, there are multiple initial observations before any treatment is given. These initial observations constitute the **baseline**, which determines the typical variation in the behavior of participants over time before any intervention. For example, perhaps we plan to give rewards for in-seat behavior in a classroom to a hyperactive child. We could measure the amount of out-of-seat behavior on a daily basis for a number of days to determine the natural amount of variation from day to day without treatment. Then, when we introduce the rewards, any changes we see after treatment can be evaluated in terms of the natural variation before treatment. In other words, the researcher would ask: Is the decrease in out-of-seat behavior after treatment greater than the natural day-to-day decreases (and increases) observed during the baseline?

EXERCISE ON TOPIC 38

1. What is the name of the design diagrammed immediately below?

O X O

O   O

2. In the design shown in Question 1, what indicates that the participants were not assigned at random to the groups?

3. If we use matching to form the two groups in the design in Question 1, would the resulting experiment be superior to a true experiment?

4. What is a major advantage of the equivalent time-samples design?

5. What is a major disadvantage of the equivalent time-samples design?

6. In psychology, what is an ABAB design?

Question for Discussion

7. Suppose you observed two classes for baseline data on calling-out behavior (i.e., calling out in class when it is inappropriate). In Class A, you observe much variation in the amount of calling out from day to day. In Class B, there is little variation (i.e., there is about the same amount from one day to the next). In which class would it be desirable to have a longer baseline? Why?

For Students Who Are Planning Research

8. If you will be conducting an experiment, will you be using a quasi-experimental design? If yes, which one? Why are you using a quasi-experimental design instead of a true experimental one? (See Topic 34.)

PART F

UNDERSTANDING STATISTICS

In this part, we will begin by examining the differences between the two major branches of statistics: descriptive statistics, which help us summarize and describe data we have collected, and inferential statistics, which help us make inferences from samples to the populations from which they were drawn. Then, we will consider basic statistical techniques used in analyzing the results of research.

Because this part is designed to prepare you to comprehend statistics reported in research reports, the emphasis is on understanding their meanings—not on computations. Thus, we will take a conceptual look at statistics and consider computations only when they are needed to help you understand concepts.

Important Note

The topics in this part are highly interrelated. Therefore, you are strongly advised to read the topics in this part of the book in the order presented.

NOTES

Descriptive statistics help us summarize data so they can easily be comprehended. For example, suppose we administered a test to all 362 freshmen enrolled in a university. It would be difficult to see even the major trends in an unordered list of these scores. However, if we prepare a **frequency distribution** such as the one in Table 1, we can easily see how the scores are distributed. For instance, the frequency distribution clearly indicates that a majority of the freshmen had scores from 14 through 16, with a scattering above and below these levels.

Table 1
Frequency Distribution with Percentages

Score (X)	Frequency (f)	Percentage
20	5	1.4
19	9	2.5
18	24	6.6
17	35	9.7
16	61	16.9
15	99	27.3
14	68	18.8
13	29	8.0
12	21	5.8
11	11	3.0
Total	362	100.0%

The **frequencies** in Table 1 are descriptive statistics. They describe how many students earned each score. The **percentages** are also descriptive. They describe how many students *per one hundred* had each score. For instance, 3.0% had a score of 11. This means that for each 100 freshmen, three of them have a score of 11. These and other descriptive statistics such as averages are described in this part of the book.

Now, suppose that in order to economize, we sampled at random (by drawing names out of a hat) only 100 freshmen to be tested (instead of testing all 362). Would we obtain exactly the same results as we would if we tested all freshmen? The answer is: in all likelihood, *no*. As you probably recall from Topics 19 through 22, random sampling produces random errors that statisticians call *sampling errors*. The purpose of **inferential statistics** is to help us draw inferences about the effects of sampling errors on the results that are described with descriptive statistics. More specifically, inferential statistics help us make generalizations about the characteristics of populations based on data obtained by studying samples.

One type of inferential statistic you may already be familiar with is a **margin of error**. When reporting the results of public opinion polls in the media, reporters frequently cite margins of error to help readers interpret results in light of sampling error. For instance, a recent poll indicated that approval of the president was at 52%, with a margin of error of ±2 (i.e., plus/minus 2) percentage points. This means we can be highly confident that the level of approval in the population is between 50% and 54% (i.e., within two points of the 52% observed in the sample).

An important family of inferential statistics consists of *significance tests*, which help us decide whether the differences in descriptive statistics we find in studies (such as differences in the reading achievement of samples of boys and girls) are reliable. The next topic will help you better understand the general purpose of significance testing, and in later sections, we will consider three popular tests of significance.

Because inferential statistics help us evaluate results in light of sampling errors, it follows that if we do *not* sample, we do *not* need inferential statistics. For instance, if we conduct a *census* (a study in which all members of a population are included), the descriptive statistics we obtain (such as percentages) are values that are free of sampling errors. Because margins of error, for instance, are designed to help us interpret results in light of sampling errors and because there are no sampling errors in the results obtained in a census, margins of error are not needed to assist in interpreting the results.

We distinguish between values obtained from a sample and values obtained from a census by using the terms **parameters** (for values from a census) and **statistics** (for values from studies in which samples were examined). Thus, descriptive statistics are referred to as parameters when they are derived from a census, but they are classified as statistics when they are based on the results obtained from a sample. As a mnemonic, remember the first letters shown here in italics:

Samples yield **S**tatistics, and
Populations yield **P**arameters.

EXERCISE ON TOPIC 39

1. Which branch of statistics ("inferential" *or* "descriptive") helps us summarize data so they can be easily comprehended?

2. According to Table 1 in this topic, how many participants had a score of 19?

3. What is the name of the statistic that describes how many participants per 100 have a certain characteristic?

4. Which branch of statistics helps us draw inferences about the effects of sampling errors on our results?

5. If we test a random sample instead of all members of a population, is it likely that the sample results will be the same as the results we would have obtained by testing the population?

6. Is a margin of error a "descriptive" *or* an "inferential" statistic?

7. Do "descriptive" *or* "inferential" statistics perform significance tests?

8. By studying populations, do we obtain "statistics" *or* "parameters"?

9. By studying samples, do we obtain "statistics" *or* "parameters"?

Question for Discussion

10. Keep your eye out for a report of a poll in which a margin of error is reported. Copy it and bring it to class for discussion.

For Students Who Are Planning Research

11. Will you be reporting descriptive statistics? (Note that statistics often are not reported in qualitative research. See Topics 9 and 10.)

12. Will you be reporting inferential statistics? Explain.

Suppose we drew random samples of engineers and psychologists, administered a self-report measure of sociability, and computed the mean (the most commonly used average) for each group. Furthermore, suppose the mean for engineers is 65.00 and the mean for psychologists is 70.00. Where did the five-point difference come from? There are three possible explanations:

1. Perhaps the population of psychologists is truly more sociable than the population of engineers, and our samples correctly identified the difference. (In fact, our *research hypothesis* may have been that psychologists are more sociable than engineers, which now appears to be supported by the data we collected.)

2. Perhaps there was a bias in procedures. By using random sampling, we have ruled out sampling bias, but other procedures, such as measurement, may be biased. For instance, maybe the psychologists were contacted during December, when many social events take place, and the engineers were contacted during a gloomy February. The only way to rule out bias as an explanation for the difference between the two means is to take *physical steps* to prevent it. In this case, we would want to make sure that the sociability of both groups was measured in the same way at the same time.

3. Perhaps the populations of psychologists and engineers are the same but the samples are unrepresentative of their populations because of random sampling errors. For example, the random draw may have given us a sample of psychologists who are more sociable, on the average, than their population purely by chance (at random).

The third explanation has a name: the **null hypothesis**. The general form in which it is stated varies from researcher to researcher. Here are three versions, all of which are consistent with each other:

Version A of the null hypothesis:

The observed difference was created by sampling error. (Note that the term *sampling error* refers only to *random errors*, not errors created

by a bias. There is no bias in sampling in our example because we sampled at random.)

Version B of the null hypothesis:

There is no true difference between the two groups. (The term *true difference* refers to the difference we would find in a census of the two populations. That is, the *true difference* is the difference we would find if there were no sampling errors.)

Version C of the null hypothesis:

The true difference between the two groups is zero.

Significance tests determine the probability that the null hypothesis is true. (We will be considering the use of specific significance tests in Topics 43–44 and 50–52.) Suppose for our example we conduct a significance test and find that the probability that the null hypothesis is a correct hypothesis is less than 5 in 100. This would be stated as $p < .05$, where p stands for the word *probability*. Of course, if the chances that something is true are less than 5 in 100, it is likely that it is *not* true. Thus, we would *reject the null hypothesis*, leaving us with only the first two explanations we started with as viable explanations for the difference.

There is no rule of nature that dictates at what probability level the null hypothesis should be rejected. However, conventional wisdom suggests that .05 or less (such as .01 or .001) is reasonable because there are low probabilities that it is true. Of course, researchers should state in their reports the probability level they used to determine whether to reject the null hypothesis.

Note that when we fail to reject the null hypothesis because the probability is greater than .05, we do just that: We "fail to reject" the null hypothesis, and it remains on our list of possible explanations. We *cannot* "accept" the null hypothesis as the only explanation for a difference based on inferential statistics because there are three possible explanations for a difference, and failing to reject one possible explanation (the null hypothesis) does *not* mean we are accepting it as the only explanation (because there are two explanations left on the list).

An alternative way to say we have rejected the null hypothesis is to state that the difference is **statistically significant**. Thus, if we state that a difference is statistically significant at the .05 level (meaning .05 or less), it is equivalent to stating that the null hypothesis has been rejected at that level.

When you read research reported in academic journals, you will find that the null hypothesis is seldom stated by researchers, who assume that readers know the sole purpose of a significance test is to test a null hypothesis. Instead, researchers report which differences were tested for significance, which significance test they used, and which differences were found to be statistically significant. It is more common to find null hypotheses stated in theses and dissertations because committee members may want to make sure the students they are supervising understand the reason they have conducted a significance test.

We will consider specific significance tests later in this part of the book.

EXERCISE ON TOPIC 40

1. How many explanations were there for the difference between psychologists and engineers in the example in this topic?

2. What does the null hypothesis say about sampling error?

3. Does the term *sampling error* refer to "random errors" *or* to "bias"?

4. The null hypothesis says the true difference equals what numerical value?

5. Significance tests are designed to determine the probabilities regarding the truth of what hypothesis?

6. The expression $p < .05$ stands for what words?

7. Do we reject the null hypothesis when the probability of its truth is "high" *or* when the probability is "low"?

8. What do we do if the probability is greater than .05?

9. What is an alternative way of saying we have rejected the null hypothesis?

10. Are you more likely to find a null hypothesis stated in a "journal article" *or* in a "dissertation"?

Question for Discussion

11. All individuals use probabilities in everyday activities to make decisions. For instance, before crossing a street with traffic, we estimate the odds that we will get across the street safely before beginning to cross it. Briefly describe one other specific use of probabilities in everyday decision-making.

For Students Who Are Planning Research

12. Will you be testing a null hypothesis in your research? Explain.

Topic 41   Scales of Measurement

There are four scales (or levels) at which we measure. The lowest level is the **nominal** level (also called the *nominal scale*). This may be thought of as the "naming" level. For instance, when we ask participants to name their marital status, they will respond with *words*—not numbers—such as "married," "single," "divorced," and so on. Notice that nominal data do not put participants in any particular mathematical order. There is no logical basis for saying that one category, such as "single," is higher or lower mathematically than any other category.

The next level is **ordinal**. At this level, the measurements place participants in order from high to low. For instance, an employer might rank applicants for a job on their professional appearance. Traditionally, we give a rank of 1 to the participant who is highest, 2 to the next highest, and so on. It is important to note that ranks do not tell us by how much participants differ. If we are told that Janet has a rank of 1 and Frank has a rank of 2, we do not know if Janet's appearance is greatly superior to Frank's or only slightly superior. To measure the *amount* of difference among participants, we use the next two levels of measurement.

Measurements at the **interval** and **ratio** levels have equal distances among the scores they yield. For example, when we say that Jill weighs 120 pounds and Sally weighs 130 pounds, we know by *how much* the two participants differ. Also, note that a 10-pound difference represents the same amount regardless of where participants are on the scale. For example, the difference between 120 and 130 pounds is the same as the difference between 220 and 230 pounds.

The ratio scale is at a higher level than the interval scale because the ratio scale has an absolute zero point that we know how to measure. Thus, *weight* is an example of the ratio scale because it has an absolute zero.

The interval scale, while having equal intervals like the ratio scale, does not have an absolute zero. The most common examples of interval scales are scores obtained using objective tests such as multiple-choice tests of achievement. It is widely assumed that each multiple-choice test item measures a single point's worth of the trait being measured and that all points are equal to all other points, making it an interval scale (just as all pounds are equal to all other pounds of weight). However, such tests do not measure at the ratio level because the zero on such tests is arbitrary, not absolute. To see this, consider someone who gets a zero on a multiple-choice final examination. Does the zero mean that the student has absolutely no knowledge of or skills in the subject area? Probably not. He or she probably has some knowledge of simple facts, definitions, and concepts, but the test was not designed to measure at the low skill level at which the student is operating. Thus, a score of zero indicates only that the student knows nothing *on that test*, not that the student has zero knowledge of the content domain. Thus, the scores are at the interval level, not the ratio level.

Here is a summary of the levels:

Lowest Level	Scale	Characteristic
	Nominal	*naming*
	Ordinal	*ordering*
⇩	**Interval**	*equal interval without an absolute zero*
	Ratio	*equal interval with an absolute zero*
Highest Level		

For those of you who like to use mnemonics, remember this environmentally friendly phrase:

No Oil In Rivers

The first letters—**NOIR**—are the first letters of the scales in order from lowest to highest.

At which level should we measure? First, some variables are inherently nominal in nature. For example, when we need to know participants' gender or state of residence, nominal data are the natural choice. Second, many novice researchers overuse the ordinal scale. For instance, if we want to measure reading ability, it would usually be much better to use a carefully constructed standardized test (which measures at the interval level) than having teachers rank students in terms of their reading ability. Remember, measuring at the interval level gives us more information than measuring at the ordinal level because the interval-level measurements tell us by *how much* students differ. In addition, as you will learn when we explore statistics, we can conduct more interesting and powerful types of analyses when we measure at the interval rather than at the ordinal level. Thus, if you are thinking in terms of having participants ranked (for ordinal measurement) when planning a research project, consider whether there is an alternative way to measure the trait at the interval level.

The choice between interval and ratio depends solely on whether it is possible to measure with an absolute zero. When it is possible, we usually do so.

For the purposes of applied statistical analyses, however, interval and ratio data are treated in the same way.

The level at which we measure has important implications for data analysis, so you will find references to scales of measurement throughout the discussion of statistics in subsequent topics in this book.

EXERCISE ON TOPIC 41

1. If we ask participants to name the country in which they were born, we are using which scale of measurement?

2. Which two scales of measurement have equal distances among the scores they yield?

3. If we have a teacher rank students according to their oral language skills, we are using which scale of measurement?

4. Which scale of measurement has an absolute zero?

5. Which scale of measurement is at the lowest level?

6. Objective, multiple-choice achievement tests are usually assumed to measure at what level?

7. If we measure in such a way that we find out which participant is most honest, which is the next most honest, and so on (without measuring to determine how much honesty each one has), we are measuring at what scale of measurement?

8. The number of minutes of overtime work that employees perform is an example of which scale of measurement?

9. Weight measured in pounds is an example of which scale of measurement?

Question for Discussion

10. Name a trait that inherently lends itself to nominal measurement. Explain your answer.

For Students Who Are Planning Research

11. List the measures you will be using in your research, and name the scale of measurement for each one.

TOPIC 42   DESCRIPTIONS OF NOMINAL DATA

We obtain *nominal data* when we classify participants according to names (words) instead of quantities. For example, suppose we asked each member of a population of 540 teachers which candidate he or she prefers for a school board vacancy and found that 258 preferred Smith and 282 preferred Jones. The 258 and 282 are *frequencies*, whose symbol is *f*. We can also refer to them as **numbers of cases**, whose symbol is *N*.

We can convert the numbers of cases into *percentages* by dividing the number who prefer each candidate by the number in the population and multiplying by 100. Thus, for Smith, the calculations are:

$$258 \div 540 = 0.478 \times 100 = 47.8\%$$

When reporting percentages, it is desirable to also report the underlying numbers of cases, which is done in Table 1.

Table 1
Teachers' Preferences

Candidate	Percentage
Jones	52.2% (N = 282)
Smith	47.8% (N = 258)
Total	100.0%

Table 1 is an example of **univariate analysis**. We are analyzing how people *vary* (hence, we use the root *variate*) on only *one* variable (hence, we use the prefix *uni-*).

We can examine a relationship between two nominal variables by conducting a **bivariate analysis**. Perhaps we want to know whether there is a relationship between teachers' gender and their preferences for candidates. Table 2 shows the results of a bivariate analysis of these variables.

The data in Table 2 clearly indicate that there is a relationship between gender and the preferences for the two candidates because a larger percentage of males than females prefers Jones, but a larger percentage of females than males prefers Smith. Another way to put this is that teachers' gender is predictive of their preferences. For instance, by knowing a teacher is male, we would predict that he is more likely to vote for Jones than to vote for Smith.

Table 2
Teachers' Preferences By Gender

Gender	Jones	Smith	Total
Male	66.4% (N = 85)	33.6% (N = 43)	100.0% (N = 128)
Female	47.8% (N = 197)	52.2% (N = 215)	100.0% (N = 412)

Note that in this population of teachers, there are many more female teachers than male teachers. When this is the case, we can be misled by examining only the numbers of cases (e.g., 85 males for Jones versus 197 females for Jones). However, in fact, a *majority* of the population of males (the smaller population) is in favor of Jones but only a *minority* of the larger population of females is in favor of him. With percentages, legitimate comparisons of groups of unequal size are possible. This is because percentages convert numbers of cases to a common scale, with a base of 100. (The percentage of 66.4% of males for Jones indicates that *for every 100 males*, 66.4 of them are in favor of Jones while the percentage of 47.8% of females for Jones indicates that *for every 100 females*, only 47.8 of them are in favor of Jones.)

In academic writing, some researchers report **proportions** instead of *percentages*. For example, a percentage of 47.8% in favor of Smith in Table 1 corresponds to a proportion of 0.478 or 0.48. (Proportions are calculated in the same way percentages are except for the multiplication by 100. That is, $258 \div 540 = 0.478 = 0.48$.) Because a proportion has a base of 1, a proportion of 0.48 means that for every *one* participant, 48 hundredths of each participant favors Smith. Clearly, proportions are harder to comprehend than percentages. When you encounter proportions in research reports, it is a good idea to convert them mentally to percentages. That is, think of the proportion of 0.48 as 48% (i.e., the percentage you get by multiplying 0.48 by 100).

In the next topic, we will consider how to analyze nominal data in studies in which we have sampled at random and need to take account of random sampling errors when interpreting univariate data. In Topic 44, we will consider the analysis of bivariate data.

EXERCISE ON TOPIC 42

1. If 400 people in a population of 1,000 are Democrats, what is the percentage who are Democrats?

2. When reporting a percentage, is it a good idea to also report the underlying number of cases?

3. Do we use "univariate" *or* "bivariate" analyses to examine relationships between two nominal variables?

4. Percentages for different groups are expressed on a common scale with what base?

5. What is the base for a proportion?

6. Are "percentages" *or* "proportions" easier for most people to comprehend?

7. When you encounter proportions in literature, it is a good idea to do what?

Question for Discussion

8. Try to locate a report in the popular press in which percentages are reported. Bring a copy to class. Be prepared to discuss whether the frequencies are also reported and whether the analysis is univariate *or* bivariate.

For Students Who Are Planning Research

9. Will you be measuring one or more variables at the nominal level? Explain.

10. Will you be reporting percentages?

11. Will you do a univariate analysis? A bivariate analysis? Explain.

TOPIC 43 INTRODUCTION TO THE CHI SQUARE TEST

Suppose we drew at random a sample of 200 members of an association of sociologists and asked them whether they were in favor of a proposed change to their bylaws. The results are shown in Table 1. Note that these *observed results* are not necessarily the *true results*[1] we would have obtained if we had questioned the entire population. Remember that the null hypothesis (see Topic 40) asserts that any observed difference was created by random sampling errors (i.e., in the population, the true difference is zero). Put another way, the null hypothesis states that the observed difference ($n = 120$ vs. $n = 80$) is an *illusion* created by random errors created by random sampling (i.e., sampling errors).

Table 1
Members' Approval of a Change in Bylaws

Response	Percentage
Yes	60.0%
	($n = 120$)
No	40.0%
	($n = 80$)
Total	100.0%

The usual test of the null hypothesis when we are considering frequencies (i.e., number of cases or *n*) is **chi square**, whose symbol is:

$$\chi^2$$

After doing some computations for the data in Table 1 (which are beyond the scope of this book), the results are:

$$\chi^2 = 4.00, df = 1, p < .05$$

What does this mean for a consumer of research who sees this in a report? The values of chi square and degrees of freedom (*df*) were calculated solely to obtain the probability that the null hypothesis is correct. In other words, chi square and degrees of freedom are *not* descriptive statistics you should attempt to interpret. Rather, think of them as substeps in the mathematical procedure for obtaining the value of *p*. Thus, a consumer of research should

concentrate on the fact that *p* is *less than* .05. As you probably recall from Topic 40, when the probability (*p*) that the null hypothesis is correct is .05 or less, we reject the null hypothesis. (Remember, when the probability that something is true is less than 5 in 100, which is a low probability, conventional wisdom suggests we should reject it.) Thus, the difference we observe in Table 1 was probably not created by random sampling errors. Therefore, we can say that the difference is *statistically significant* at the .05 level.

So far, we have concluded that the difference we observed in the sample was *probably not* created by sampling errors. So where did the difference come from? These two possibilities remain:

1. Perhaps there was a bias in procedures, such as the interviewer asking the question in the survey leading the respondents by talking enthusiastically about the proposed change in the bylaws. Thus, the sample would no longer be representative of the population because the interviewer biased the respondents.

   If we are convinced that adequate measures were taken to prevent procedural bias, we are left only with the next possibility as a viable explanation.

2. Perhaps the *population* of sociologists is, in fact, in favor of the proposed change, and this fact is correctly identified by studying the random sample.

Now, consider some results from a survey in which the null hypothesis was *not* rejected. Table 2 shows the numbers and percentages of participants in a random sample from a population of teachers who prefer each of three methods for teaching reading.

Table 2
Teachers' Preferences for Methods

Method A	Method B	Method C
$n = 30$	$n = 27$	$n = 22$
(37.97%)	(34.18%)	(27.85%)

In Table 2, there are three differences: **(1)** 30 preferring A versus 27 preferring B, **(2)** 30 preferring A versus 22 preferring C, and **(3)** 27 preferring B versus 22 preferring C. The null hypothesis says that this *set of three differences* was created by ran-

---

[1] We are using the term *true results* here to stand for the results of a census of the entire population. The results of a census are *true* in the sense that they are free of *sampling errors*.

dom sampling errors. In other words, it says that there is no true difference in the population—that we have observed a difference only because of sampling errors. The results of the chi square test for the data in Table 2 are:

$$\chi^2 = 1.214, \, df = 2, \, p > .05$$

Note that p is *greater than* (>) .05. Using the decision rule that p must be equal to or less than .05 to reject the null hypothesis, we will *not* reject the null hypothesis (i.e., fail to reject it), which is called a *statistically insignificant* result. In other words, the null hypothesis must remain on our list as a viable

explanation for the set of differences we observed by studying a sample. Put another way, the probability that sampling error created the difference is too great for us to reject it as a possibility.

In this topic, we have considered the use of chi square in a *univariate analysis* in which we classify each participant in only one way (such as which candidate each prefers). In the next topic, we will consider its use in *bivariate analysis* in which we classify each participant in two ways (such as which candidate each prefers *and* the gender of each) in order to examine a relationship between the two nominal variables.

EXERCISE ON TOPIC 43

1. When we study a sample, are the results called the "true results" *or* the "observed results"?

2. According to the null hypothesis, what created the difference in Table 1 in this topic?

3. What is the name of the test of the null hypothesis used in this topic?

4. As a consumer of research, should you try to interpret the value of *df*?

5. What is the symbol for *probability*?

6. If you read that a chi square test of a difference yielded a *p* of less than 5 in 100, on the basis of conventional wisdom, what should you conclude about the null hypothesis?

7. Does "*p* < .05" *or* "*p* > .05" usually lead a researcher to declare a difference to be statistically significant?

8. If we fail to reject a null hypothesis, is the difference in question statistically significant?

9. If we have a statistically insignificant result, does the null hypothesis remain on our list of viable hypotheses?

Question for Discussion

10. Briefly describe a hypothetical study in which it would be appropriate to conduct a chi square test for univariate data.

For Students Who Are Planning Research

11. Will you be conducting a univariate chi square test in your research? Explain.

Topic 44   A Closer Look at the Chi Square Test

In this topic, we will examine the use of the chi square test in a *bivariate analysis* (i.e., an analysis in which each participant is classified in terms of two variables in order to examine the relationship between them). Consider an example. Suppose we conducted an experiment in which three methods of job training were tried with welfare recipients. Random samples of recipients were drawn for each method, and the number who obtained jobs by the end of the training sessions was determined. The resulting data are shown in Table 1.

Table 1
Training Methods and Job Placement

Job?	Method A	Method B	Method C
Yes	$n = 20$	$n = 15$	$n = 9$
	(66.7%)	(51.7%)	(31.0%)
No	$n = 10$	$n = 14$	$n = 20$
	(33.3%)	(48.3%)	(69.0%)

Clearly, the statistics in Table 1 suggest there is a relationship between which method of job training was used and the outcome (whether or not participants got jobs); that is because we have observed that Method A is superior to Methods B and C and that Method B is superior to Method C. A stumbling block in our interpretation of these results is the *null hypothesis*, which says there is no true difference (i.e., if all members of the population had been studied, we would have found no differences among the three methods). For example, quite by the luck of the random draw, recipients who were more employable to begin with (before treatment) were assigned to Method A, while the less employable, by chance, were assigned to the other two methods. We can test the null hypothesis by using the chi square test.

For the data shown in Table 1, this result would be shown in a report on the experiment:

$$\chi^2 = 7.54, df = 2, p < .05$$

As you know from the previous topics, we reject the null hypothesis when the odds that it is true are equal to or less than .05 (i.e., $p < .05$). Thus, for this data, we reject the null hypothesis and declare the result to be significant at the .05 level. In other words, we have concluded that the observed differences that suggest a relationship between method of training and job placement are too great to be attributed to random errors (i.e., sampling errors).

Now we will consider what we mean by "the .05 level" in more detail than we have up to this point. When we reject the null hypothesis at exactly the .05 level (i.e., $p = .05$), there are 5 chances in 100 that the null hypothesis is correct. Thus, we are taking 5 chances in 100 of being *wrong* by rejecting the null hypothesis at this level. Note that we can never be certain we have made the correct decision when rejecting the null hypothesis. It is always possible that the null hypothesis is true (in this case, there are 5 in 100 chances that it is true) and that we are making a mistake by rejecting it. This possibility is called a **Type I Error**. When we use the .05 level, the odds of making a Type I Error are 5 in 100; when we use the .01 level, the odds of making this type of error are 1 in 100; and when we use the .001 level, the odds of making it are 1 in 1,000.

When we fail to reject the null hypothesis, as we did in Topic 43 for the data in Table 2, we are also taking a chance that we are wrong. That is, perhaps the null hypothesis should have been rejected, but the significance test failed to lead us to the correct decision. This mistake is called a **Type II Error**.

In review, these are the two types of errors that researchers make:

Type I Error: Rejecting the null hypothesis when it is in fact a correct hypothesis.

Type II Error: Failing to reject the null hypothesis when it is in fact an incorrect hypothesis.

At first, this discussion of errors may make significance tests such as chi square seem weak because we can be wrong no matter what decision we make. However, consider the big picture. Having decided to sample at random (the desirable way to sample because it is free from bias), it is likely that random error will affect our results—at least to some extent. In light of this, we can never be *certain* about decisions based on the observed differences. Instead, we must use *probabilities* to make decisions. We use them in such a way that we *minimize* the probability that we are wrong. To do this, we usually emphasize minimizing the probability of a Type I error by using a low probability such as .05 or less. By using a low probability, we will infrequently be wrong in rejecting the null hypothesis.

EXERCISE ON TOPIC 44

1. What is the name of the type of analysis in which each participant is classified in terms of two variables in order to examine the relationship between the two variables?

2. What decision should we make about the null hypothesis if a chi square test leads us to the conclusion that the observed differences that suggest a relationship between two variables are unlikely to be due to random errors?

3. If $p = .05$ for a chi square test, chances are how many in 100 that the null hypothesis is true?

4. When we use the .01 level, what are the odds of making a Type I Error?

5. What is the name of the error we make when we fail to reject the null hypothesis when it is in fact an incorrect hypothesis?

6. What is the name of the error we make when we reject the null hypothesis when it is in fact a correct hypothesis?

7. Why is random sampling desirable even though it creates errors?

Questions for Discussion

8. Are both variables in Table 1 in this topic nominal? Explain.

9. Briefly describe a hypothetical study in which it would be appropriate to conduct a chi square test on bivariate data.

For Students Who Are Planning Research

10. Will you be using a chi square test in a bivariate analysis? Explain.

TOPIC 45 SHAPES OF DISTRIBUTIONS

One way to describe quantitative data is to prepare a *frequency distribution* such as that shown in Topic 39. It is easier to see the shape of the distribution if we prepare a figure called a **frequency polygon**. Figure 1 is a frequency polygon for the data in Topic 39.

Figure 1. Frequency polygon for data on page 97.

A frequency polygon is easy to read. For example, a score of 20 has a frequency (*f*) of 5, which is why the curve is low at a score of 20. A score of 15 has a frequency of 99, which is why the curve is high at 15.

Notice that the curve in Figure 1 is fairly symmetrical, with a high point in the middle and dropping off on the right and left. When very large samples are used, the curve often takes on an even smoother shape, such as the one shown in Figure 2.

Figure 2. The normal curve.

The smooth, bell-shaped curve in Figure 2 has a special name: the **normal curve**. Many variables in nature are normally distributed, such as the weights of grains of sand on a beach, the heights of women (or men), the annual amounts of rainfall in most areas, and so on. The list is almost limitless. Many

social and behavioral scientists also believe that mental traits of humans are probably also normally distributed.[1]

Some distributions are **skewed** (i.e., they have a tail on one side and not the other). Figure 3 shows a distribution that is *skewed to the right* (i.e., the tail is to the right). It is said to have a **positive skew**. An example of a distribution with a positive skew is income. Most people earn relatively small amounts, so the curve is high on the left. Small numbers of rich and very rich people create a tail to the right.

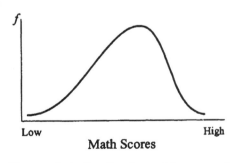

Figure 3. A distribution with a positive skew.

Figure 4 is *skewed to the left*; it has a **negative skew**. We would get a negative skew, for example, if we administered a test of basic math skills to a large sample of college seniors. Most would do very well and get almost perfect scores, but a small scattering would get lower scores for a variety of reasons, such as misunderstanding the directions for marking their answers, not feeling well the day the test was administered, and so on.

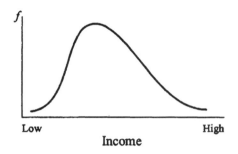

Figure 4. A distribution with a negative skew.

While there are other shapes, the three shown here are the ones you are most likely to encounter.

---

[1] Because measures of mental traits are far from perfect, it is not possible to show conclusively that mental traits are normally distributed.

Whether a distribution is normal (or close to normal) *or* skewed affects how quantitative data at the interval and ratio levels are analyzed (see Topic 41). We will consider this issue in the next topic.

To make the proper associations with the names "positive skew" and "negative skew," keep in mind a number line on which zero is in the middle. The negative values are to the left of zero. Thus, when the tail of a curve points to the left, we say it has a *negative skew*. Because the positive values on a number line are to the right, when the tail points to the right, we say the curve has a *positive skew*. Sometimes, researchers merely say "skewed to the left" to indicate a "negative skew" and "skewed to the right" to indicate a "positive skew."

EXERCISE ON TOPIC 45

1. According to Figure 1, about how many participants had a score of 16?

2. In Figure 1, are the frequencies on the "vertical" *or* "horizontal" axis?

3. What is the name of the curve that is symmetrical?

4. If a distribution has some extreme scores on the right (but not on the left), it is said to have what type of skew?

5. If a distribution is skewed to the left, does it have a "positive" *or* "negative" skew?

6. In most populations, income has what type of skew?

7. Does a distribution with a tail to the right have a "positive" *or* "negative" skew?

Question for Discussion

8. Name a population and a variable you think might have a positive skew.

For Students Who Are Planning Research

9. Do you anticipate that any of your distributions will be highly skewed? Explain.

TOPIC 46 THE MEAN, MEDIAN, AND MODE

The most frequently used average is the **mean**, which is the *balance point* in a distribution. Its computation is simple: Sum (add up) the scores and divide by the number of scores. The most common symbol for the mean in academic journals is *M* (for the mean of a population) or *m* (for the mean of a sample). The symbol preferred by statisticians is

$\overline{X}$, which is pronounced "X-bar."

Consider the formal definition of the mean: It is *the value around which the deviations sum to zero.* This definition is illustrated in Table 1, in which the mean of the scores is 4.0. When we subtract this mean from each of the other scores, we get the deviations (whose symbol is lowercase *x*). Notice that if we sum the deviations, we get zero, as shown in the last column of Table 1.

Table 1
Scores and Deviation Scores

X	minus	M	equals	x
1	–	4.0	=	–3.0
1	–	4.0	=	–3.0
1	–	4.0	=	–3.0
2	–	4.0	=	–2.0
2	–	4.0	=	–2.0
4	–	4.0	=	0.0
6	–	4.0	=	2.0
7	–	4.0	=	3.0
8	–	4.0	=	4.0
8	–	4.0	=	4.0
Sum of the deviations (x) = 0.0				

Note that if you take *any set of scores*, compute their mean, and follow the steps in Table 1, the sum of the deviations will always equal zero.[1] In other words, the mean always has this defining characteristic. If the deviations do not sum to zero, the statistic is not the mean (or a mistake was made in the computation of the mean).

Considering the formal definition, you can see why we also informally define the mean as the *balance point* in a distribution. This is because the positive and negative deviations *balance* each other out, causing the deviations to "balance out" to zero.

A major drawback of the mean is that it is drawn in the direction of extreme scores (i.e., in the direc-

tion of the skew). Consider the following two sets of scores and their means.

Scores for Group A: 1, 1, 1, 2, 3, 6, 7, 8, 8
M = 4.11

Scores for Group B: 1, 2, 2, 3, 4, 7, 9, 25, 32
M = 9.44

Notice that there are nine scores in both sets of scores, and the two distributions are very similar except for the scores of 25 and 32 in Group B, which are much higher than the others and thus create a skewed distribution. (To review skewed distributions, see Topic 45.) Also, notice that the two very high scores (i.e., 25 and 32) have greatly pulled up the mean for Group B. In fact, the mean for Group B is more than twice as high as the mean for Group A because of just the two high scores. Because seven of the nine scores for Group B are 9 or less, a mean of 9.44 is not a good estimate of the typical or "center score."

While the mean is the most frequently used average, when a distribution is highly skewed, researchers use a different average: the **median**. The median is defined as the *middle score*. To get an *approximate median*, put the scores in order from low to high as they are for Groups A and B above (from low on the left to high on the right), and then count to the middle. Because there are nine scores in Group A, the median (middle score) is 3 (five scores up from the bottom). For Group B, the median (middle score) is 4 (also five scores up from the bottom). For Group B, an average of 4 is more representative of the center of this skewed distribution than the mean, which we noted was 9.44. Thus, an important use of the median is to describe the averages of skewed distributions. Another use is to describe the average of ordinal data, which we will explore in Topic 48.

A third average, the **mode**, is simply the *most frequently occurring score*. For Group B, there are more scores of 2 (i.e., two 2s) than any other score. Thus, 2 is the mode. The mode is sometimes used in informal reporting but is very seldom used in formal reports of research. This is because the mode is unstable (i.e., unreliable). For instance, if just two individuals with scores of 9 joined the group, the mode would jump all the way from 2 to 9 because there would then be three 9s. Note that large movements in the value of an average when the

---

[1] It might be slightly off from zero if you use a rounded mean such as using 20.33 when its precise value is 20.3333333333.

sample changes slightly indicate its instability. Also, note that the mode does not always have a unique value. For instance, if one individual with a score of 3 joined Group B, there would be two modes: (a) 2 because there are two 2s and (b) 3 because there would also be two 3s. Note that the mean and median, unlike the mode, always have only one value for a given set of scores (i.e., they have unique values).

Because there is more than one type of average, it is vague to make a statement such as, "The *aver-age* is 4.11." Instead, researchers indicate the specific type of average being reported with statements such as, "The *mean* is 4.11."

Note that a synonym for the term **averages** is **measures of central tendency**. Although this term is seldom used in reports of scientific research, you will often encounter it in other research and statistics textbooks when averages are discussed.

EXERCISE ON TOPIC 46

1. Which average is defined as the *most frequently occurring score*?

2. Which average is defined as the *balance point* in a distribution?

3. Which average is defined as the *middle score*?

4. What is the formal definition of the mean?

5. How is the mean calculated?

6. Should the mean be used for highly skewed distributions?

7. Should the median be used for highly skewed distributions?

8. Which average is described in this topic as being *unstable*?

9. What is a synonym for the term *averages*?

Question for Discussion

10. Suppose a fellow student gave a report in class and said, "The average was 25.88." For what additional information should you ask? Why?

For Students Who Are Planning Research

11. Do you anticipate calculating measures of central tendency? If so, name them. Explain your choice(s).

TOPIC 47   THE MEAN AND STANDARD DEVIATION

Often, a distribution of scores is described with only two statistics: the **mean** to describe its *average* and the **standard deviation** (whose symbol is *S* or *SD* for a population, and *s* or *sd* for a sample) to describe its *variability*. The term "variability" refers to the amount by which participants *vary* or differ from each other. Let us see what this means by considering the scores of three groups, all of which have the same mean but different standard deviations.

Group A: 0, 5, 10, 15, 20, 25, 30
$M = 15.00$, $S = 10.00$

Group B: 14, 14, 14, 15, 16, 16, 16
$M = 15.00$, $S = 0.93$

Group C: 15, 15, 15, 15, 15, 15, 15
$M = 15.00$, $S = 0.00$

Although Groups A, B, and C are the same on the average, as indicated by the mean, they are very different in terms of variability. Notice that the differences among the scores of Group A (a score of 0 vs. a score of 5 vs. a score of 10 vs. a score of 15, and so on) are much greater than the differences among the scores of Group B (a score of 14 vs. a score of 14 vs. a score of 14 vs. a score of 15, and so on). At the extreme, when all the scores are the same, as in Group C, there is no variability. As a result, the standard deviation equals zero. Thus, as a rule, the smaller the variability, the smaller the standard deviation.[1]

The standard deviation has a special relationship to the normal curve (see Topic 45). *If a distribution is normal, 68% of the participants in the distribution lie within one standard-deviation unit of the mean.*[2] For example, if you read in a report that $M = 70$ and $S = 10$ for a normal distribution, you would know that 68% of the participants have scores between 60 and 80 (i.e., $70 - 10 = 60$ and $70 + 10 = 80$). This is illustrated in Figure 1.

In Figure 2, the mean is also 70, but the standard deviation is only 5. The smaller standard deviation in Figure 2 is reflected by the fact that the curve is narrower than in Figure 1. Yet in both distributions,

68% of the cases lies within one standard deviation unit of the mean because they are both normal.

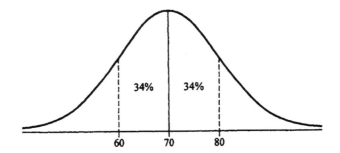

Figure 1. Normal curve with a mean of 70 and a standard deviation of 10.

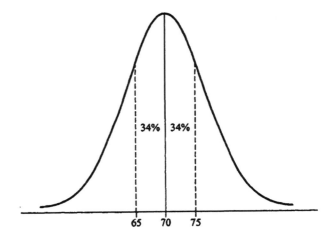

Figure 2. Normal curve with a mean of 70 and a standard deviation of 5.

Note that the middle area of Figure 2 is more narrow *but taller* than the middle area of Figure 1. This additional height in Figure 2 makes it possible for it to have the same percentage (68%) of cases as the middle area of Figure 1 has.

At first, this may seem like magic. Regardless of the value of the standard deviation, 68% of the cases lies within one standard-deviation unit in a normal curve. Actually, it is not magic but a property of the normal curve. When you are calculating the standard deviation, you are actually calculating the number of points that one must go out from the mean to capture 68% of the cases. This 68% rule does *not* strictly apply if the distribution is *not* normal. The less normal it is, the less accurate the rule is. Put another way, if the middle area of a distribution does not contain approximately 68% of the cases, the distribution is not normal.

---

[1] For those of you who are mathematically inclined, the computation of the standard deviation is illustrated in Appendix F. Considering the method of computation may give you a better understanding of its meaning.
[2] Note that *within* means on *both sides of the mean* (i.e., the mean plus/minus the standard deviation).

Note that the normal curve (see Topic 45) is not an invention of statisticians. Instead, it is a curve that has been observed with great frequency in nature. Statisticians derived the standard deviation in order to have a standardized method for describing the variability of normal distributions.

EXERCISE ON TOPIC 47

1. Which average is usually reported when the standard deviation is reported?

2. What is meant by the term *variability*?

3. Is it possible for two groups to have the same mean but different standard deviations?

4. If all individuals in a group have the same score, what is the value of the standard deviation for the scores?

5. What percentage of the participants lies within one standard-deviation unit of the mean (i.e., on both sides of the mean) in a normal distribution?

6. The middle 68% of the participants in a normal distribution have scores between what two values if the mean equals 100 and the standard deviation equals 15?

7. If the mean of a normal distribution equals 50 and the standard deviation equals 5, what percentage of the participants have scores between 45 and 50?

8. Does the 68% rule strictly apply if a distribution is *not* normal?

9. If the standard deviation for Group X is 14.55 and the standard deviation for Group Y is 20.99, which group has less variability in their scores?

10. Refer to Question 9. Does "Group X" *or* "Group Y" have a narrower curve?

Question for Discussion

11. Locate a journal article in which the researcher reports a mean and standard deviation. Does the researcher indicate whether the underlying distribution being described is normal in shape? Do you think the 68% rule strictly applies? Explain.

For Students Who Are Planning Research

12. Will you be reporting means and standard deviations? Explain.

TOPIC 48   THE MEDIAN AND INTERQUARTILE RANGE

As you know from Topic 46, the **median** is the *middle score* in a distribution. Being in the middle, it always has 50% of the scores above it and 50% of the scores below it. For the scores in Figure 1, the median is 6.5 (halfway between the middle two scores of 6 and 7).

1, 1, 1, 2, 3, 4, 5, 6, 7, 8, 8, 9, 10, 11, 11, 12

⇧

6.5

Figure 1. Scores for Group A and their median.

The median is used instead of the mean when a distribution is highly skewed (see Topic 45). It also is used to describe the average when the data are *ordinal* (i.e., data that put participants in *order* from high to low but do not have equal intervals among them; see Topic 41).[1]

When the **median** is reported as the average, it is customary to report the **range** or **interquartile range** as a measure of variability. You should recall from Topic 47 that *variability* refers to the amount by which participants *vary* or differ from each other.

The *range* is simply the highest score minus the lowest score. For the scores shown above, it is 12 – 1 = 11 (or we can say that the scores *range from* 1 *to* 12). For reasons that are beyond the scope of this discussion, measurement theory indicates that the more extreme the score, the more unreliable it is. In other words, the more extreme the score, the more likely that it has errors in it. (This is true in the natural sciences as well as the social and behavioral sciences.) Because the range is based on the two most extreme scores, it is an unreliable statistic. To get around this problem, we often use a modified version of the range, which is called the *interquartile range*. Because *inter-* means *between* and *-quartile* refers to *quarters*, interquartile range refers to the *range between quarters*. Specifically, it is the range of the middle two quarters. To calculate it, first divide the distribution into quarters, as

shown in Figure 2 (e.g., the first quarter consists of scores 1, 1, 1, and 2). As you can see, the middle 50% of the participants are between the values of 2.5 and 9.5. Because the formal definition of the *interquartile range (IQR)* is the *range of the middle 50% of the participants*, we can calculate it as follows: 9.5 – 2.5 = 7.0. Thus, *IQR* = 7.0.[2]

1, 1, 1, 2, 3, 4, 5, 6, 7, 8, 8, 9, 10, 11, 11, 12

⇧   ⇧   ⇧

2.5   6.5   9.5

Figure 2. Scores for Group A divided into quarters.

To see how the *IQR* helps us understand the variability in sets of data, consider Figure 3, where the median is 43.0 and the interquartile range is 71.0 (i.e., 83.5 – 12.5 = 71.0).

0, 5, 7, 10, 15, 22, 30, 41, 45, 57, 67, 78, 89, 92, 95, 99

⇧   ⇧   ⇧

12.5   43.0   83.5

Figure 3. Scores for Group B divided into quarters.

Thus, for Groups A and B, we might find the data presented in a research report as illustrated in Table 1.

Table 1
Medians and Interquartile Range for Two Groups

Group	Median	Interquartile Range
A	6.5	7.0
B	43.0	71.0

As you can see, Table 1 indicates two things. First, Group A has a lower average than Group B (as indicated by the median of 6.5 for Group A vs. the median of 43.0 for Group B). Second, Group A has less variability (as indicated by an interquartile range of 7.0 for Group A vs. 71.0 for Group B). Reconsideration of the scores shown in Figures 2

---

[1] It is inappropriate to use the *mean* to describe ordinal data because the mean is the point around which the differences sum to zero. If the differences are unequal in size (as they are with ordinal data), it makes no sense to use a statistic based on the values of the differences. See Topics 41 and 46.

[2] Some researchers report the value of the *semi-interquartile range*. Because "semi-" means "half," the semi-interquartile range is half of the interquartile range. In our example, the semi-interquartile range for Group A equals half of 7.0 (i.e., 7.0/2 = 3.5).

and 3 indicates that these results make sense. The middle score for Group A is much lower than the middle score for Group B, and the differences among the scores for Group A (1 vs. 1 vs. 1 vs. 2 vs. 3, etc.) are much smaller than the differences among the scores for Group B (0 vs. 5 vs. 7 vs. 10 vs. 15, and so on), indicating less variability in Group A than Group B.

In summary, the median describes the average (i.e., the central tendency) of a set of scores while the interquartile range describes their variability. When the median is reported as the average (or measure of central tendency), it is customary to report the interquartile range as the measure of variability.

EXERCISE ON TOPIC 48

1. If the median for a group of participants is 25.00, what percentage of the participants have scores above a score of 25.00?

2. Should the "mean" *or* the "median" be used with ordinal data?

3. How do you calculate the range of a set of scores?

4. Is the "range" *or* the "interquartile range" a more reliable statistic?

5. The *interquartile range* is the range of what?

6. Suppose you read that for Group X, the median equals 55.1 and the *IQR* equals 30.0, while for Group Y, the median equals 62.9 and the *IQR* equals 25.0. Which group has the higher average score?

7. Based on the information in Question 6, the scores for which group are more variable?

8. Which statistics discussed in this topic are measures of variability?

9. Which two statistics mentioned in this topic are averages (i.e., measures of central tendency)?

10. When the median is reported as the measure of central tendency, it is customary to report which measure of variability?

Question for Discussion

11. Name two circumstances under which the median is preferable to the mean.

For Students Who Are Planning Research

12. Do you anticipate reporting medians and interquartile ranges? Explain.

TOPIC 49 THE PEARSON CORRELATION COEFFICIENT

When we want to examine the relationship between two quantitative sets of scores (at the interval or ratio levels; see Topic 41), we compute a correlation coefficient. The most widely used coefficient is the **Pearson product-moment correlation coefficient**, whose symbol is r (usually called the **Pearson r**).

Consider the scores in Table 1. As you can see, the employment test scores put participants in *roughly* the same order as the ratings by supervisors. In other words, those who have high employment test scores (e.g., Joe and Jane) have high supervisors' ratings, *and* those who have low test scores (e.g., John and Jake) have low supervisors' ratings. This illustrates what we mean by a **direct relationship** (also called a **positive relationship**).

Table 1
Direct Relationship; r = .89

Employee	Employment Test Scores	Supervisors' Ratings
Joe	35	9
Jane	32	10
Bob	29	8
June	27	8
Leslie	25	7
Homer	22	8
Milly	21	6
Jake	18	4
John	15	5

Notice that the relationship in Table 1 is not perfect. For example, although Joe has a higher employment test score than Jane, Jane has a higher supervisors' rating than Joe. If the relationship were perfect, the value of the Pearson r would be 1.00. Being less than perfect, its actual value is .89. As you can see in Figure 1, this value indicates a strong, direct relationship.

In an **inverse relationship** (also called a **negative relationship**), those who are high on one variable are low on the other. Such a relationship exists between the two sets of scores in Table 2. Individu-als who are high on self-concept (such as Joe and Jane) are low on depression while those who are low on self-concept (such as Jake and John) are high on depression. However, the relationship is not perfect. The value of the Pearson r for the relationship in Table 2 is –.86.

Table 2
Inverse Relationship; r = –.86

Employee	Self-Concept Scores	Depression Scores
Joe	10	2
Jane	8	1
Bob	9	0
June	7	5
Leslie	7	6
Homer	6	8
Milly	4	8
Jake	1	9
John	0	9

The relationships in Tables 1 and 2 are strong because they are near 1.00 and –1.00, but in each case, there are exceptions, which make the Pearson rs less than 1.00 and –.100. As the number and size of the exceptions increase, the values of the Pearson r become closer to 0.00. A value of 0.00 indicates the complete absence of a relationship. (See Figure 1 below.)

It is important to note that a Pearson r is *not* a proportion and *cannot* be multiplied by 100 to get a percentage. For example, a Pearson r of .50 does not correspond to 50% of any characteristic of the data. To think about correlation in terms of percentages, we must convert Pearson rs to another statistic called the **coefficient of determination**, whose symbol is r^2, which indicates how to compute it: simply square r. Thus, for an r of .50, r^2 equals .25. If we multiply .25 by 100, we get 25%. What does this mean? Simply this: A Pearson r of .50 is 25% better than a Pearson r of 0.00. Table 3 on the next page shows selected values of r, r^2, and the percentages you should think about when interpreting a value of r.[1]

–1.00	INVERSE RELATIONSHIP			0.00	DIRECT RELATIONSHIP			1.00
⇧	⇧	⇧	⇧	⇧	⇧	⇧	⇧	⇧
perfect	strong	moderate	weak	none	weak	moderate	strong	perfect

Figure 1. Values of the Pearson r.

---

[1] Note that the procedure for computing a Pearson r is beyond the scope of this book.

Table 3
Selected Values of r and r²

r	r²	Percentage better than zero[1]
.90	.81	81%
.50	.25	25%
.25	.06	6%
−.25	.06	6%
−.50	.25	25%
−.90	.81	81%

[1]Also called *percentage of variance accounted for* or *percentage of explained variance*.

EXERCISE ON TOPIC 49

1. "Pearson *r*" stands for what words?

2. When the relationship between two variables is perfect and inverse, what is the value of *r*?

3. Is it possible for a negative relationship to be strong?

4. Is an *r* of −.90 stronger than an *r* of .50?

5. Is a relationship "direct" *or* "inverse" when those with high scores on one variable have high scores on the other *and* those with low scores on one variable have low scores on the other?

6. What does an *r* of 1.00 indicate?

7. For a Pearson *r* of .60, what is the value of the coefficient of determination?

8. What do we do to a coefficient of determination to get a percentage?

9. A Pearson *r* of .70 is what percentage better than a Pearson *r* of 0.00?

Question for Discussion

10. Name two variables between which you would expect to get a strong, positive value of *r*.

For Students Who Are Planning Research

11. Will you be reporting Pearson *r*s? If so, name the two variables that will be correlated for each value of *r*.

TOPIC 50   THE *t* TEST

Suppose we have a *research hypothesis* that says "homicide investigators who take a short course on the causes of HIV will be less fearful of the disease than investigators who have not taken the course" and test the hypothesis by conducting an experiment in which a random sample of investigators is assigned to take the course and another random sample is designated as the control group that does not take the course.[1] Suppose that at the end of the experiment, the experimental group has a mean of 16.61 on a fear-of-HIV scale and the control group has a mean of 29.67 (where the higher the score, the greater the fear of HIV). These means support the research hypothesis. However, can we be certain that our research hypothesis is correct? If you have been reading the topics on statistics in this book in order from the beginning, you already know the answer is "no" because of the *null hypothesis*, which says that there is no *true* difference between the means. That is, it says the difference was created merely by the chance errors created by random sampling. (These errors are known simply as *sampling errors*.) Put another way, unrepresentative groups may have been assigned to the two conditions quite at random, creating the difference between the two means.

The *t test* is often used to test the null hypothesis regarding the observed difference between two means.[2] For the example we are considering, a series of computations, which are beyond the scope of this book, would be performed to obtain a value of *t* (in this case, it is 5.38) and a value of degrees of freedom (which, in this case, is $df = 179$). The values of *t* and *df* are not of any special interest to consumers of research because they are merely substeps in the mathematical procedure used to get the *probability* (*p*) that the null hypothesis is true. In this particular case, *p* is less than .05. Thus, in a research report, you may read a statement such as this:

The difference between the means is statistically significant ($t = 5.38$, $df = 179$, $p < .05$).[3]

As you know from Topic 40, the term *statistically significant* indicates that the null hypothesis has been rejected. You should recall that when the probability that the null hypothesis is true is .05 or less (such as .01 or .001), we reject the null hypothesis. (When something is unlikely to be true because it has a low probability of being true, we reject it.)

Having rejected the null hypothesis, we are in a position to assert that our research hypothesis is probably true (assuming no procedural bias was allowed to affect the results, such as testing the control group immediately after a major news story on a famous person with AIDS while testing the experimental group at an earlier time).

What can cause a *t* test to yield a low probability? Three factors:

1. *Sample size.* The larger the sample, the less likely that an observed difference is due to sampling errors. (You should recall from the topics on sampling that larger samples provide more precise information.) Thus, when a sample is large, we are more likely to reject the null hypothesis than when the sample is small.

2. *The size of the difference between means.* The larger the difference, the less likely the difference is due to sampling errors. Thus, when the difference between the means is large, we are more likely to reject the null hypothesis than when the difference is small.

3. *The amount of variation in the population.* You should recall from Topic 24 that when a population is very heterogeneous (has much variability), there is more potential for sampling error. Thus, when there is little variation (as indicated by the standard deviations of the sample), we are more likely to reject the null hypothesis than when there is much variation.

A special type of *t* test is also applied to correlation coefficients. Suppose we drew a random sample of 50 students and correlated their hand size with their GPAs and got an *r* of 0.19 on the Pearson *r* scale with possible values ranging from 1.00 to

---

[1] You probably recall that we prefer random sampling because (1) it precludes any bias in the assignment of participants to the groups and (2) we can test for the effect of random errors with significance tests while we cannot test for the effects of bias.

[2] To test the null hypothesis between two *medians*, the *median test* is used. It is a specialized form of the chi square test, whose results you already know how to interpret (see Topics 43 and 44).

[3] Sometimes, researchers leave out the abbreviation *df* and present the result as $t(179) = 5.38$, $p < .05$.

−1.00. The null hypothesis says that the *true* correlation in the population is 0.00. In other words, it says that we obtained 0.19 merely as the result of sampling errors. For this example, the *t* test indicates that $p > .05$. Because the probability that the null hypothesis is true is greater than 5 in 100, we do *not* reject the null hypothesis; we have a statistically insignificant correlation coefficient. (In other words, for $n = 50$, an *r* of 0.19 is not significantly different from an *r* of 0.00.) When reporting the results of the *t* test for the significance of a correlation coefficient, it is conventional *not* to mention the value of *t*. Rather, researchers usually indicate only whether or not the correlation is significant at a given probability level.

EXERCISE ON TOPIC 50

1. What does the null hypothesis say about the difference between two sample means?

2. Are the values of *t* and *df* of any special interest to consumers of research?

3. Suppose you read that $t = 2.000$, $df = 20$, $p > .05$ for the difference between two means. Using conventional standards, should you conclude that the null hypothesis should be rejected?

4. Suppose you read that $t = 2.859$, $df = 40$, $p < .01$ for the difference between two means. Using conventional standards, should you conclude that the null hypothesis should be rejected?

5. Based on the information in Question 4, should you conclude that the difference between the means is statistically significant?

6. When we use a large sample, are we "more" *or* "less" likely to reject the null hypothesis than when we use a small sample?

7. When the size of the difference between means is large, are we "more" *or* "less" likely to reject the null hypothesis than when the size of the difference is small?

8. If we read that for a sample of 92 participants, $r = .41$, $p < .001$, should we reject the null hypothesis?

9. Is the value of *r* in Question 8 statistically significant?

Question for Discussion

10. Of the three factors that lead to a low probability when *t* tests are conducted, which one is most directly under the control of a researcher?

For Students Who Are Planning Research

11. Will you be conducting *t* tests? Explain.

TOPIC 51   ONE-WAY ANALYSIS OF VARIANCE

In the previous topic, you learned that the *t* test may be used to test the null hypothesis for the observed difference between two sample means. An alternative test for this problem is **analysis of variance** (often called **ANOVA**).[1] Instead of *t*, it yields a statistic called *F*, as well as degrees of freedom (*df*), sum of squares, mean square, and a *p* value, which indicates the probability that the null hypothesis is correct. As with the *t* test, the only value of interest to the typical consumer of research is the value of *p*. By convention, when *p* equals .05 or less (such as .01 or .001), we reject the null hypothesis and declare the result to be *statistically significant*.

Because the *t* test and ANOVA are based on the same theory and assumptions, when we compare two means, both tests yield exactly the same value of *p* and, hence, lead to the same conclusion regarding significance. So for two means, both tests are equivalent. Note, however, that a single *t* test can compare only two means, but a single ANOVA can compare a number of means, which is a great advantage.

Suppose, for example, we try three drugs designed to treat depression in an experiment and obtain the means in Table 1.

Table 1
Posttest Means: Depression Scores for Three Drugs

Drug A	Drug B	Drug C
M = 6.00	*M* = 5.50	*M* = 2.33

Note that the higher the score, the greater the depression. Inspection of the means shows that there are three observed differences:

1. Drug C is superior to Drug A.
2. Drug C is superior to Drug B.
3. Drug B is superior to Drug A.

The null hypothesis says that this *entire set* of three differences was created by sampling error. Through a series of computations that are beyond the scope of this book, an ANOVA for these data was conducted and this is the result: $F = 10.837$, $df = 2, 15$, $p < .05$. This result might be stated in a sentence or presented in a table such as Table 2, which is called an ANOVA table.

Table 2
ANOVA for Data in Table 1

Source of Variation	df	Sum of Squares	Mean Square	F
Between Groups	2	47.445	23.722	10.837*
Within Groups	15	32.833	2.189	
Total	17	80.278		

*$p < .05$

While Table 2 contains many values, which were used to arrive at the probability in the footnote to the table, the typical consumer of research is only interested in the end result, which is the value of *p*. As you know, when the probability is .05 or less (as it is here), we reject the null hypothesis. This means that the *entire set* of differences is statistically significant at the .05 level. Note that the ANOVA does *not* tell us which of the three differences we listed are significant. In fact, it could be that only one, *or* only two, *or* all three are significant. This needs to be explored with additional tests known as *multiple comparisons tests*. There are a number of such tests based on different assumptions, which usually yield the same result. (There is still some controversy over which multiple comparisons test is most appropriate.) For the data we are considering, application of Scheffé's test (a popular multiple comparisons test) yields these probabilities:

1. for Drug C vs. A, $p < .05$
2. for Drug C vs. B, $p < .05$
3. for Drug B vs. A, $p > .05$

Thus, we have found that Drug C is significantly better than Drugs A and B because the probabilities are less than .05, but that Drugs B and A are not significantly different from each other because the probability is greater than .05.

In review, an ANOVA tells us whether a set of differences, *overall*, is significant. If so, we can use a multiple comparisons test to determine which individual pairs of means are significantly different from each other.

In this topic, we have been considering a **one-way ANOVA** (also known as a **single-factor ANOVA**). It is called this when the participants have been classified in only one way. In this case, they were classified only in terms of which drug they took (A, B, or C). In the next topic, we will consider the use of ANOVA when participants are classified in two ways.

---

[1] Because it yields a value of *F*, it is sometimes called an *F* test.

EXERCISE ON TOPIC 51

1. ANOVA stands for what words?

2. If we compare two means for significance, will ANOVA and the t test yield the same probability?

3. If an ANOVA yields $p < .001$, should the null hypothesis be rejected?

4. If an ANOVA yields $p > .05$, is/are the difference(s) statistically significant?

5. If we have four means on an achievement test for samples of students in four states, can we determine whether the set of differences, overall, is statistically significant by using ANOVA?

6. For the information in Question 5, could we use a t test for the same purpose?

7. Should the typical consumer of research be concerned with the values of the sum of squares?

8. In an ANOVA table, which statistic is of the greatest interest to the typical consumer of research?

9. If an overall ANOVA for three or more means is significant, it can be followed up with what type of test to determine the significance of the differences among the individual pairs of means?

Questions for Discussion

10. Very briefly describe a hypothetical study in which it would be appropriate to conduct a one-way ANOVA but it would *not* be appropriate to conduct a t test.

11. If you have means for four groups (named A, B, C, and D), you have how many individual pairs of means to be compared with a multiple comparisons test?

For Students Who Are Planning Research

12. Will you be conducting a one-way ANOVA? Explain.

TOPIC 52 TWO-WAY ANALYSIS OF VARIANCE

In the previous topic, we saw how **ANOVA** can be used to test for the overall significance of a set of means when participants have been classified in only one way. Often, however, it is desirable to look at a two-way classification, such as (1) which drug was taken and (2) how long participants have been depressed. Table 1 shows the means for such a study.[1] Because higher depression scores indicate more depression, a low mean is desirable.

Table 1
Means for a Study of Depression: Drugs and Length of Depression Comparisons

Length of Depression	Drug A	Drug B	Row Mean
Long Term	$M = 8.11$	$M = 8.32$	$M = 8.22$
Short Term	$M = 4.67$	$M = 8.45$	$M = 6.56$
Col. Mean	$M = 6.39$	$M = 8.38$	

Although the participants are classified in two ways, the statistics in the table answer *three* questions. First, by comparing the column means of 6.39 and 8.38, we can see that overall, those who took Drug A are less depressed. It is important to notice that the mean of 6.39 for Drug A is based on both those who have long-term *and* those who have short-term depression. The same is true of the column mean of 8.38 for Drug B. Thus, by comparing the column means, we are answering the question of which drug is more effective *in general without regard to how long participants have been depressed*. In analysis of variance, this is known as a **main effect**.

Each way in which participants are classified yields a main effect in analysis of variance. Thus, because participants were also classified in terms of their length of depression, there is a main effect for short-term vs. long-term depression, which can be seen by examining the row means of 8.22 and 6.56. This main effect indicates that overall, those with short-term depression were less depressed at the end of the experiment than those with long-term depression.

In this example, the most interesting question is the question of an **interaction**. The question is simply this: "Is the effectiveness of the drugs dependent, in part, on the length of depression?" By examining the individual cell means (those *not* in bold in Table 1), we can see that the answer is "yes." Drug A is more effective for short-term than long-term depression (4.67 vs. 8.11) while Drug B is about equally effective for both types of depression (8.32 vs. 8.45). What is the practical implication of this interaction? The overall effectiveness of Drug A is almost entirely attributable to its effectiveness for short-term depression. In other words, if a person has short-term depression, Drug A is indicated, but if a person has long-term depression, either drug is likely to be about equally effective. Thus, the two classification variables *interact*: The best drug to take is dependent on the length of the depression.

For the data in Table 1, it turns out that $p < .05$ for both main effects and the interaction. Thus, we can reject the null hypotheses that say the differences we are considering are the result of random errors. Of course, it does not always turn out this way. It is possible for one or two of the main effects to be significant but the interaction to be not significant. It is also possible for neither main effect to be significant while the interaction is significant, which is the case for the data in Table 2.

Table 2
Means for a Study of Depression: Drugs and Gender Comparisons

Gender	Drug A	Drug B	Row Mean
Female	$M = 8.00$	$M = 5.00$	$M = 6.50$
Male	$M = 5.00$	$M = 8.00$	$M = 6.50$
Col. Mean	$M = 6.50$	$M = 6.50$	

Notice that the column means (6.50 vs. 6.50) in Table 2 indicate no main effect for Drug A vs. Drug B. Likewise, the row means (6.50 vs. 6.50) indicate no main effect for gender. However, there is one very interesting finding: There is an interaction of drug type and gender, which indicates that for females, Drug B is superior, but for males, Drug A is superior. Note that if we had compared the two drugs in a one-way ANOVA without also classifying the participants according to gender (as we did here in a two-way ANOVA), we would have missed this important interaction. By examining interactions using ANOVA, researchers are one step closer to examining the effects of various traits in complex ways (not just one at a time).

---

[1] For instructional purposes, only two types of drugs are shown. However, we may use ANOVA when there are more than two.

EXERCISE ON TOPIC 52

1. Suppose we drew random samples of urban, suburban, and rural children, tested them for creativity, and obtained three means. Should we use a one-way or two-way ANOVA to test for significance? Explain.

2. Do the following means on a performance test indicate an interaction between type of reward and age?

Age Level	Praise Reward	Monetary Reward	Row Mean
Young Adults	$M = 50.00$	$M = 60.00$	$M = 55.00$
Older Adults	$M = 60.00$	$M = 50.00$	$M = 55.00$
Col. Mean	$M = 55.00$	$M = 55.00$	

3. Do the means for Question 2 indicate a main effect for type of reward?

4. Do the following means on an achievement test indicate an interaction between the method of instruction (A vs. B) and the aptitude of the students (high vs. low)?

Aptitude	Method A	Method B	Row Mean
High Aptitude	$M = 100.00$	$M = 85.00$	$M = 92.50$
Low Aptitude	$M = 100.00$	$M = 85.00$	$M = 92.50$
Col. Mean	$M = 100.00$	$M = 85.00$	

5. Do the means for Question 4 indicate a main effect for method of instruction?

6. Do the means for Question 4 indicate a main effect for aptitude?

7. If $p > .05$ for an interaction in an analysis of variance, should we reject the null hypothesis?

Question for Discussion

8. Very briefly describe a hypothetical study in which it would be appropriate to conduct a two-way ANOVA but it would *not* be appropriate to conduct a one-way ANOVA.

For Students Who Are Planning Research

9. Will you be conducting a two-way ANOVA? Explain.

Topic 53 Practical Significance of Results

As you know from previous topics, **statistical significance** tells us whether a difference is reliable in light of random errors. Assume, for example, that we assigned students at random to two groups: one that was taught a mathematics lesson with new instructional software (the experimental group) and one that was taught using a traditional lecture/textbook approach (the control group). Let us assume, furthermore, that use of the instructional software *in truth* is very slightly superior to the lecture/textbook approach (i.e., it really produces a superior outcome in math achievement, but the superiority is quite small). With a very large sample, randomization should give us experimental and control groups that are very similar at the beginning of the experiment (i.e., on the pretest). Because larger samples have less sampling error than smaller ones, a significance test such as a t test for the difference between the two posttest means may be able to detect the reliability of this small difference and allow us to declare it to be *statistically significant* at some probability level such as $p < .05$. Thus, we arrive at an important principle: Even a small difference can be a statistically significant difference.[1] This is true because statistical significance determines only the likelihood that a difference is due to random errors, not whether it is large.

While determining the statistical significance of a difference is the first step, determining the **practical significance** is the next step. Determining practical significance involves five considerations.

The first consideration is the cost in relation to the benefit, which is often referred to as a **cost-benefit analysis**. While there are mechanical, statistical means for conducting such an analysis, for most purposes, common sense and good judgment can give us a good answer to the question of whether the results are of practical significance in terms of cost. Consider the example we started with above. Suppose all students already have access to

computers for their math lessons and the software is being donated (or is highly subsidized by some foundation). In this case, the low cost might make the small difference practically significant. On the other hand, if expensive computers and software would need to be purchased and the teachers would need extensive (and, therefore, expensive) training in its use, we might forgo using the experimental method in everyday instruction in order to achieve the very small increase in math performance that was detected in the experiment.

As you have just seen, even a small difference can be of both statistical and practical significance if the cost is low. In addition, a small, statistically significant difference can be of practical significance—even if it is costly—if it is **a crucial difference** (*the second consideration*). A crucial difference is one that results in a crucial increase or decrease. Consider an extreme example. Suppose an experiment in which very expensive computerized simulations that teach how to conduct a delicate form of surgery reduces the death rate from such surgery from 2 in 100,000 to 1.8 in 100,000. In this case, we might decide that even this small difference is worth the high cost because saving even a very small number of lives during surgery is crucial. This is a less extreme example: If a school needs just a few points' increase (on the average) to cross a crucial threshold such as having the average student score at or above the 50th percentile rank on a standardized math test in order to obtain substantial increases in state funding for instruction, crossing this threshold might be considered crucial by teachers, parents, and students.

The third consideration in determining practical significance is **client acceptability**. In school settings, students are clients. If students greatly dislike a statistically superior computerized technique for improving math achievement, using the technique might cause students to develop negative attitudes toward math. If so, the statistically significant difference might be of little practical significance because of the *negative side effect* (i.e., development of negative attitudes).

The fourth consideration is **public and political acceptability**. For instance, studies suggest that stem cell research might be fruitful in curing a number of debilitating and deadly diseases. Yet large segments of the public (at the time of this writing) are opposed to it, calling into question its

---

[1] As you know from Topic 50, the t test is more likely to lead to significance if the difference between the two means is large. However, if there is little variation among the participants and if a large enough sample is used, even small reliable differences can be reliably detected and declared statistically significant. Note that a small difference can be of great practical importance. For instance, in a national election, having only one vote more than the competing candidate out of millions of votes can lead to victory.

practical significance as a line of research that scientists should continue to pursue.

Fifth, we need to consider the **ethical and legal implications** of a statistically significant result. No matter how much benefit and no matter how low the cost, some treatments that have been shown to produce statistically superior results may violate the ethical standards of a profession or impinge on legal requirements such as the laws that govern the operation of schools.

As you can see, determining practical significance should not be done mechanically. If there is any question as to the practical significance of the results of a study, representative groups of potential providers of the treatments (such as teachers or psychologists, their clients, the public, and politicians) may need to be consulted. In addition, legal counsel may be needed to help in the determination of practical significance.

EXERCISE ON TOPIC 53

1. Is it possible for a small difference to be statistically significant?

2. This topic describes *how many* types of considerations for determining practical significance?

3. If the cost is very low, might a very small statistically significant difference be of practical significance?

4. Does a crucial difference need to be numerically large to be of practical significance?

5. According to this topic, should the acceptability of a treatment to the clients be considered when determining practical significance?

6. "According to this topic, ethical considerations should play no role in the interpretation of the results of a study." Is this statement true *or* false?

7. Should the determination of the practical significance of the results of a study be a mechanical process?

Questions for Discussion

8. In addition to the three examples in this topic, name a hypothetical result that you would favor implementing even if it were costly because it might make a *crucial difference*.

9. Consider the last research report you read that had statistically significant results. Did the researcher who wrote the article discuss the practical significance of his or her results? Explain.

For Students Who Are Planning Research

10. Can you anticipate any considerations that might limit the practical significance of the results you hope to obtain in your study? Explain.

PART G

EFFECT SIZE AND META-ANALYSIS

In this part of the book, you will learn about a statistical tool called effect size, which helps us evaluate the size of a difference, such as the difference between two means. In addition, you will learn how a statistical technique named meta-analysis can be used to combine results across diverse studies on a given topic.

NOTES

TOPIC 54 INTRODUCTION TO EFFECT SIZE (*d*)

To understand the need to consider the **effect size** of a difference, let us consider a practical problem in interpreting research. Suppose that Experimenter A administered a new treatment for depression (Treatment X) to an experimental group while the control group received a standard treatment. Furthermore, suppose that Experimenter A used a 20-item true–false depression scale (with possible raw scores from 0 to 20) and obtained the results on the posttest shown in Table 1.[1] Note that the difference between the two means is 5 raw-score points.

Table 1
Statistics Obtained in Experiment A (Treatment X)

Group	*m*	*sd*
Experimental group (*n* = 50)	12.00	4.00
Control group (*n* = 50)	7.00	4.00
Difference between two means	5.00	

Suppose that Experimenter B administered Treatment Y to an experimental group while treating the control group with the standard treatment. Furthermore, suppose Experimenter B used a 30-item scale with choices from "Strongly agree" to "Strongly disagree" with possible scores from 0 to 120 and obtained the results in Table 2, which shows a difference of 10 raw-score points in favor of the experimental group.

Table 2
Statistics Obtained in Experiment B (Treatment Y)

Group	*m*	*sd*
Experimental group (*n* = 50)	80.00	14.00
Control group (*n* = 50)	70.00	14.00
Difference between two means	10.00	

Which treatment is superior? Treatment X, which resulted in a 5-point raw-score difference between the two means, *or* Treatment Y, which resulted in a 10-point raw-score difference between the two means? Of course, the answer is not clear because the two experimenters used different measurement scales (0 to 20 versus 0 to 120).

To make the results of the two studies comparable, we need to *standardize* them so that both differences can be expressed on the same scale. The most straightforward way to do this is to express both differences in terms of their *standard-deviation units* (instead of their raw-score units).[2] In Experiment A, *one standard-deviation unit* equals 4.00 raw score points. By dividing the difference between the means (5.00) by the size of the standard-deviation unit for Experiment A (4.00 points), we obtain an answer of 1.25. This value is known as *d* and is obtained by the following formula in which m_e stands for the mean of the experimental group, and m_c stands for the mean of the control group:

$$d = \frac{m_e - m_c}{sd} = \frac{12.00 - 7.00}{4.00} = 1.25$$

The result tells us that the experimental group exceeded the control group by 1.25 (one and one-quarter) standard-deviation units. For all practical purposes, there are only three standard-deviation units on each side of the mean. Thus, *d* is expressed in standard-deviation units and has an effective range from 0.00 (no difference between the means) to 3.00 (the maximum difference between the means).[3] Thus, for Experiment A, the experimental group is one and one-quarter standard deviations above no difference (0.00) on a standardized scale that ranges from 0.00 to only 3.00. On such a limited scale, a value of *d* of 1.25 indicates that the difference is substantially above 0.00.

Using the formula for Experiment B, we divide the difference between the means by the standard deviation (10.00/14.00) and obtain *d* = 0.71, which is almost three-quarters of the way above 0.00 on the three-point scale. The following is what we now know about the differences in the two experiments when both are expressed on a common (i.e., standardized) scale called *d*. Clearly, the difference in Experiment A (1.25) is greater than the difference in Experiment B (0.71).

0.00 0.50 0.75 1.00 1.50 1.75 2.00 2.50 2.75 3.00
　　　　↑　　　　↑
　　　Exp. B　Exp. A

Table 3 summarizes the differences. Remember that the two raw-score differences are not directly

---

[1] Note that in both tables, *higher* mean scores indicate *less* depression.

[2] See Topic 47 to review the meaning of the standard deviation.

[3] If a control group has a higher mean than the experimental group, the value of *d* will be negative.

comparable because different measurement scales were used (0 to 20 points versus 0 to 120 points). By examining the standardized values of d, which range from 0.00 to 3.00, we can make a meaningful comparison of the results of the two experiments.

In each of the two examples in this topic, the two standard deviations are equal. When they are unequal, a special averaging procedure that results in the "pooled standard deviation" should be used. See Appendix G for more information.

Now for an important definition: *Effect size* refers to the *magnitude* (i.e., size) of a difference when it is expressed on a standardized scale. The statistic d is one of the most popular statistics for describing the effect size of the difference between two means. In the next topic, you will learn more about the interpretation of d. In Topic 56, you will learn about another statistic for expressing effect size.

Table 3
Differences Expressed in Raw Scores and in Values of d

Group	Raw-score difference	Standardized differences (d)
Experimenter A	5 points	1.25
Experimenter B	10 points	0.71

EXERCISE ON TOPIC 54

1. In this topic, which experimenter had the smaller range of possible raw scores? Explain.

2. In this topic, the raw-score differences between the means (5 for Experimenter A and 10 for Experimenter B) were standardized by dividing each of them by what statistic?

3. When comparing the results of two experiments, is it possible for the experiment with the smaller raw-score difference to have a larger difference when the differences are expressed as d?

4. Suppose a researcher obtained a value of d of 2.95. Would you characterize this as representing a large difference? Explain.

5. Suppose you read that the mean for an experimental group is 20.00 and the mean for the control group is 22.00. Based on this information alone, can you calculate the value of d? Explain.

6. Suppose you conducted an experiment on improving algebra achievement, and your experimental post-test raw-score mean equaled 500.00 ($sd = 100.00$), and your control group raw-score mean equaled 400.00 ($sd = 100.00$). What is the value of the effect size for your experiment?

7. What is the definition of *effect size*?

Question for Discussion

8. In your own words, briefly explain why it is desirable to compute d when comparing the results of two experiments that use different measurement scales.

For Students Who Are Planning Research

9. Do you plan to report value(s) of d in the results section of your research report? Explain.

TOPIC 55 INTERPRETATION OF EFFECT SIZE (d)

In the previous topic, you learned about d as a statistic that expresses effect size. The two examples in that topic had values of d of 0.71 and 1.25. Obviously, the experiment with a value of 1.25 had a larger effect than the one with a value of 0.71.

While there are no universally accepted standards for describing values of d in words, it seems safe to say that many researchers use Cohen's (1992)[1] suggestions: (1) a value of d of about 0.20 (one-fifth of a standard deviation) is "small," (2) a value of 0.50 (one-half of a standard deviation) is "medium," and (3) a value of 0.80 (eight-tenths of a standard deviation) is "large." (Keep in mind that in terms of values of d, an experimental group can rarely exceed a control group by more than 3.00 because the effective range of standard-deviation units is only three on each side of the mean. Thus, for most practical purposes, 3.00 [or –3.00] is the maximum value of d.)[2]

Extrapolating from Cohen's suggestions, we might call a value of 1.10 "very large," and a value of 1.40 or more "extremely large." Values that are this large are rarely found in social and behavioral research.

Table 1 summarizes the new material that we have covered so far in this topic.

Table 1
Labels for Values of d

Value of d	Label
0.20	Small
0.50	Medium
0.80	Large
1.10	Very Large
1.40+	Extremely Large

Using the labels in Table 1, the value of d of 0.71 in the previous topic would be described as being closer to "large" than "medium," while the value of 1.25 would be described as being between "very large" and "extremely large."

---

[1] Cohen, J. (1992). A power primer. *Psychological Bulletin, 112*, 155–159.

[2] A negative is obtained when the control group's mean is higher than the experimental group's mean. Note that less than one-half of one percent of a normal distribution lies above +3.00 and below –3.00, which means that it is technically possible—but highly unlikely—to obtain values larger than +3.00 and –3.00.

Cohen (1992), who proposed the labels for the first three values in Table 1, noted that he originally established them subjectively but that they subsequently have been found to be useful by other researchers in various fields of study.

The labels we have been discussing should not be used arbitrarily without considering the full context in which the values of d are obtained and the possible implications of the results. This brings us to two principles: (1) a small effect size might represent an important result and (2) a large effect size might represent an unimportant result.

Consider the *first principle*. Suppose that researchers have been frustrated by consistently finding values of d well below 0.20 when trying various treatments for solving an important problem (such as treatments for a new and deadly disease). If a subsequent researcher finds a treatment that results in a value of about 0.20, this might be considered a very important finding. At this low level (0.20), the effect of the treatment is small, but it might be of immense importance to ill individuals helped by the treatment—however small the effect. In addition, the results might point the scientific community in a fruitful direction for additional research on treatments for the problem in question.

The *second principle* is that a large value of d—even one above 1.40—might be of limited importance. This is most likely when the results lack practical significance in terms of cost, public and political acceptability, and ethical and legal concerns. (See Topic 53 for considerations in determining the practical significance of research results.)

Here are three steps for interpreting the difference between two means. First, determine whether the difference is statistically significant at an acceptable probability level such as $p < .05$. If it is not, the difference should usually be regarded as unreliable and should be interpreted as such. Second, consider the value of d and consider the labels in Table 1 for describing the magnitude of the difference. Third, consider the implications of the difference for validating any relevant theories as well as the practical significance of the results.

Of course, before beginning to follow the three steps outlined in the previous paragraph, you should consider the adequacy of the research methodology employed by the researcher. Woefully inadequate sampling (such as a very biased sample), clearly invalid instrumentation (such as a test that measures a variable other than the one the researcher wanted to study), and/or a very poor research design (such as a design that will not answer the research question) would lead to very serious questions regarding the validity of the results. In such cases, consideration of values of d might be meaningless.

EXERCISE ON TOPIC 55

1. Are there universally accepted standards for describing effect sizes?

2. What is the "effective range" of standard deviation units on both sides of the mean? Explain.

3. If the value of d for the difference between two means equals 1.00, the experimental group's mean is how many standard-deviation units higher than the control group's mean?

4. What value of d is associated with the label "extremely large"?

5. According to Cohen, what label should be attached to a value of d of 0.80?

6. Under what circumstance will a negative value of d be obtained?

7. Should a test of statistical significance be conducted "before" *or* "after" computing d and interpreting its value using labels?

Questions for Discussion

8. As noted in this topic, a small value of d might be associated with an important result. Name a specific problem that is currently confounding researchers and for which even a small value of d might indicate a result of great practical importance.

9. Is it possible for a large value of d to be associated with a difference that is unimportant? Explain.

For Students Who Are Planning Research

10. Will you be comparing the difference between two means in your analysis? If so, do you expect to find a statistically significant difference? Do you expect to find a large value of d? Explain.

TOPIC 56 EFFECT SIZE AND CORRELATION (r)

Cohen's *d* is so widely used as a measure of effect size that some researchers inaccurately use the term "effect size" and "*d*" interchangeably—as though they are synonyms. However, "effect size" refers to any statistic that *describes the size of a difference on a standardized metric*. For instance, *d* describes the size of the difference between two means.[1] Furthermore, *d* is *standardized* because regardless of what variables are being studied and regardless of what raw-score scale is being used to express the difference, the value of *d* is always expressed on a standard-deviation scale that almost always ranges only from –3.00 to +3.00.[2]

In addition to *d*, a number of other measures of effect size have been proposed. One that is very widely reported is "effect-size *r*," which is simply the Pearson correlation coefficient (*r*) that you learned about in Topic 49. As you probably recall, *r* indicates the direction and strength of a relationship between two variables expressed on a scale that ranges from –1.00 to +1.00, where 0.00 indicates no relationship. We interpret values of *r* by first squaring them (r^2). For instance, when $r = 0.50$, $r^2 = .25$ (i.e., $0.50 \times 0.50 = 0.25$). Then, we multiply the value of r^2 by 100%. In our example, $0.25 \times 100\% = 25\%$. Thus, we can say that the value of *r* of 0.50 is 25% greater than 0.00 on a scale that extends up to a maximum possible value of 1.00.

In simple, straightforward studies, the choice between reporting *means* and the associated values of *d* (which can range from –3.00 to 3.00) and reporting *correlation coefficients* and the associated values of r^2 (which can range from –1.00 to 1.00) is usually quite straightforward. If a researcher wants to determine which of two groups is superior *on the average*, a comparison of means using *d* is usually the preferred method of analysis. On the other hand, if there is one group of participants with two scores per participant and if the goal is to determine the *degree of relationship between the two sets of scores*, then *r* and r^2 should be used. For instance, if a group of students was administered a vocabulary knowledge test and a reading comprehension test, it

would not be surprising to obtain a correlation coefficient as high as 0.70, which indicates a substantial degree of relationship between two variables (i.e., there is a strong tendency for students who score high on vocabulary knowledge to score high on reading comprehension). As you learned in Topic 49, for interpretative purposes, 0.70 squared equals 0.49, which is equivalent to 49%. Knowing this allows us to say that the relationship between the two variables is 49% higher than a relationship of 0.00.

When reviewing a body of literature on a given topic, you will sometimes find that some studies present means and values of *d* while other studies on the topic present values of *r*, depending on the specific research purposes and research designs. When interpreting such a set of studies, you may find it useful to think in terms of the equivalence of *d* and *r*. Table 1 permits you to do this for selected values.

Table 1
Equivalent Values of d, r, and r^2

d	r	r^2	% for r^2
0.20	0.100	0.010	1.0%
0.50	0.243	0.059	5.9%
0.80	0.371	0.138	13.8%
1.20	0.514	0.264	26.4%
1.50	0.600	0.360	36.0%
2.00	0.707	0.500	50.0%

Let us consider an example that illustrates the usefulness of Table 1. Suppose you were examining the literature on anxiety and depression and found a study in which one group was administered scales that measured the two variables, and $r = 0.37$ was obtained. Suppose that in another study, an experimental group was administered a treatment designed to induce anxiety while the control group received a neutral treatment. Then, all participants were administered a depression scale (to see whether anxiety induces depression). Further, suppose that the experimenter reported that $d = 0.80$ for the difference between the posttest means for the two groups. Using Table 1, you can determine that the effect sizes (i.e., magnitude of the differences) in the two studies are the same (i.e., for a value of *d* of 0.80 in the first column, the corresponding value of *r* in the second column is 0.371).

For values not shown in Table 1, it is often sufficient to locate the closest values and make mental

---

[1] If the means of two groups are identical, $d = 0.00$.

[2] Once again, note that it is mathematically possible for *d* to exceed 3.00 because a very tiny percentage of the cases lies above three standard deviations above the mean. Such values are seldom seen in the social and behavioral sciences.

approximations. To obtain more precise equivalent values of d and r, use the formulas provided near the end of Appendix G.

EXERCISE ON TOPIC 56

1. According to this topic, what are the two measures of effect size that are very widely reported?

2. Correlation coefficients are expressed on a standard scale that always ranges from -1.00 up to what value?

3. A value of r should be interpreted by doing what?

4. A value of r equal to 0.40 is what percentage of the distance above zero?

5. If there is one group of participants and a researcher wants to determine the strength of the relationship between two sets of test scores, which measure of effect size would typically be the more appropriate?

6. A value of d of 1.20 corresponds to what value of r^2?

7. A value of r of 0.600 corresponds to what value of d?

Question for Discussion

8. Briefly describe a hypothetical study in which it would be more appropriate to compute a value of d instead of a value of r as a measure of effect size.

For Students Who Are Planning Research

9. In this topic, there is an example of an experiment and an example of a correlational study. Will you be conducting either type of study? Explain.

Meta-analysis is a set of statistical methods for combining the results of previous studies.[1] To understand its basic premise, consider the following example. Suppose a researcher (named W) randomly assigned 50 students to an experimental group that received one-on-one remedial tutorial reading instruction. The remaining 50 children were the controls. At the end of the experiment, the experimental group had a mean of 22.00, and the control group had a mean of 19.00 on a standardized reading test. Subsequently, three other experimenters conducted strict replications of the first experiment using the same research methods, the same type of tutorial reading instruction, and the same number of second-grade students drawn at random from the same pool of students (e.g., second-graders in a particular school district). The posttest means of the four experiments are shown in Table 1.

Table 1
Results of a Meta-Analysis of Two Experiments

	Experimental Group	Control Group	Mean Difference
Exp. W	$m = 22.00$	$m = 19.00$	$m_{difference} = 3.00$
Exp. X	$m = 20.00$	$m = 18.00$	$m_{difference} = 2.00$
Exp. Y	$m = 23.00$	$m = 17.00$	$m_{difference} = 6.00$
Exp. Z	$m = 15.00$	$m = 16.00$	$m_{difference} = -1.00$

As you can see, there are differences in the results from study to study. The differences could be caused by one or more of the following types of errors:

1. Random sampling errors created by assigning participants at random to the two groups such as having more motivated students assigned (quite at random) to the experimental group in one or more of the experiments.
2. Random errors of measurement such as participants guessing on the multiple-choice test,

and some students not feeling well on the day the test was administered.

3. Systematic errors known to one or more of the researchers such as the unavailability of experienced tutors for one or more of the experiments.
4. Systematic errors of which one or more of the researchers are unaware such as tutors not following the curriculum when the researcher or researchers were not present.

All four types of errors are possible in any experiment. Hence, the results of any one experiment should be interpreted with caution. However, in this particular example, we have four experiments, which should give us more confidence in any conclusions we reach. In a *traditional, subjective narrative review of these studies*, it would be reasonable to synthesize these four experiments with a statement such as, "Three of the four experiments on the tutorial instruction showed positive results, with one experiment showing a six-point difference in favor of the experimental group. However, the one negative case in which the control group exceeded the experimental group by one point reduces confidence in the effectiveness of this program."

In a *meta-analysis*, a reviewer might make comments such as the one in the previous paragraph. However, the main thrust of the conclusions in a meta-analysis is based on a *mathematical synthesis* of the statistical results of the previous studies. In this case, we can average the results by summing the four mean differences (3.00 + 2.00 + 6.00 − 1.00 = 10.00) and then dividing the sum by four because there were four studies (10.00/4.00 = 2.50). Thus, in a meta-analysis, the author would state that the best estimate of the effectiveness of the program is 2.50 points.[2]

At this point, you should recognize that a meta-analysis estimate of 2.50 points has two important characteristics. The first one is that a statistical result (2.50) that we are considering is based on a sample of 400 students. (Note that each of the four individual studies had 50 in each group for a total of 100 in each study.) Statistics based on larger sam-

---

[1] The prefix "meta" means occurring later and/or being later and more highly organized. Meta-analysis is conducted on previous results and mathematically organizes them.

[2] For reasons that you will learn about in the next topic, those who conduct meta-analyses usually convert their results to one or more measures of effect size (such as *d* or *r*), which were discussed in the previous three topics.

ples (such as 400 versus 100) yield more *reliable results*.

It is important to note that *reliable results* are not necessarily *valid results*. A systematic bias that skews the results (such as the experimental group having access to the answer key for the test) will yield invalid results no matter how large the sample is.

The second important characteristic of meta-analysis is that it typically synthesizes the results of studies conducted by *independent* researchers (i.e., researchers who are not working together). Thus, if one researcher makes a *systematic error* (such as using poorly trained tutors), the effects of his or her erroneous results will have less of an effect on the overall result when they are averaged with the results obtained by other independent researchers who have not made the same error.

In short, the process of averaging when conducting a meta-analysis tends to decrease the effects of both the random and systematic errors listed earlier in this topic.

EXERCISE ON TOPIC 57

1. What is the meaning of the prefix "meta" as used in this topic?

2. Meta-analysis is a "set of statistical methods" for doing what?

3. Two types of random errors tend to be canceled out in the process of conducting a meta-analysis. What are the two types of random errors discussed in this topic?

4. In the report of a meta-analysis, the "main thrust of the conclusions" is based on what?

5. Very briefly state the "second important characteristic" of meta-analysis.

Question for Discussion

6. Based on what you have learned about meta-analysis in this topic, to what extent do you think that it is a good method for advancing knowledge on a topic? Explain.

For Students Who Are Planning Research

7. Some institutions (and journals) consider a meta-analysis to be a work of original research even though it is based on a reanalysis of the research results created by others. If you are planning to conduct research, would you be interested in conducting a meta-analysis as your research project (based on what you know about it at this point)? Explain. (Note: After reading the next two topics, reconsider your answer to this question.)

For instructional purposes, the example in the previous topic illustrated a meta-analysis on four studies that were as similar as possible (i.e., a study by Researcher W plus three strict replications). In practice, it would be difficult to find even one perfectly strict replication of a study. One very important way that various studies on a given topic often differ is that various researchers frequently use a number of different measures of the same variable. To see how important this issue is in conducting and interpreting a meta-analysis, consider the values in Table 1, which are based on a study in which Experimenter A used a test with possible score values from 200 to 800 (like the *SAT*) while Experimenter B used a test with possible score values from 0 to 50.

Table 1
Results Used in Conducting a Meta-Analysis

	Experimental Group	Control Group	Mean Difference
Exp. A $n = 50$	$m = 500.00$ $sd = 200.00$	$m = 400.00$ $sd = 200.00$	$m_{difference}$ $= 100.00$
Exp. B $n = 50$	$m = 24.00$ $sd = 3.00$	$m = 22.00$ $sd = 3.00$	$m_{difference}$ $= 2.00$

If we compute the average of the mean differences as we did in the last topic, we get a result that lacks meaning ($100.00 + 2.00 = 102.00/2 = 51.00$) because the results are expressed on different scales. In other words, the answer of 51.00 does *not* refer specifically to the scale that goes from 200 to 800 *nor* does it refer specifically to the scale that goes from 0 to 50. As we locate more studies on the same topic, we are likely to find additional tests that have other possible score-value points, making the simple average of the mean differences entirely uninterpretable.

The solution to the problem we are considering is to use a measure of *effect size*. One of the most popular is Cohen's *d*, which is expressed on a standardized scale that typically ranges from –3.00 to +3.00. (This statistic was discussed in Topics 54 through 56.) If we calculate *d* for all studies that we want to synthesize in a meta-analysis, we can average the values of *d* to get a meaningful result.

As you may recall, to obtain *d*, divide the difference between the means by the standard deviation. For Experiment A, $d = 100.00/200.00 = \textbf{0.50}$. For Experiment B, $d = 2.00/3.00 = \textbf{0.67}$. When the re-

sults of the two experiments are expressed on a common scale (*d*), we can now see that Experiment B (with a *d* of 0.67) had a larger effect than Experiment A (with a *d* of 0.50), which was not clear by a simple inspection of Table 1.

To proceed with the meta-analysis, we can now average the two values of *d* to get a mathematical synthesis of the results [$(0.67 + 0.50)/2 = 0.58$]. Thus, **0.58** is our best estimate of the effect. Referring to Table 1 in Topic 55, we can say that the overall result of the meta-analysis is somewhat above medium in strength.

In our example in this topic, the standard deviations for both groups in each experiment were the same. In reality, they will almost always be at least somewhat different. Those who plan to conduct a meta-analysis and want more information on several possible solutions to this problem should consult Appendix G.

Also in our example, the two experiments had the same number of participants ($n = 50$ in each). Suppose we now locate an additional published experiment (Experiment C) in which 300 participants were used. We would, of course, calculate *d* for this experiment (let us assume that $d = 0.90$, which is "large" according to Table 1 in Topic 55). If we simply sum the three values of *d* and divide by 3 (the number of studies), we are giving each study an equal weight. In other words, we are treating the three values of *d* as though they were equally important even though the value of *d* for Experiment C is based on a much larger sample than that of the other two experiments. Using statistical methods that are beyond the scope of this book, researchers can "weight" the average value of *d* to take account of the varying numbers of participants, giving more weight to those studies with more participants in the final average. As a consumer of research, you should look to see whether a meta-analysis is based on "weighted averages," which is almost always desirable.

As you know from Topic 56, *r* is also a measure of effect sizes. Like *d*, it is expressed on a standard, common scale. However, the scale for *r* has values that can range from –1.00 to 1.00. Like *d*, values of *r* reported in various studies can be averaged while weighting the average to take account of varying sample sizes. (The mathematics of the weighting procedure for *r* are beyond the scope of this book.)

In this topic and the previous one, very simple examples were used to help you understand the purposes of meta-analysis and its interpretation. These simple examples may have failed to impress on you the importance of meta-analysis because of their limited size, so let us briefly consider two published meta-analytic studies. First, in one meta-analysis, researchers located 29 studies that reported on the effectiveness of supplementary one-on-one reading instruction for elementary school students judged to be at risk for reading failure. Combined, these studies contained a total of 1,539 students. By averaging the effect sizes across the 29 studies, the researchers found an overall weighted mean value of d of 0.41, which is close to "medium" in strength according to Table 1 in Topic 55.[1] As you can see, this result is based on a large number of studies and a large combined sample size.

In another meta-analysis, researchers reported a weighted average value of r of −0.24 for the relationship between neuroticism and leadership qualities based on 48 studies involving 8,025 participants. With such a large sample, the result of this meta-analysis is highly reliable.[2]

In conclusion, meta-analysis provides a statistical method that can contribute to our understanding of the results of multiple studies on a given topic. Thus, meta-analytic studies are an important adjunct to traditional, more subjective narrative reviews of literature, which are largely non-mathematical (i.e., reviews of literature in which some particular statistics may be mentioned but the results of the studies being reviewed are not mathematically synthesized).

EXERCISE ON TOPIC 58

1. According to this topic, is it easy to find perfectly strict replications of previous studies?

2. What is "one very important way" that various studies on a given topic differ?

3. Computing a grand mean difference across studies that use measurement scales that have different possible numbers of score points is meaningless. What is suggested in this topic to overcome this problem?

4. What needs to be done when the studies to be used in a meta-analysis have different sample sizes?

5. Is d the only standardized measure of effect size used in meta-analytic studies? Explain.

Question for Discussion

6. In this topic, a meta-analytic study that reported a weighted average value of r of −0.24 for the relationship between neuroticism and leadership qualities was cited. Based on what you know about correlation, how would you interpret the direction and strength of this relationship?

For Students Who Are Planning Research

7. Reconsider your answer to Question 7 in the previous topic in light of what you learned in this topic. Has your answer changed? Explain.

---

[1] Source: Elbaum, B., Vaughn, S., Hughes, M. T., & Moody, S. W. (2000). How effective are one-on-one tutoring programs for elementary students at risk for reading failure? A meta-analysis of the intervention research. *Journal of Educational Psychology, 92*, 605–619.

[2] Source: Judge, T. A., & Bono, J. E. (2002). Personality and leadership: A qualitative and quantitative review. *Journal of Applied Psychology, 87*, 765–780.

Topic 59 Meta-Analysis: Strengths and Weaknesses

Meta-analysis has both strengths and weaknesses. A major strength mentioned in the previous topic is that it produces results based on large combined samples—sometimes very large samples. The previous topic cited a meta-analysis of 48 studies that produced a mathematical synthesis involving 8,025 participants, which is very much larger than the typical number used in research reports in academic journals. You also learned in the last topic that very large samples usually yield very reliable (although not necessarily valid) results. However, if the studies subjected to a meta-analysis have serious methodological flaws (resulting in a lack of validity), then the mathematical synthesis of their results will also lack validity.

You also know from Topic 57 that a strength of meta-analysis is that it can be used to synthesize the results of studies conducted by *independent* researchers (i.e., researchers who are not working together). Whether or not meta-analysis is used, independent confirmation of results is an important standard that is applied when assessing the validity of the results reported on a given research topic.

An additional strength of meta-analysis is the objectivity of its conclusions.[1] After making subjective judgments regarding how to define a topic, how to search for relevant studies, and what criteria should be used to select studies from the available pool of potential studies, the remaining steps in a meta-analysis are mathematical, leading to an objectively obtained result (such as *d* or *r*). Note that in a traditional qualitative literature review (i.e., a review that consists of a narrative discussion without averaging measures of effect size), the conclusions are expressed in words. The phrasing, emphasis, and other characteristics of written communication used to express the conclusions in a non-mathematical, traditional review are not "objective" from a mathematical point of view.

A potential weakness occurs if a researcher is not careful in the selection of studies to include in a meta-analysis. Poor selection might produce results that are difficult to interpret (at best) or meaningless

(at worst). For instance, a meta-analysis involving all studies of tutoring in reading regardless of grade level (from first grade through high school) would not be very helpful in reaching conclusions that have implications for program implementation at any given grade level. This is because different types of results might be obtained at different levels (e.g., tutoring might be more helpful at the primary levels than at the high school level). When combined into one grand mean, the poor effectiveness at the high school level might cancel out much of the effectiveness at the primary level (by pulling the grand mean down).

One way to handle the problem of diversity across a set of studies is to establish criteria for the inclusion of a subset of studies on a topic in a meta-analysis. For instance, a researcher might include only those that meet criteria such as employment of teachers as tutors, use of tutoring sessions that last at least 30 minutes per session, and tutoring of only primary-grade students.

Another solution to the problem of diversity is to conduct multiple meta-analyses within a single meta-analytic project. For instance, a researcher might conduct three separate analyses: one for studies involving primary-grade students, one for those involving middle-school students, and a third for high school students. Comparing results of the three analyses would provide insights into the effectiveness of the programs at different grade levels.

In a report in which separate analyses are conducted for various subgroups, the variable on which the studies were divided into subgroups (e.g., the various grade levels) is called a *moderator variable* because it may moderate the results so that the results for subgroups are different from the grand combined result. The use of moderator variables is very common in published reports of meta-analyses.

A final potential weakness of meta-analysis stems from what is known as "publication bias." Typically, researchers are looking for significant differences (and relationships). When they fail to find them, they may be inclined *not* to write reports on such studies for submission for publication. It is also possible that some journal editors may have a bias such that they tend to reject studies with insignificant results for publication. Hence, the body of published research available on a topic for a meta-analysis might be biased toward studies that have

---

[1] Quantitative researchers value and strive for objectivity, while qualitative researchers tend to question whether objectivity is obtainable. For this and other philosophical reasons, qualitative researchers challenge the feasibility and desirability of seeking complete objectivity in scientific research.

statistically significant results. (A researcher conducting a meta-analysis, of course, wants to include all relevant studies whether the differences are significant or not in order to get an *overall* estimate of effectiveness.) A partial solution to this problem is for those conducting meta-analyses to search for studies that might be reported in dissertations, convention papers, government reports, and other non-journal sources, where there might not be as much bias against studies with statistically insignificant results.

Despite the potential weaknesses, meta-analysis is an important tool for gaining mathematical perspectives on the results of the studies on a research topic. It shows what can be obtained "objectively," which can be compared and contrasted with more subjective qualitative literature reviews on the same research topic.

Exercise on Topic 59

1. What was the sample size for the meta-analysis of the 48 studies mentioned in this topic?

2. According to this topic, is a "meta-analysis" *or* a "review" consisting of a narrative discussion of the literature more objective?

3. Even if a meta-analysis yields highly reliable results based on objective mathematical procedures, are its results necessarily valid? Explain.

4. What is the name of the "final potential weakness of meta-analysis"?

5. What is a partial solution to the problem you named in your response to Question 4?

Question for Discussion

6. Is meta-analysis completely objective? Explain.

For Students Who Are Planning Research

7. Based on what you know about meta-analysis, would you be interested in conducting one in the near future? At some later point in your professional career? Explain.

PART H

QUALITATIVE RESEARCH

In Topics 9 and 10 in the first part of this book, you learned about some of the major distinctions between quantitative and qualitative research. In this part, techniques used by qualitative researchers are explored in more detail. Topics 60 and 61 describe sampling in qualitative research, Topics 62 and 63 describe methods used to collect data, and Topic 64 describes specific techniques qualitative researchers use to ensure the quality of their research. This part ends with Topics 65 and 66, which describe two frequently used general approaches to the analysis of qualitative data.

NOTES

In Part C of this book (i.e., Topics 19 through 24), the emphasis was on sampling from the point of view of quantitative researchers. However, Topic 22 briefly described **purposive sampling**, which was widely used by qualitative researchers. To select a purposive sample, a researcher must first identify a research topic of interest and then seek individuals who are likely to have relevant information. This is sometimes described as seeking individuals who will be "rich sources of information." In other words, qualitative researchers make subjective judgments regarding the individuals to select based on the likelihood that they will be able to provide the needed information. Example 1 illustrates purposive sampling in which department chairs are asked to nominate potential participants. In the example, notice that the department chairs were asked to use their "judgment" rather than some objective criteria such as GPAs.

EXAMPLE 1
Purposive sampling: To identify a sample of Asian American college students majoring in clinical psychology who have the potential to become highly successful clinicians, letters were sent to chairs of departments of psychology soliciting nominations. The letters asked the chairs to nominate Asian American students who, in the chairs' judgment, had the greatest potential for success as clinical psychologists, without regard to the students' grades or test scores.

Purposive sampling is the correct term to use when the researchers seek participants who fit into some broad category such as "Asian American students with the greatest potential to succeed as clinical psychologists." In contrast, when there are a number of criteria to be applied in the selection of a sample, the sampling technique is more properly called **purposive criterion sampling**. This is illustrated in Example 2.

EXAMPLE 2
Purposive criterion sampling: To identify a sample of distinguished elementary school teachers, a list of all elementary school teachers in a school district who had received merit raises in the past five years was obtained. From those on the list, teachers were selected who met these criteria: (1) at least three years of teaching experience at the elementary school level, (2) hold full credentials issued by the state in which they taught, (3) hold Master's degrees in education,

and (4) had supervised at least one student teacher in the past three years. The last criterion was included because student teachers are typically assigned only to experienced teachers that school administrators believe to be master teachers.

Sometimes, qualitative researchers seek diversity in their samples. Thus, for instance, in Example 2, the researchers might purposively select teachers who are diverse in their ages, ethnic/racial backgrounds, and in their majors as undergraduates in college. Using a diverse sample introduces additional variables that might need to be accounted for during the analysis of participants' responses. Hence, some qualitative researchers seek fairly homogeneous samples in order to simplify their research.

Regardless of whether diversity is sought while sampling, qualitative researchers should collect demographic information that will help consumers of research "see" the participants. Example 3 lists the demographics collected for a qualitative study on the working lives of women living in a shelter due to domestic abuse. Note that these demographics were *not* a basis for selecting the women. The demographic data were collected at the onset of the study (after the participants were selected) so that the sample could be described in detail for consumers of the research.

EXAMPLE 3
Demographics of a sample: The demographic variables were: (1) age (e.g., average age was 35.4 years), (2) race/ethnicity, (3) marital status, (4) number of children, (5) highest educational level achieved, (6) type of employment, and (7) length of employment.[1]

Sometimes, qualitative researchers are silent on the issue of how their samples were selected and provide little demographic information in their research reports. For instance, they might simply say, "Fifteen male students enrolled in an introductory sociology class were interviewed." When this is encountered, it should be considered a serious flaw.

---

[1] Wettersten, K. B. et al. (2004). Freedom through self-sufficiency: A qualitative examination of the impact of domestic violence on the working lives of women in shelter. *Journal of Counseling Psychology, 51*, 447–462.

Exercise on Topic 60

1. Is purposive sampling widely used by "qualitative researchers" *or* by "quantitative researchers"?

2. Qualitative researchers make subjective judgments regarding the individuals to select based on the likelihood of what?

3. What is the proper name for purposive sampling when there are a number of criteria to be applied in the selection of a sample?

4. Do all qualitative researchers seek diversity in their samples?

5. In a qualitative study, is the sole purpose for collecting demographic data to assist in the selection of participants?

Question for Discussion

6. Name a general topic on which a qualitative researcher might conduct research. Then, name at least four demographic variables for which it would be appropriate to collect data in light of the topic. At least two of them should be variables other than those mentioned in Example 3.

For Students Who Are Planning Research

7. If you are planning to conduct qualitative research, do you plan to use "purposive sampling" *or* "purposive criterion sampling"? Explain your choice. If you plan to use purposive criterion sampling, name some of the criteria you plan to apply.

Sometimes, qualitative researchers are interested in researching a problem that exists in a particular location or institution. For instance, they might want to understand why few women on the campus at which they teach are majoring in engineering. For such a study, sampling women only from that campus would be appropriate.

When qualitative researchers are interested in results that may have broader applications, they should seek participants from a variety of sources. For instance, college women might be solicited from several different colleges in order to study why so few major in engineering. The use of participants from *diverse sources* is a methodological strength of a qualitative study when the researcher has a broader interest than just a single source (such as a single college campus). Example 1 illustrates how one group of researchers sought participants from diverse sources for a qualitative study.

EXAMPLE 1
Obtaining participants from diverse sources: A questionnaire assessing self-handicapping and defensive pessimism (see Martin, 1998) was administered to 584 first-year education students enrolled in three universities in metropolitan Sydney (Australia). Included in the questionnaire was an invitation for students to record their names and phone numbers if they were willing to be interviewed at a later time. In total, 134 students volunteered this information.[1]

One method to obtain data from diverse sources is to rent a list of names and addresses of potential participants.[2] For instance, most major professional associations, such as the American Sociological Association, will rent lists for a reasonable fee to individuals who are conducting legitimate research. Their lists are segmented so that, for instance, a list of only those who belong to a particular interest group within the organization can be rented. Example 2 illustrates the use of a rented list to reach out to diverse sources for participants.

EXAMPLE 2
Obtaining participants from diverse sources using a rented list: Participants were selected based on purposive criterion sampling from a list, purchased[3] by the research team, that consisted of professionals who had managerial positions in business, governmental, or nongovernmental organizations in a western Canadian city. The criteria for participation included....[4]

Qualitative researchers usually use fewer participants than quantitative researchers. A brief survey of sample sizes in a random sample of quantitative and qualitative research articles in five journals published by the American Psychological Association was conducted by this writer. The results of the survey are shown in Example 3.[5]

EXAMPLE 3
Sample sizes in five journals, each of which publishes both quantitative and qualitative research:
For qualitative research: Sample sizes ranged from 10 to 36, with a median (i.e., average) of 13.
For quantitative research: Sample sizes ranged from 25 to 766, with a median (i.e., average) of 82.

The major reason qualitative researchers use smaller samples than quantitative researchers is that qualitative data collection methods are often more expensive (including the expense of labor) and time-consuming than quantitative ones. For instance, a questionnaire for quantitative research can be distributed to hundreds of students in an auditorium relatively inexpensively. In contrast, individual interviews with students, each of which might last an hour or more, might make it possible to use only a dozen students, unless the researcher has funding for the research.

---

[1] Martin, A. J., Marsh, H. W., Williamson, A., & Debus, R. L. (2003). Self-handicapping, defensive pessimism, and goal orientation: A qualitative study of university students. *Journal of Educational Psychology*, 95, 617–628.

[2] To locate specialized lists, use the term "list broker" (including the quotation marks) in a computer search using any major search engine. At the time of this writing, 80,800 Web sites for list brokers were identified by conducting such a search.

[3] While some lists can be "purchased" for unlimited use, typically they are "rented" for a specific purpose and for a specific number of times that they may be used.

[4] Iwasaki, Y., MacKay, K. J., & Ristock, J. (2004). Gender-based analyses of stress among professional managers: An exploratory qualitative study. *International Journal of Stress Management*, 11, 56–79.

[5] The journals are: *Journal of Counseling Psychology*, *Journal of Educational Psychology*, *Cultural Diversity and Ethnic Minority Psychology*, *American Journal of Orthopsychiatry*, and *Professional Psychology: Research and Practice*.

In addition, quantitative researchers often hope for statistically significant results using significance tests such as the *t* test. As you may recall from Topic 50, the larger the sample, the more likely the results will be statistically significant. Qualitative researchers almost never test for statistical significance, and thus are not under pressure to use large samples for this purpose.

A criterion many qualitative researchers use for determining their sample size is called **saturation**. Briefly, this is how it is applied: As the data are collected (such as while conducting interviews), the qualitative researcher conducts a preliminary, informal analysis, noting the major and minor themes that are emerging. At the point at which several additional participants fail to respond with new information that leads to the identification of additional themes, the researcher might conclude that the data collection process has become "saturated." At that point, no additional participants are studied because new types of information are unlikely to be obtained by increasing the sample size. Thus, the "point of saturation" may determine the final sample size.

EXERCISE ON TOPIC 61

1. Are qualitative researchers always interested in problems that extend beyond one location or institution?

2. The use of participants from *diverse sources* is a methodological strength of a qualitative study when the researcher has what?

3. How might a qualitative researcher obtain names for a national sample?

4. Based on the brief survey reported in this topic, what was the average sample size for qualitative studies?

5. Do "qualitative researchers" *or* "quantitative researchers" tend to use more expensive data collection methods?

6. At what point might a qualitative researcher conclude that the data collection process has become "saturated"?

Question for Discussion

7. Are you surprised by the results reported in Example 3 on the previous page? Explain.

For Students Who Are Planning Research

8. If you are planning to conduct qualitative research, do you plan to sample from diverse sources? Will you collect data until you reach "saturation"? Explain.

Semi-structured interviews are by far the most widely used instrument for collecting data for qualitative research. Typically, these are face-to-face interviews, which are often tape recorded. The obvious advantages of tape recording the interviews are that they can be examined carefully at a later date and can be examined by other researchers who are collaborating on the research project.

There should be an **interview protocol** consisting of written directions for conducting the interview as well as a standard set of predetermined questions to be asked of all participants. Ideally, the questions should be pilot-tested with at least a few individuals who will not be participants in the study. Based on the pilot test, they should be revised, if necessary. Also, when possible, the predetermined questions should be reviewed by experts in the area being investigated and revised accordingly.

The initial questions should be designed to *establish rapport*. Example 1 shows three of the nine questions researchers asked in order to establish rapport with first-year university students at the beginning of an interview. Notice that the questions are quite general and do not deal with the direct topic of the research (i.e., self-handicapping, defensive pessimism, and goal orientation). These might also be thought of as "warm-up" questions.

EXAMPLE 1
Sample interview questions to establish rapport with first-year university students:

So now that you're at the university, what do you think?

Is the university what you expected?

Are you the enjoying university?[1]

Example 2 shows how a research team described their use of predetermined questions. Notice that they commenced with "broad, open-ended questions," followed by increasingly specific questions as the data collection progressed.

EXAMPLE 2
Use of predetermined questions in a semi-structured interview: A set of predetermined questions guided but did not limit the conversation. Interviews were about half an hour in length and commenced with broad, open-ended questions inviting participants to describe in their own words what assisted or impeded recovery during the 6 months immediately following discharge from treatment. As data collection progressed and emerging categories became apparent, participants were asked increasingly specific questions. In addition, summary statements and reflections were frequently made to validate responses and verify accurate understanding.[2]

"Semi-structured" refers to the fact that the interviewer does not need to ask only the predetermined questions. First, if a participant does not seem to understand a question, it can be reworded by the interviewer. Second, if a response is too terse, the interviewer can ask additional questions such as "Can you tell me more about it?" Third, the interviewer can probe with additional questions (in addition to the predetermined questions) in order to explore unexpected, unusual, or especially relevant material revealed by a participant.

It is especially important that qualitative interviewers be skilled in interviewing because they are not sticking to a predetermined script. This skill is acquired through practice. A novice who is planning qualitative research should conduct some practice interviews with individuals who will not be participants in the study. If possible, these practice interviews should be observed by an experienced qualitative researcher, who provides feedback to the novice.

It is also important that an interviewer be unbiased. An interviewer can achieve an unbiased attitude through the process of **self-disclosure**. This refers to considering the research problem in relation to the interviewer's background and attitudes before conducting the interviews. For instance, if a qualitative researcher is planning to study child-rearing practices of recent emigrants from Asia, he or she should consciously think about how they themselves were raised, their own experiences raising children, and any attitudes they have toward

---

[1] Martin, A. J., Marsh, H. W., Williamson, A., & Debus, R. L. (2003). Self-handicapping, defensive pessimism, and goal orientation: A qualitative study of university students. *Journal of Educational Psychology, 95,* 617–628.

[2] Cockell, S. J., Zaitsoff, S. L., & Geller, J. (2004). Maintaining change following eating disorder treatment. *Professional Psychology: Research and Practice, 35,* 527–534.

Asian Americans that might predispose them to skew the interview. The purpose of self-disclosure is to "clear the air" as well as to "clear the mind" before conducting the interviews. In some published reports of qualitative research, brief summaries of the researchers' self-disclosures are described.

Note that some of the predetermined questions should ask for **demographic information** (i.e., background information such as age, highest level of education), which will allow the researcher to describe the participants in a research report.

The next topic explores additional issues in data collection in qualitative research.

EXERCISE ON TOPIC 62

1. Are semi-structured interviews widely used for collecting data in qualitative research?

2. An "interview protocol" consists of what?

3. With whom should a pilot-test of the interview questions be conducted?

4. The initial questions should be designed to do what?

5. In a semi-structured interview, is it ever acceptable for an interviewer to ask questions not included in the list of predetermined questions?

6. What is the name of the process through which an interviewer can "clear the air" and "clear the mind"?

Question for Discussion

7. In your opinion, does the flexibility afforded by semi-structured interviewing open the possibility that the interviewer might bias the interview so that the interviewer obtains results along the lines that he or she already expected to find? Do you think that fully structured interviews (with only predetermined questions) might provide more valid data?

For Students Who Are Planning Research

8. If you are planning to conduct qualitative research, do you consider yourself to be a "novice"? If yes, how do you plan to gain experience before conducting your research? Explain.

Basic characteristics of semi-structured interviews were described in the previous topic. This topic explores some additional issues regarding them and then describes other measurement methods used in qualitative research.

The use of interview data to explore complex issues raises the issue of "reality." For instance, when participants describe how they were treated in some situation, the interview primarily exposes how participants "perceive" these matters. To many quantitative empiricists, *perception* is important but may not be as important as "reality." To most qualitative researchers, however, "objective factual reality"[1] is not as interesting or informative as participants' perceptions. Examining perceptions is known as a **phenomenological approach** to acquiring knowledge. Almost all qualitative researchers are in some sense "phenomenologists."[2,3]

In addition to one-on-one semi-structured interviews, qualitative researchers sometimes use **focus groups**. A focus group usually consists of six to twelve participants who are gathered to discuss a topic. The group is led by a **facilitator,**[4] as opposed to an "interviewer." The facilitator describes the topic to be discussed and tries to create a nonthreatening environment in which all group members feel free to express their opinions, attitudes, and experiences even if they differ from those of other participants. The facilitator should have a predetermined set of questions (also known as a "questioning route") to ensure that all relevant aspects of the topic are discussed. In addition, the facilitator should probe for additional information when needed.

Typically, a focus group lasts for about an hour. Also, it is typical to use two or more focus groups in a given research project.

A clear advantage of using focus groups is that it reveals *the evolution of perceptions in a social context*. It is interesting to note that the focus group method began as a business marketing research tool when marketing researchers realized that the perceptions of an individual in isolation may be different from their perceptions as they develop in a social context. For instance, a new product that initially seems satisfactory to an individual may be seen as less desirable after discussing it with other individuals who may have different perspectives on it.

Example 1 shows a brief description of how data were collected using the focus group method in a study on stress.

EXAMPLE 1
Description of data collection using focus groups: The moderator followed a focus group questioning route...developed by the research team and guided by the research objectives. The questioning route outlined opening comments about the topic of stress, introductory questions to engage the participants in the topic, transition questions related to evaluations of stress, key questions on the causes of stress and coping strategies, and ending questions to summarize the discussions and confirm main points.... At each stage of questioning, the moderator gave sufficient time for all the participants to share their views....[5]

Appendix A at the end of this book shows the "question route" used by the authors of Example 1. Notice that the questions in the appendix move logically from broad to more specific questions, with the exception of the "ending questions," which are broad.

Although it is widely discussed in research methodology textbooks, the use of direct, physical observation is seldom used in published qualitative research reports in the social and behavioral sciences. Nevertheless, direct observation can provide valuable data. In qualitative observational studies, an important distinction is made between **nonparticipant observation** and **participant observation**. In *nonparticipant observation*, the qualitative re-

---

[1] Both qualitative and quantitative researchers realize that "objective factual reality" is elusive. The distinction here is in whether the researchers strive to obtain it.

[2] Both qualitative and quantitative researchers are interested in "perceptions." The distinction here is in the degree to which the two types of researchers rely on perceptions for understanding a research topic.

[3] A full discussion of these issues is beyond the scope of this book. However, it is helpful to consider a trial in a court of law, in which a jury attempts to determine the reality of a situation, often relying heavily on witnesses' perceptions and recollections as well as any physical evidence.

[4] Facilitators are also sometimes called **moderators**.

---

[5] Iwasaki, Y., MacKay, K. J., & Ristock, J. (2004). Gender-based analyses of stress among professional managers: An exploratory qualitative study. *International Journal of Stress Management, 11*, 56–79.

searcher observes individuals as an outsider such as by sitting at the back of a classroom to observe student/teacher interactions. A particular concern with this type of observation is that the participants' behavior may change from its normal course because the participants know they are being observed.

In *participant observation*, the researcher becomes (or already is) a member of the group being researched, and thus makes his or her observations as an insider. For instance, a teacher who is also a researcher who wants to study a high school that is widely known for academic achievement might ar-range to teach at the school, providing an opportunity to observe while participating. It is important to note that making participant observations without revealing to those who are being observed that research is being conducted raises serious ethical problems.

Researchers who use observational methods often refer to their research as **field research**, which has historical roots in the field of anthropology. When the focus is on cultural issues, the research may be referred to as **ethnography**.

EXERCISE ON TOPIC 63

1. Examining perceptions is known as what type of "approach" to acquiring knowledge?

2. A focus group usually consists of about how many participants?

3. What are the two names for the individual who leads a focus group?

4. According to this topic, what is a "clear advantage" of using focus groups?

5. What is the name of the type of observation in which the researcher observes as an outsider?

6. When the emphasis in field research is on cultural issues, the research may be referred to as what?

Question for Discussion

7. Do you think that it would be easier to analyze and interpret data from "individual interviews" *or* from "focus group discussions"? Explain.

For Students Who Are Planning Research

8. If you are planning to conduct qualitative research, do you anticipate using focus groups? Explain.

TOPIC 64 QUALITY CONTROL IN QUALITATIVE RESEARCH

This topic describes some of the specific techniques that qualitative researchers use to establish the dependability and trustworthiness of their data.[1]

One technique is to use multiple sources for obtaining data on the research topic. The technical name for this is **data triangulation**. For instance, for a qualitative study of discrimination in an employment setting, a researcher might interview employees, their supervisors, and the responsible personnel officers. To the extent that the various sources provide similar information, the data can be said to be corroborated.

The methods used to collect data can also be triangulated. For instance, a researcher might conduct individual interviews with parents regarding their child-rearing practices and then have the same participants provide data via focus groups. This would be an example of **methods triangulation**.

Note that in *data triangulation*, typically two or more types of participants (such as employees and supervisors) are used to collect data on a research topic. In contrast, in *methods triangulation*, only one type of participant (such as parents) is used to provide data but two or more methods are used to collect the data.

An important technique to assure the quality of qualitative research is to form a *research team*, with each member of the team participating in the collection and analysis of data. This can be thought of as **researcher triangulation**, which reduces the possibility that the results of qualitative research represent only the idiosyncratic views of one individual researcher.

Sometimes, it is helpful to form a **team of researchers with diverse backgrounds**. For instance, for a study on the success of minority students in medical school, a team of researchers that consists of both medical school instructors and medical school students might strengthen the study by providing more than one perspective when collecting and analyzing the data.

The issue of having diversity in a research team is addressed in Example 1, which is from a qualitative research report on gender issues. The researchers point out that gender diversity in their research team helps to provide a "comprehensive view."

EXAMPLE 1
Diversity in a research team: Gender and sexuality issues were analyzed by all three researchers. That our research team included one man and two women probably helped us have a comprehensive view of the different meanings of gender issues.[2]

Oral interviews and focus groups are typically audiotaped and then transcribed. Sometimes, transcription is difficult because certain participants might not speak distinctly. In addition, transcribers sometimes make errors. Therefore, checking the accuracy of a transcription helps to ensure the quality of the data. In Example 2, a sample of segments was checked.

EXAMPLE 2
Checking the accuracy of transcriptions: Each audiotaped session was transcribed verbatim. Segments of the transcriptions were checked randomly against the audiotapes for accuracy.[3]

In the analysis of data, which is covered in the next two topics in more detail, each member of a research team should initially work independently (without consulting each other) and then compare the results of their analyses. To the extent that they agree, the results are more dependable. This technique examines what is called **interobserver agreement**.[4] When there are disagreements, often they can be resolved by having the researchers discuss their differences until they reach a consensus. This process is described in more detail in Topic 66.

The use of an outside expert can also help to ensure the quality of the research. A researcher's peer (such as another experienced qualitative researcher) can examine the process used to collect data, the resulting data and the conclusions, and then provide feedback to the researcher. This process is called **peer review**. Under certain circumstances, the peer

---

[1] The terms "dependability" and "trustworthiness" in qualitative research loosely correspond to the terms "reliability" and "validity" in quantitative research.

[2] Rasera, E. F., Vieira, E. M., & Japur, M. (2004). Influence of gender and sexuality on the construction of being HIV positive as experienced in a support group in Brazil. *Families, Systems, & Health, 22,* 340–351.

[3] Lukens, E. P., Thorning, H., & Lohrer, S. (2004). Sibling perspectives on severe mental illness: Reflections on self and family. *American Journal of Orthopsychiatry, 74,* 489–501.

[4] In qualitative research, this is sometimes called *intercoder agreement*. In quantitative research, this concept is called *interobserver reliability*.

who provides the review is called an **auditor**, which is discussed in Topic 66.

The dependability of the results can also be enhanced by a process called **member checking**. This term is based on the idea that the participants are "members" of the research team. By having the participants/members review the results of the analysis, researchers can determine whether their results "ring true" to the participants. If not, adjustments can be made in the description of the results.

EXERCISE ON TOPIC 64

1. Suppose a researcher interviewed participants and then observed the behavior of the same participants. Is this an example of "data triangulation" *or* an example of "methods triangulation"?

2. In data triangulation, how many types of participants are used?

3. What is the name of the type of triangulation that reduces the possibility that the results of qualitative research represent only the idiosyncratic views of one individual researcher?

4. Is it ever desirable for a team of researchers to consist of individuals with diverse backgrounds?

5. In "peer review," what is a peer?

6. Who are the "members" in "member checking"?

Question for Discussion

7. Name a research topic for qualitative research for which it might be helpful to have a team of researchers with diverse backgrounds. Explain why it might be helpful for the research topic you name.

For Students Who Are Planning Research

8. If you are planning to conduct qualitative research, which of the techniques described in this topic, if any, do you plan to use? Explain your choice(s).

To guide their data analysis, qualitative researchers usually select a general, overarching approach. Perhaps the most frequently used approach is **grounded theory**. At first, the term "theory" in "grounded theory" can be a bit misleading because it does not refer to an existing theory of human behavior. Instead, it refers to an *inductive method* of analysis that can lead to theories of behavior. In the inductive approach, which is characteristic of all qualitative research, the results (including resulting "theories") emerge through consideration and analysis of the data. In other words, qualitative researchers start with the data and develop theories based on the data (i.e., grounded in the data). In contrast, many quantitative researchers start with an existing theory or deduce a new one from existing information and collect data to test the theory; they typically do not look to the data they have collected to develop new theories. Thus, quantitative researchers use a *deductive method*.

To put it more simply, quantitative researchers deduce theories from what is known and test the theories with research. In contrast, qualitative researchers collect data and analyze it in order to derive theories that explain the patterns noted in the responses of participants. In their seminal work on how to use the grounded theory approach, Strauss and Corbin said:

> It is through careful scrutiny of data, line by line, that researchers are able to uncover new concepts and novel relationships and to systematically develop categories in terms of their properties and dimensions.[1]

The grounded theory approach starts with **open coding**. In this stage, segments of the transcripts of the interviews are examined for distinct, separate segments (such as ideas or experiences of the participants) and are "coded" by identifying them and giving each type a name. For instance, in a study of adolescent delinquents, each statement referring to overt aggression by the participant might be coded with a certain color highlighter. Subcategories should also be developed, when possible. For instance, "overt aggression" might have two subcategories: "overt aggression toward peers" and "overt aggression toward adults, including parents and teachers."[2] Preliminary notes on any overarching themes noticed in the data should also be made at this point.

The second step in the grounded theory approach to data analysis is called **axial coding**. At this stage, the transcripts of the interviews and any other data sources, such as memos written during data collection, are reexamined with the purpose of identifying relationships between the categories and themes identified during open coding. Some important types of relationships that might be noted are (1) temporal (X usually precedes Y in time), (2) causal (X caused participants to do Y),[3] (3) associational (X and Y usually or always occur at about the same time but are not believed to be causally connected), (4) valence (participants have stronger emotional reactions to X than to Y), and (5) spatial (X and Y occur in the same place *or* X and Y occur in different places).

In the final stages of the grounded theory approach to analysis, qualitative researchers develop a **core category**, which is the main overarching category under which the other categories and subcategories belong. They also attempt to describe the *process* that leads to the relationships identified in the previous stage of the analysis. A process description should describe how the categories work together (or in opposition to each other) in order to arrive at the conditions or behaviors contained in the core category.

A key element throughout the analysis of data using the grounded theory approach is **constant comparison**, which is a technical term that refers to constantly comparing each new element of the data with all previous elements that have been coded in order to establish and refine categories. While this is being done, the analysis focuses on similarities

---

[1] Strauss, A. L., and Corbin, J. (1998). *Basics of Qualitative Research: Techniques and Procedures for Developing Grounded Theory* (2nd ed.). Thousand Oaks, CA: Sage.

[2] In keeping with the inductive approach, categories and subcategories should be suggested by the data during data analysis, not developed prior to analyzing the data. Categories and subcategories developed at this stage should be regarded as preliminary and subject to change during the remainder of the analysis using the grounded theory approach.

[3] Participants' claims that "X caused me to do Y" should be viewed with caution because participants sometimes are not sufficiently insightful into the causes of their behavior.

and differences in the data that might be accounted
for by a core idea.

EXERCISE ON TOPIC 65

1. In the term "grounded theory," does the term "theory" refer to a theory that existed prior to conducting the research?

2. Does the grounded theory approach use the "inductive approach" *or* does it use the "deductive approach"?

3. The grounded theory approach starts with what type of coding?

4. What is the name of the second step in the grounded theory approach?

5. In which type of coding is there an emphasis on identifying relationships?

6. What is the technical term that refers to constantly comparing each new element of the data with all previous elements that have been coded in order to establish and refine categories?

Question for Discussion

7. Do you think that the inductive approach (such as grounded theory) *or* the deductive approach (such as quantitative research) are more likely to yield important information? Are they equally likely to do so? Explain.

For Students Who Are Planning Research

8. If you are planning to conduct qualitative research, do you anticipate using the grounded theory approach? Explain. How prepared do you feel to use it? If poorly prepared, how do you plan to learn more about it?

As you learned in the previous topic, qualitative researchers usually select a general, overarching approach to the analysis of their data. In the previous topic, the grounded theory approach was described. In this topic, **consensual qualitative research (CQR)** is described.[1] Like all qualitative research, both approaches are *inductive* (see the previous topic).

As its name implies, CQR aims for having a team of researchers arrive at a consensus on the meaning of the data collected (such as interview transcripts).

The first step in the CQR method is to **code into domains**. This refers to segmenting the data (such as interview transcripts) into groups according to the topics they cover. After each member of the research team has done this, they meet and discuss and refine the domains until they reach unanimous agreement on them.

The next step is to **develop core ideas within domains**. This is done by writing short summaries (i.e., abstracts) that reduce the original ideas of participants into fewer words. Notice that initially, the researchers work independently in developing core ideas.

The third step in CQR is called **cross-analysis**. In this step, the core ideas are grouped into categories based on similarities. This results in a higher level of generalization (i.e., the results are becoming less specific and more general).

Example 1 shows how one team of researchers described the above three steps.

EXAMPLE 1
Description of the use of CQR by a research team:
…the consensual qualitative research (CQR) method was developed by Hill et al. (1997) with the understanding that complex issues discussed during interviews often involve "multiple perspectives and levels of awareness" (p. 523). Consequently, CQR requires that researchers on a team openly discuss any ambiguities in meanings that may exist in the data obtained during the interviews. This open discussion allows for clarification and often promotes more accurate conceptualizations of the data. CQR directs researchers to group data into domains (clusters of similar topics), constructs core ideas (summaries of

domain content), and conducts cross-analyses (identification of the themes in the core ideas across the cases) to determine the categories in which the core ideas fit.[2]

In CQR there may be an external **stability check**, which can be done by examining data in addition to the interview transcripts (perhaps eyewitness accounts or physical evidence), if available.

Internal stability is examined in CQR by determining the extent to which each category was general, typical, or variant. Typically, domains that apply to all the participants are called **general**; those that apply to half or more of the participants are called **typical**; and those that apply to less than half but more than two are called **variant**. When writing up the results, those who use CQR usually use these labels throughout their results sections. Emphasis on enumerating the number of participants to which each domain applies is a distinctive feature of CQR. Example 2 shows a portion of the results section of a CQR study in which there is enumeration.

EXAMPLE 2
Enumeration in the results of a CQR study (bold added for emphasis):
Results for European American therapists yielded one **typical** and two **variant categories** (neither of the variant categories emerged for the African American sample). As a **typical category**, these participants stated that, like their African American counterparts, they would address race when they deemed it relevant to the therapy process or relationship.… In the first **variant category**, these participants reported that if a client raised the topic of race, the therapist would respond.…[3]

The CQR method requires the use of an **auditor**, who is an outside expert. The auditor usually re-

---

[1] For more information on CQR, see Hill, C. E., Thompson, B. J., & Williams, E. N. (1997). A guide to conducting consensual qualitative research. *The Counseling Psychologist, 25,* 517–572.

[2] DiGiorgio, K. E., Arnkoff, D. B., Glass, C. R., Lyhus, K. E., & Walter, R. C. (2004). EMDR and theoretical orientation: A qualitative study of how therapists integrate eye movement desensitization and reprocessing into their approach to psychotherapy. *Journal of Psychotherapy Integration, 14,* 227–252.

[3] Knox, S., Burkard, A. W., Johnson, A. J., Suzuki, L. A., & Ponterotto, J. G. (2003). African American and European American therapists' experiences of addressing race in cross-racial psychotherapy dyads. *Journal of Counseling Psychology, 50,* 466–481.

views the work of the research team after each major step in a study, not just at its conclusion. In a report on a CQR study, the following should be briefly described: the credentials of the auditor, the steps at which the auditor supplied feedback, and whether changes were made on the basis of the auditors' feedback. If changes were made, the types of changes made should be mentioned.

EXERCISE ON TOPIC 66

1. "Unlike the grounded theory approach in Topic 65, CQR is *deductive*." Is this statement true *or* false?

2. What is the first step in analyzing data using the CQR approach?

3. Which step includes writing short summaries of participants' ideas?

4. What is done in the cross-analysis?

5. In CQR, what term is used for domains that apply to all the participants?

6. Does the auditor review the work of the research team only at the conclusion of the study?

Question for Discussion

7. Do you think that CQR (as you understand it from this topic) is likely to produce studies that yield important and valuable information? Explain.

For Students Who Are Planning Research

8. If you are planning to conduct qualitative research, do you anticipate using CQR? Explain. How prepared do you feel to use it? If poorly prepared, how do you plan to learn more about it?

APPENDIX A
OUTLINE OF QUESTION ROUTE FOR A FOCUS GROUP STUDY OF STRESS[1]

Opening comments:

Welcome and statements regarding the purpose of the study, focus group procedures, and ethical issues.

Opening comment:

"Please tell us a little bit about yourself."

Introductory question:

"Stress is prevalent in our everyday lives because many people feel stressed. In thinking about your daily life, what does stress mean to you?"

Transition questions:

"Is stress a negative factor in your life? If so, explain how it is negative."
"Is stress a positive factor in your life? If so, in what ways is it positive?"
  Subprobe: "What is it about stress that makes it good or bad?"

Key questions:

"What are the things that contribute to stress in your life?"
  Subprobe: (a) "How does this work? Does one thing contribute to stress more than others, or does the combination of many things contribute to stress?" (b) "Do you have any particular health concerns that contribute to your feelings of stress? Can you tell us more about this?" (c) "Besides possible health concerns, is there anything else that adds to your feelings of stress?" (d) "Does being a manager contribute to your feelings of stress? If so, describe how."

Ending questions:

"All things considered, what would you say is the major cause of stress in your life?"
"Is there anything about stress that we haven't talked about that you would like to raise before we leave tonight?"

---

[1] Reprinted from page 62 of Iwasaki, Y., MacKay, K. J., & Ristock, J. (2004). Gender-based analyses of stress among professional managers: An exploratory qualitative study. *International Journal of Stress Management, 11*, 56–79.

NOTES

Appendix B
Excerpts from Literature Reviews

The following are excerpts from literature reviews that appeared in the introductions to research reports published in academic journals. They constitute the stimulus material for Questions 8 through 19 in Topic 17 of this book.

Excerpt 1: Emotion Control in the Performance of Salespeople

To better perform their tasks, salespeople conduct themselves with customers in friendly, positive, and professional ways. However, things often happen unexpectedly in customer–salesperson interactions to produce negative emotions (e.g., anxiety, embarrassment, frustration, guilt, shame) that threaten to disrupt the relationship (e.g., Fine, Shepherd, & Josephs, 1994; George, 1998; Verbeke & Bagozzi, 2000). As a consequence, salespeople attempt to manage their relationships with customers so as to prevent dysfunctional effects of negative emotions (e.g., Hochschild, 1983). An important part of the management of relationships is the self-regulation of emotions. Frijda (1994) defines this process as one of emotion control or inhibition: "Inhibitory control is the means whereby emotions get attuned to the seriousness of their cause...inhibition is primarily regulated by anticipation of the aversive consequences of the response to be controlled" (p. 120).

References

Fine, L., Shepherd, D., & Josephs, S. (1994). Sexual harassment in the sales force: The customer is NOT always right. *Journal of Personal Selling and Sales Management, 14,* 15–30.

Frijda, N. H. (1994). Emotions are functional, most of the time. In P. Ekman & R. J. Davidson (Eds.), *The nature of emotions: Fundamental questions* (pp. 112–122). New York: Oxford University Press.

George, J. M. (1998). Salesperson mood at work: Implications for helping customers. *Journal of Personal Selling and Sales Management, 18,* 23–30.

Hochschild, A. R. (1983). *The managed heart: Commercialization of human feeling.* Berkeley, CA: University of California Press.

Verbeke, W. J., & Bagozzi, R. P. (2000). Sales call anxiety: Exploring what it means when fear rules a sales encounter. *Journal of Marketing, 64,* 88–101.

Source

Bagozzi, R. P., Verbeke, W., & Gavino, J. C., Jr. (2003). Culture moderates the self-regulation of shame and its effects on performance: The case of salespersons in the Netherlands and the Philippines. *Journal of Applied Psychology, 88,* 219–233. (Excerpt from page 219.) Copyright 2003 by American Psychological Association. Reprinted with permission.

Notes:

_____

_____

_____

_____

_____

Excerpt 2: Social Workers' Perceptions of Working Women

If the move to professionalization preoccupied social workers, was it at the expense of ignoring serious social issues? Bartlett (1958) acknowledged that the social work profession had often been in the position of taking action after problems had reached an acute state. As she stated, "social, economic, and political trends are of major importance in influencing the development of social work practice" (p. 9). However, the only social issue she identified as a perceived problem was one of the rising numbers of working mothers. She seemed unaware that in many minority communities, particularly African American, most mothers had to work, not for personal fulfillment but for their family to survive.

Reference

Bartlett, H. M. (1958). Towards clarification and improvement of social work practice. *Social Work, 3*(2), 3–9.

Source

O'Brian, C. (2003). Resource and educational empowerment: A social work paradigm for the disenfranchised. *Research on Social Work Practice, 13,* 388–399. (Excerpt from page 389.) Copyright 2003 by Sage Publications, Inc. Reprinted with permission.

Notes:

_____

_____

_____

_____

_____

Excerpt 3: Benefits of Group Work for Survivors of Childhood Abuse

Group work is highly recommended for adult survivors of childhood abuse as a part of this recovery process (Ferrara, 2002; Harris, 1998; Harrison, 2001; Randall, 1995; Shaffer, Brown, & McWhirter, 1998; Werner & Kurpius-Robinson, 1995; Zaidi, 1999). Groups are beneficial to survivors in a number of ways. First, groups serve as a support system and help members develop a sense of belonging, thereby reducing their sense of isolation (Armsworth & Stronck, 1999; Draucker, 1999; Zaidi, 1999) and instilling a sense of hope (Gorey et al., 2001). Developing relationships within the group reduces the mistrust of others that survivors often experience, and this opportunity helps them begin to form more meaningful relationships with others (Ainscough & Toon, 1993; Draucker, 1999; Lubin et al., 1998). As members identify with other survivors' experiences, their reactions and perceptions of the abuse are normalized (Shaffer et al., 1998). Survivors are also able to gain self-esteem as their experiences are validated (Draucker, 1999; Ferrara, 2002).

Second, the group process can enhance members' self-awareness concerning how current beliefs and coping strategies are connected to the abuse in the past (Ainscough & Toon, 1993; Shaffer et al., 1998). Groups enable members to challenge and modify maladaptive beliefs related to safety, trust, power, self-esteem, and intimacy (Ainscough & Toon, 1993; Owens et al., 2001; Thomas et al., 1994; Zaidi, 1999). Third, group work can be an effective venue for learning interpersonal skills and anxiety management strategies and can provide a safe environment for members to practice new skills and behaviors (Corey & Corey, 2001; Ferrara, 2002; Shaffer et al., 1998; Zaidi, 1999). Finally, groups offer survivors the opportunity to help other members, providing an altruistic experience in which they view themselves as useful and capable (Courtois, 1988; Harrison, 2001).

References

Ainscough, C., & Toon, K. (1993). *Breaking free: Help for survivors of child sexual abuse.* London: Sheldon Press.

Armsworth, M. W., & Stronck, K. (1999). Intergenerational effects of incest on parenting: Skills, abilities, and attitudes. *Journal of Counseling and Development, 77,* 303–314.

Corey, M. S., & Corey, G. (2001). *Groups: Process and practice* (6th ed.). Pacific Grove, CA: Brooks/Cole.

Courtois, C. A. (1988). *Healing the incest wound: Adult survivors in therapy.* New York: Norton.

Draucker, C. B. (1999). *Counseling survivors of childhood sexual abuse.* London: Sage.

Ferrara, F. F. (2002). *Childhood sexual abuse: Developmental effects across the lifespan.* Pacific Grove, CA: Brooks/Cole.

Gorey, K. M., Richter, N. L., & Snyder, E. (2001). Guilt, isolation, and hopelessness among female survivors of childhood sexual abuse: Effectiveness of a group work intervention. *Child Abuse & Neglect, 25,* 347–355.

Harris, M. (1998). *Trauma recovery and empowerment: A clinician's guide for working with women in groups.* New York: Free Press.

Harrison, R. (2001). An application of Adlerian principles in counseling survivors of sexual abuse. *Journal of Individual Psychology, 57,* 94–101.

Lubin, H., Loris, M., Burt, J., & Johnson, D. R. (1998). Efficacy of psychoeducational group therapy in reducing symptoms of posttraumatic stress disorder among multiple traumatized women. *American Journal of Psychiatry, 155,* 1172–1177.

Owens, G. P., Pike, J. L., & Chard, K. L. (2001). Treatment effects of cognitive processing therapy on cognitive distortions of female child sexual abuse survivors. *Behavior Therapy, 32,* 413–424.

Randall, D. A. (1995). Curative factor rankings for female incest groups: A summary of three studies. *Journal for Specialists in Group Work, 20,* 232–239.

Shaffer, J., Brown, L. L., & McWhirter, J. J. (1998). Survivors of child sexual abuse and dissociative coping: Relearning in a group context. *Journal for Specialists in Group Work, 23,* 74–94.

Thomas, M. C., Nelson, C. S., & Sumners, C. M. (1994). From victims to victors: Group process as the path to recovery for males molested as children. *Journal for Specialists in Group Work, 19,* 102–111.

Werner, N., & Kurpius-Robinson, S. (1995). *Shattered innocence: A practical guide for counseling women survivors of childhood sexual abuse.* Washington, DC: Taylor and Francis.

Zaidi, L. (1999). Group treatment for adult survivors of childhood abuse. In B. H. Young & D. D. Blake (Eds.), *Group treatment for PTSD: Conceptualizations, themes, and processes* (pp. 201–220). London: Brunner/Mazel.

Source

Choate, L. H., & Henson, A. (2003). Group work with adult survivors of childhood abuse and neglect: A psychoeducational approach. *The Journal for Specialists in Group Work, 28,* 106–121. (Excerpt from page 108.) Copyright 2003 by Sage Publications, Inc. Reprinted with permission.

Notes:

_____

_____

_____

_____

_____

Excerpt 4: Reasons for Interpersonal Conflict

Conflict has been defined as "perceived divergence of interest, or a belief that the parties' current aspirations cannot be achieved simultaneously" (Rubin, Pruitt, & Kim, 1994, p. 5). Many conflict analysts attribute interpersonal conflict to incompatible goals (Hocker & Wilmot, 1995; Laue, 1987). Others cite problems with communication (Folger, Poole, & Stutman, 2001; Grimshaw, 1990) resulting from different styles of communication (Tannen, 1993) or from cultural differences (Folger et al., 2001). C. Moore (1996) attributed interpersonal conflict to five sources, consisting of (a) data conflicts—related to lack of or incorrect information; (b) interest conflicts—concerned with procedure or content; (c) structural conflicts—involved with unequal power or resources; (d) value conflicts—influenced by diverse goals or ideals; and (e) relationship conflicts—related to poor communication or uncontrolled emotions. Conflict and the sources of conflict for parents were confirmed in a previous analysis (J. Moore & Kordick, 2003).

References

Folger, J., Poole, M., & Stutman, S. (2001). *Working through conflict strategies for relationships, groups, and organizations* (4th ed.). New York: Longman.

Grimshaw, A. D. (Ed.). (1990). *Conflict talk: Sociolinguistic investigations of arguments in conversations*. Cambridge, UK: Cambridge University Press.

Hocker, J. L., & Wilmot, W. W. (1995). *Interpersonal conflict* (4th ed.). Madison, WI: Brown & Benchmark.

Laue, J. (1987). The emergence and institutionalization of third party roles in conflict. In D. J. Sandole & I. Sandole-Staroste (Eds.), *Conflict management and problem solving: From interpersonal to international applications* (pp. 17–29). New York: New York University Press.

Moore, C. W. (1996). *The mediation process: Practical strategies for resolving conflict*. San Francisco: Jossey-Bass.

Moore, J. B., & Kordick, M. F. (2003). *Conflict between families and health care providers: Experiences of children with cancer and their parents*. Manuscript submitted for publication.

Rubin, J. Z., Pruitt, D. G., & Kim, S. H. (1994). *Social conflict: Escalation, stalemate, and settlement* (2nd ed.). New York: McGraw-Hill.

Tannen, D. (1993). *Framing in discourse*. New York: Oxford University Press.

Source

Moore, J. B., & Beckwitt, A. E. (2003). Parents' reactions to conflict with health care providers. *Western Journal of Nursing Research*, *25*, 30–44. (Excerpt from page 31.) Copyright 2003 by Sage Publications, Inc. Reprinted with permission.

Notes:

_____

_____

_____

_____

Excerpt 5: Prevalence of Alcohol Use by Adolescents

During the transition from adolescence to adulthood, developmental activities such as testing limits, becoming independent, and making autonomous decisions may be manifest in alcohol use (Baumrind, 1987). Indeed, most initiation of alcohol use occurs during adolescence (Daughton, Daughton, & Patil, 1997). In a survey of 284 high school seniors, 84% reported a history of alcohol use (Daughton et al., 1997). Chen and Kandel (1995) found that by age 19, 88% of students reported alcohol use. According to Johnston, O'Malley, and Bachman (1989, 1991), 90% of students have consumed alcohol by the time they are seniors in high school. In a study of more than 1,000 students, Kelly and Edwards (1998) found that 62% of 7th-grade, 87% of 9th-grade, and 95% of 11th-grade students reported having consumed alcohol.

References

Baumrind, D. (1987). A developmental perspective on adolescent risk taking in contemporary America. In C. Irwin (Ed.), *Adolescent social behavior and health*: *New directions for child development* (No. 37, pp. 93–125). San Francisco: Jossey-Bass.

Chen, K., & Kandel, D. (1995). Natural history of drug use from adolescence to the mid-thirties in a general population sample. *American Journal of Public Health*, *85*, 41–47.

Daughton, J., Daughton, D., & Patil, K. (1997). Self-recognition of alcohol and cigarette dependency among high school seniors. *Perceptual and Motor Skills*, *85*, 115–120.

Johnston, L., O'Malley, P., & Bachman, J. (1989). *Drug use, drinking and smoking: National survey results from high school, college and young adult population 1975–1988*. Rockville, MD: National Institute on Drug Abuse.

Johnston, L., O'Malley, P., & Bachman, J. (1991). *Trends in drug use and associated factors among American high school students, college students, and young adults: 1975–1989*. Ann Arbor, MI: Institute for Social Research, University of Michigan.

Kelly, K., & Edwards, R. (1998). Image advertisements for alcohol products: Is their appeal associated with adolescents' intention to consume alcohol? *Adolescence*, *33*(129), 47–59.

Source

Workman, J. E. (2003). Alcohol promotional clothing items and alcohol use by underage consumers. *Family and Consumer Sciences Research Journal*, *31*, 331–354. (Excerpt from page 331.) Copyright 2003 by Sage Publications, Inc. Reprinted with permission.

Notes:

_____

_____

_____

_____

_____

Excerpt 6: High School Reform and Black Male Students

Despite efforts to improve ineffective schools and raise academic achievement, there is a well-documented, lingering achievement gap between affluent and poor students as well as between white and black students (Grissmer & Flanagan, 2001; Jencks & Phillips, 1998). Moreover, there is growing evidence that low socioeconomic students of color are disproportionately taught by less qualified teachers and attend deteriorated schools that are racially and socioeconomically isolated (Darling-Hammond, 1997). In the report *What Matters Most: Teaching for America's Future*, Darling-Hammond and her colleagues (National Commission of Teaching and America's Future, 1996) contended that students enrolled in high-poverty and racially isolated high schools are unlikely to have classroom teachers with certification or college degrees in their field. Such students, they reported, have less than a 50% probability of taking a course with a math or science teacher holding a state-issued license and undergraduate degree in the field she or he teaches (National Commission of Teaching and America's Future, 1996).

References

Darling-Hammond, L. (1997). Teachers and teaching: Testing policy hypotheses from a national commission report. *Education Researcher, 27,* 5–15.

Grissmer, D., & Flanagan, A. (2001). *The role of federal resources in closing the achievement gaps of minority and disadvantaged students.* Santa Monica, CA: RAND.

Jencks, C., & Phillips, M. (Eds.). (1998). *The Black–White Test score gap.* Washington, DC: Brookings Institution.

National Commission of Teaching and America's Future. (1996). *What matters most: Teaching for America's future.* New York: Author.

Source

Jordan, W. J., & Cooper, R. (2003). High school reform and Black male students: Limits and possibilities of policy and practice. *Urban Education, 38,* 196–216. (Excerpt from page 197.) Copyright 2003 by Sage Publications, Inc. Reprinted with permission.

Notes:

_____

_____

_____

_____

_____

APPENDIX C
ELECTRONIC DATABASES FOR LOCATING LITERATURE

Access Note

Access to all the following electronic databases can usually be obtained free of charge through your college or university library, which probably maintains license agreements with the database publishers. Consult with your reference librarian for information on their availability at your library. Note that the *ERIC* database and *MEDLINE* database are available free of charge to all individuals via the Internet.

Databases Discussed in Topic 15

The *ERIC* database contains more than one million abstracts of unpublished documents and published journal articles on educational research and practice. The *AskERIC* version of the database can be accessed on the Internet free of charge by any individual. A unique, free feature of this database is the "Ask an ERIC Expert" feature, which allows users to pose free-form questions and receive information based on bibliographic sources in response. Visit www.eric.ed.gov for more information.

PsycINFO indexes and abstracts journal articles from more than 1,800 journals, which constitute more than 77% of the database. Books, dissertations, and university and government reports are also included. An online thesaurus is available. Members of the public can access this database via the Internet for a daily service charge (charged to a credit card) at www.apa.org. Consult with the reference librarian at your college or university for information on accessing this database free of charge through your library's license agreement.

PsycARTICLES (a database that is related to *PsycINFO*) contains more than 3,100 full-text articles (not just abstracts) from more than 50 journals and selected chapters from books published by the American Psychological Association. Members of the public can access this database via the Internet for a daily service charge (charged to a credit card) at www.apa.org. Consult with the reference librarian at your college or university for information on accessing this database free of charge through your library's license agreement.

Sociological Abstracts indexes and abstracts (i.e., summarizes) articles in 1,900 international journals, and indexes and abstracts books and chapters in books. *Sociological Abstracts* indexes dissertations, book reviews, film reviews, and game reviews. An online thesaurus is available. Consult with the reference librarian at your college or university for information on accessing this database free of charge through your library's license agreement.

Other Electronic Databases

The *ABI/Inform* (*ProQuest*) database is a business and management database with abstracts and many full-text articles from over 1,000 U.S. and international publications. Topics include advertising, marketing, economics, human resources, finance, taxation, and computers.

The *Chicano Database* identifies all types of material about Chicanos. It incorporates the *Spanish Speaking Mental Health Database*, which covers psychological, sociological, and educational literature. Also included (1992 to the present) are the broader Latino experiences of Puerto Ricans, Cuban Americans, and Central American immigrants.

Child Development Abstracts and Bibliography includes abstracts from professional periodicals and book reviews related to the growth and development of children from 1927 to the present. It is divided into seven sections: biology, health, and medicine; cognition, learning, and perception; education; psychiatry and clinical psychology; social psychology and personality; theory, methodology, and book reviews; and book notices.

Contemporary Women's Issues provides full-text access to journals, hard-to-find newsletters, reports, pamphlets, fact sheets, and guides on a broad array of gender-related issues published since 1992.

Criminal Justice Periodical Index contains full-text articles from criminology and criminal justice journal articles on law enforcement, corrections administration, social work, drug rehabilitation, criminal and family law, industrial security, and other related fields. There is also indexing and abstracts for 150 U.S. and international journals.

Dissertation Abstracts Online is a definitive subject, title, and author guide to virtually every American dissertation accepted at an accredited institution since 1861. Selected master's theses have been included since 1962. The electronic version indexes doctoral records from July 1980 (*Dissertation Abstracts International*, Volume 41, Number 1) to the present. Abstracts are included for master's theses from Spring 1988 (*Master's Abstracts*, Volume 26, Number 1) to the present. This database has very wide subject matter coverage including, but not limited to, business and economics, education, fine arts and music, geography, health sciences, political science, language and literature, library and information science, psychology, and sociology.

Family Studies contains citations and abstracts for journal articles, books, popular literature, conference papers, and government reports in the fields of family science, human ecology, and human development since 1970.

International Index to Black Periodicals Full Text (*IIBP Full Text*) draws its current content from more than 150 international scholarly and popular periodicals. It covers a wide array of humanities-related disciplines including art, cultural criticism, economics, education, health, history, language and literature, law, philosophy, politics, religion, and sociology, among others. All records in the current file (1998 forward) contain abstracts.

MEDLINE is the National Library of Medicine's (NLM) premier bibliographic database covering the fields of medicine, nursing, dentistry, veterinary medicine, the health care system, and the preclinical sciences. *MEDLINE*, the primary subset of *PubMed*, is available on the Internet through the NLM home page at http://www.nlm.nih.gov and can be searched free of charge. No registration is required. Additional *MEDLINE* services are also provided by organizations that lease the database from NLM. Access to various *MEDLINE* services is often available from medical libraries and many public libraries.

Social Sciences Citation Index (*SSCI*®) and *Social SciSearch*® provide access to current and retrospective bibliographic information, author abstracts, and cited references found in over 1,700 of the world's leading scholarly social sciences journals covering more than 50 disciplines. They also cover individually selected, relevant items from approximately 3,300 of the world's leading science and technology journals. Note that the *Citation Index* lists cited authors and their works together with all authors who have discussed the cited works in their publications. This can be very helpful in conducting a literature search if you start with a classic older article that is highly relevant to your topic. By searching for all publications in which it was subsequently cited, you can quickly build a collection of references that are likely to be very specific to your topic. Examining these sequentially permits you to trace the history of thought on a topic or theory.

APPENDIX D
ELECTRONIC SOURCES OF STATISTICAL INFORMATION[1]

When writing literature reviews, writers need up-to-date information. Because of the ease of electronic publishing, the Web usually has more up-to-date information than conventionally printed materials. (Note that it is not uncommon for a journal article or book to be published a year after it was written.)

It is often a good idea to begin literature reviews with current statistics on how many people (and/or the percentage of people) have a certain characteristic or a particular problem. Suppose, for instance, that your general topic for a literature review is cigarette smoking by pregnant women. Examine Box A, which shows two possible first sentences for a review. The second one, which cites current statistics found on the Web, is stronger and more compelling than the first one.[2]

Box A
The beginning of two possible first paragraphs for a literature review. The second one cites recent statistics found on the Web.

1. Many pregnant women continue to smoke despite warnings from the medical community. This makes it important to review literature to identify effective programs that....

2. Approximately 17 percent of pregnant women smoked cigarettes within the last month, according to a recent national survey (NHSDA, 1999).[3] This makes it important to review literature to identify... effective programs that....

Even if you do not begin your literature review with statistics, including specific statistics (e.g., "5,421 students" and "55.6% of the students") at some point in your literature review will make it more convincing than a review in which only vague references to statistics are made (e.g., "many individuals" and "a majority").

Note that many sources on the Web post the latest available information, which may not be completely up-to-date. For instance, the information in Box A was the most current available (for 1999) when retrieved in 2002 for use in this book. Nevertheless, a journal article or book published in 1999 would probably contain even older statistics given the publication lag in conventional, hard-copy publishing.

Note that Web addresses (i.e., URLs) frequently change, Web sites are often discontinued, and access that might be free at the time of this writing might not be free by the time you try to access them. If you have difficulties locating Web sites given in this book, use a general search engine such as www.Google.com to locate newer sites, additional free sites, and so on.

✍ Guideline 1 FedStats.gov is one of the most valuable sources of statistical information on the Web.

At www.FedStats.gov, you will be able to access statistics from more than 100 Federal agencies.[4] Prior to the establishment of this Web site, writers needed to search for statistics agency by agency. While the Fed-Stats site still allows you to search within only selected agencies, you can also search by *topic* and the Fed-Stats search engine will automatically search all agencies for relevant links to federal statistics. This is im-

---

[1] This appendix was adapted from Chapter 4 of *Preparing Literature Reviews*: *Qualitative and Quantitative Approaches* by M. Ling Pan (pp. 44–50). Copyright © 2003 by Pyrczak Publishing. All rights reserved.
[2] Using simple, compelling statistics is appropriate in both qualitative and quantitative reviews.
[3] Retrieved at http://www.samhsa.gov/oas/2k2/PregAlcTob/PregAlcTob.htm on September 19, 2002.
[4] Be sure to go to www.FedStats.*gov* and *not* www.FedStats.*com*. The latter is *not* a government site. Also be sure to type www. Although it is possible to access many sites on the Web without the prefix "www," this site is not one of them.

portant for two reasons: (1) you do not have to search each agency separately and (2) an agency that you are not aware of (or did not think of) may have statistics relevant to your topic.

For example, a topic search conducted by first going to www.FedStats.*gov* and clicking on Topic links – A to Z produced a screen with a row of letters of the alphabet underlined followed by a list of categories for each letter. (Web links to other sites are usually underlined and/or are sometimes identifiable by other means, such as the use of a different color for a link.) By clicking on the letter C in the row of letters, the extensive set of links shown in Box B was obtained. By clicking on the Breast link (the second link from the top), the links in Box C (on the next page) were obtained.

Box B
FedStats links for the letter C.

Cancer:
-- *Atlas of Cancer Mortality in the United States*
-- Breast
-- Cervical
-- Lung
-- Mortality maps
-- Prostate
Charitable trusts
Children:
-- Administration for Children programs and services
-- Adoption
-- Aid to Families with Dependent Children
-- *America's Children* (ChildStats)
-- Behavior and social environment indicators
-- Child care
-- Child support enforcement
-- Cigarette smoking
-- Delinquency and victimization
    -- Delinquency case records
    -- Juvenile arrests
    -- Juveniles as offenders
    -- Juveniles as victims
    -- Juveniles in court
    -- Juveniles in detention and corrections
-- Drug use
-- Economic security indicators
-- Education indicators
-- Foster care
-- HeadStart
Health:
-- Child and infant
-- Indicators
-- Insurance
-- Population and family characteristics
-- Nutrition
-- WIC
Civil justice statistics
Coal
Commodity flow
Common cold
Communications:
-- Broadcast radio and television
-- Cable television providers by community served
-- Telephone industry and telephone usage
-- Wireless communications services
Computer and Internet use
Construction
Industry tax statistics:
-- Corporations
-- Exempt organizations' unrelated business
-- Partnerships
-- Sole proprietorship

Consumer Credit
Consumer product safety
Consumer Price Indexes
Consumption, energy
Corporations
Country profiles
Crime (See also *Law enforcement*):
-- Characteristics of crime
-- Children
-- Crime in schools
-- Crimes reported to the police
-- Criminal offenders
-- Drugs
-- Firearms
-- Hate
-- Homicide
-- Prison inmates
-- Terrorism
-- Victims
-- Violent
Criminal justice:
-- Corrections
    -- Capital punishment
    -- Inmates
    -- Jails
    -- Prisons
    -- Probation and parole statistics
-- Courts and sentencing
    -- Court organization
    -- Criminal case processing
    -- Pretrial release and detention
    -- Sentencing
-- Criminal record systems
-- Employment and expenditure
-- Federal justice statistics
-- Indigent defense statistics
-- Law enforcement
    -- Campus law enforcement
    -- Federal law enforcement
    -- State and local law enforcement
-- Prosecution
Crops:
-- Crop progress and weather, weekly
-- Data by county
-- Data by state, historic
-- Field
-- Fruits and nuts
-- Vegetables

Box C
A large sample of the links obtained by clicking on Breast, which is the second link in Box B (under the main heading "Cancer").

Treatment
Information about treatment, including surgery, chemotherapy, radiation therapy, immunotherapy, and vaccine therapy
• Breast Cancer Treatment
[patients] [health professionals]
• Male Breast Cancer Treatment
[patients] [health professionals]
• Breast Cancer and Pregnancy
[patients] [health professionals]
• More Information

Prevention, Genetics, Causes
Information related to prevention, genetics, risk factors
• Breast Cancer Prevention
[patients] [health professionals]
• Genetics of Breast and Ovarian Cancer
• Postmenopausal Hormone Use
• Long Island Breast Cancer Study Project
• More Information

Screening and Testing
Information about methods of cancer detection, including new imaging technologies, tumor markers, and biopsy procedures
• Breast Cancer Screening
[patients] [health professionals]
• NCI Statement on Mammography Screening
• HHS Affirms Value of Mammography
• More Information

Clinical Trials
Information on clinical trials and current news on trials and trial-related data
• Breast Cancer Updates
• Search for Clinical Trials

Cancer Literature
Resources available from the CANCERLIT® database
• Search CANCERLIT®
• CANCERLIT® Topic Searches: Breast Cancer
• CANCERLIT® Topic Searches: Cancer Genetics

Related Information
Other information, including reports about NCI priorities for cancer research and initiatives
• Breast Cancer Progress Review Group

Statistics
Information related to cancer incidence, mortality, and survival
• Probability of Breast Cancer in American Women
• Breast - U.S. Racial/Ethnic Cancer Patterns
• Data Sources

☙ Guideline 2 State and local governments and their agencies (including state-supported universities) often post very current statistics on the Web.

While you can obtain information at the local level at FedStats, you can sometimes obtain more current statistical information from nonfederal governmental sources. This is true for two reasons: (1) the federal government collects data periodically, with years intervening in some cases, and (2) local agencies must report in a very timely manner to their superiors such as city councils and mayors. Example 2.1 shows the latest statistics on property crimes in Buffalo, New York, posted on FedStats at the time of this writing as well as the latest ones obtained by going directly to the City of Buffalo Web site.[5]

Example 2.1

Table 1
Property-Crime Statistics for Buffalo, New York, from Federal and Local Sources

Year	FedStats Web Site	City of Buffalo Web Site
2001	not available	16,185
2000	not available	16,591
1999	17,436	17,436

---

[5] Retrieved September 19, 2002, from www.city-buffalo.com/Files/1_2_1/Police/Crime%20Statistics.htm

✎ Guideline 3   Use the raw statistics from governmental agencies—not statistics filtered by politicians or others with special interests.

Government statistics are usually collected by civil service employees (not political appointees). While there may be errors in their work, there is no more reason to suspect them of deliberately biasing the data collection than to suspect any other type of researcher. However, some politicians may understandably be selective (and perhaps misleading) in choosing which statistics to report. Hence, it is usually best to obtain the original government reports either in print or via the Web rather than relying on secondhand reports of government statistics presented by politicians or special-interest groups and organizations. However, as you will see in Guideline 5, those with vested interests in statistical information sometimes provide useful links or primary-source information (via the Web), which can be helpful when writing literature reviews.

Note that in some cases, it is appropriate to present original government statistics in a literature review *and* discuss how they are interpreted by individuals and organizations with varying political points of view.

✎ Guideline 4   Consider consulting the Library of Congress's Virtual Reference Shelf on the Web.

The Library of Congress maintains a Web site titled the "Virtual Reference Shelf." It is an excellent site for general references such as dictionaries, general history, abbreviations, genealogy, and so on. It can be found at www.loc.gov/rr/askalib/virtualref.html.[6] Box D shows the main links at that site. Although these links take you to a wide variety of types of information, they often include statistics on various topics. At the bottom of the home page (not shown in the box but clearly visible on the Web site) is a link for "Ask a Librarian," which can be a very useful service if you are struggling to find specialized statistical information to use in your literature review.

Box D
Links on the home page of the Library of Congress's Virtual Reference Shelf.

Internet Public Library Reference Center
Librarian's Index to the Internet Refdesk

• <u>Abbreviations</u>	• <u>Education</u>
• <u>Almanacs and Fast Facts</u>	• <u>Encyclopedias</u>
• <u>Associations</u>	• <u>Genealogy, Biography, and Archaeology</u>
• <u>Awards/Prizes</u>	• <u>General History</u>
• <u>Books, Periodicals, and Publishing</u>	• <u>Health/Medical</u>
• <u>Business</u>	• <u>Language and Literature</u>
• <u>Calculators</u>	• <u>Law</u>
• <u>Clocks/Times</u>	• <u>Libraries</u>
• <u>Consumer Information</u>	• <u>Maps/Driving Directions</u>
• <u>Current Events on the Web</u>	• <u>Political Science and Government</u>
• <u>Dictionaries/Thesauri</u>	• <u>Quotations</u>
• <u>Directories</u>	• <u>Statistics</u>
• <u>Domestic Arts</u>	• <u>Technology and Engineering</u> (Weather)

<u>Selected Subject Feature</u> * <u>Other Reference Sites</u> * <u>In the News</u>

✎ Guideline 5   Consider accessing information posted on the Web by a variety of nongovernmental agencies, such as businesses, professional associations, and advocacy groups.

A wide variety of associations post information (and statistics) on the Web. Following the link called "Associations" in the Virtual Reference Shelf (see Box D), you can identify hundreds of associations, many

---

[6] Rather than typing (and risk mistyping) long URLs, it is sometimes faster to do a quick search on a major search engine such as www.Google.com using a term such as "Virtual Reference Shelf." Use the quotation marks around the terms (e.g., "Virtual Reference Shelf") to conduct an exact phrase match and exclude other Web sites that might have only one of the words such as "virtual."

of which are quite specialized. For instance, there are employee associations such as the Southern California Association of Fingerprint Officers at www.scafo.org, which publishes an on-line journal titled *The Print* in which there are original articles as well as reprints of articles from other sources. In contrast, there are political lobbying and advocacy associations such as the Web site for the American Civil Liberties Union at www.aclu.org, which publishes a newsletter and sells inexpensive special reports such as *Unequal, Unfair, and Irreversible: The Death Penalty in Virginia*, which cites relevant statistics.

Be cautious when citing information found on Web sites maintained by advocacy groups such as unions and political-interest groups. Nevertheless, because of their special interest in topics related to their missions, advocacy groups may have more information than other sources because they have sought it out more thoroughly than others have or because they have conducted their own unpublished studies. Note that you might want to compare and contrast the points of view of opposing advocacy groups in your literature review. For instance, you might point out how the Republican candidate for an office interprets a change in unemployment statistics and compare it with how the Democratic candidate interprets the same statistics. Note that while the statistics cited by politicians (and others) are secondary-source material, the *interpretations* of the statistics are primary sources of information.

You should also consider accessing information posted on the Web by businesses and corporations. Suppose you are writing a literature review on allergies for a health education class. Going to the home page for the prescription drug Flonase® will provide you with a reference to an article on allergies in an academic journal.

Keep in mind that complete objectivity in research cannot be achieved. All agencies sponsoring research (even nonprofit ones that have special tax status) have points of view that might influence what is researched, how questions are worded, how the sample is drawn, how the information is presented, and so on. It is your responsibility to try to understand their points of view and identify information on the Web that is reliable and useful for the purposes of your literature review.

NOTES

APPENDIX E
OTHER METHODS OF DETERMINING RELIABILITY

In addition to interobserver, test–retest, and parallel-forms reliability (see Topic 30), we may also examine the **split-half reliability** of a test. To do this, we can treat a test administered just once to a group of examinees as two tests by scoring the even-numbered items separately from the odd-numbered items. This yields two scores per examinee. Calculating a correlation coefficient for them yields what is called a *split-half reliability coefficient*. Like other reliability coefficients, it ranges from 0.00 to 1.00. There are two problems with it, however. First, it is an estimate of the reliability of a test only *half as long* as the whole test. (You may recall from Topic 29 that the longer the test, the higher the reliability.) A statistical adjustment, known as the **Spearman-Brown Prophecy Formula**, may be used to estimate the reliability of the *whole test* based on the split-half reliability of the half test. As you know from Topic 29, longer tests tend to be more reliable than shorter tests, so it is important to use the Spearman-Brown formula.

The second problem is that the interpretation of split-half reliability coefficients is complicated by the fact that its values are dependent on the extent to which the odd-numbered items measure the same traits as the even-numbered items. Thus, the result is referred to by some as **internal consistency reliability** and by others as merely **internal consistency** (without the term *reliability*).

Somewhat analogous results can be obtained by using either **coefficient alpha** or **Kuder-Richardson Formula 20** or **21**, all of which indicate the extent to which all the items on a test measure the same trait. Once again, these are *internal consistency* measures that also range from 0.00 to 1.00.

Information from these procedures, all of which require only one administration of a test, is of value if we want to know whether the content of a test is homogeneous (as indicated by a high coefficient). However, if we want to judge reliability as it is classically defined, the methods described in Topic 30 are preferable.

For detailed information on the assumptions underlying the various methods of examining reliability, see any introductory measurement textbook such as Thorndike, R. M. (1996). *Measurement and evaluation in psychology and education*. New York: Prentice-Hall.

NOTES

APPENDIX F
A CLOSER LOOK AT THE STANDARD DEVIATION

In this appendix, we will consider some rules for interpreting the standard deviation in relation to the normal curve as well as how to compute the standard deviation.

You learned in Topic 47 that if you go out one standard-deviation unit on both sides of the mean, you capture 68% of the cases in a normal distribution. It turns out that if you go out two units on both sides of the mean, you capture approximately 95% of the cases.[1] For the distribution we considered with $M = 70$ and $S = 10$, we noted that 68% lies between scores of 60 and 80. If we go out $2 \times 10 = 20$ points (which is two standard-deviation units), we come to scores of 50 and 90 (i.e., the mean of 70 *minus* 20 = 50, and the mean of 70 *plus* 20 = 90). This is illustrated in Figure 1.

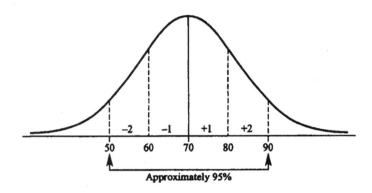

Figure 1. Normal curve illustrating approximate 95% rule.

If we go out three standard-deviation units, we capture 99.7% of the cases, which is essentially all of them. Thus, there are about three standard-deviation units on both sides of the mean in a normal distribution.

Considering how the standard deviation is calculated should give you a feeling for the meaning of the standard deviation. As the formula below indicates, it is the *square root of the mean squared deviation from the mean*. Thus, the larger the deviations from the mean, the larger the standard deviation. Conversely, the smaller the deviations from the mean, the smaller the standard deviation.

The formula that defines the standard deviation is:

$$S = \sqrt{\frac{\sum x^2}{N}}$$

The lowercase x stands for the deviation of a score from the mean of its distribution. To obtain it, first calculate the mean (in this case, 78/6 = 13.00) and subtract the mean from each score, as shown in Example 1 on the next page. Then, square the deviations and sum the squares, as indicated by the symbol Σ. Then, enter this value in the formula along with the number of cases (N) and perform the calculations as indicated in Example 1 on the next page.

---

[1] To capture precisely 95%, go out 1.96 (a little less than 2.00) standard deviations. If we go out 2.58 standard deviations, we capture 99% of the cases.

EXAMPLE 1

Scores (X)	Deviations ($X - M$)	Deviations Squared (x^2)
10	$10 - 13.00 = -3$	9.00
11	$11 - 13.00 = -2$	4.00
11	$11 - 13.00 = -2$	4.00
13	$13 - 13.00 = 0$	0.00
14	$14 - 13.00 = 1$	1.00
19	$19 - 13.00 = 6$	36.00
		$\Sigma x^2 = 54.00$

Thus, for these data:

$$S = \sqrt{\frac{54}{6}} = \sqrt{9.00} = 3.00$$

APPENDIX G
A CLOSER LOOK AT EFFECT SIZE

Reporting effect sizes in research reports has become common only in recent years, and they still are not universally reported. Hence, consumers of research (who typically do not need to compute statistics) may find it beneficial to be able to calculate some simple statistics that will allow them to interpret more accurately results in which effect sizes have been omitted in research reports.

In Topic 54, the calculation of Cohen's d was illustrated in the examples in which the two standard deviations were equal. When they are not equal, most researchers divide the difference between means by the "pooled standard deviation," which is a special type of average standard deviation that can be obtained using the following formula. Its use is illustrated for an experiment in which the experimental group's standard deviation is 10.00 (with 15 participants, $n = 15$), and the control group's standard deviation is 14.00 (with 12 participants, $n = 12$). Note that for an experiment, the subscript "1" designates the experimental group, and the subscript "2" designates the control group.

$$sd_{pooled} = \sqrt{\frac{(n_1 - 1)sd_1^2 + (n_2 - 1)sd_2^2}{n_1 + n_2 - 2}} = \sqrt{\frac{(15 - 1)10.00^2 + (12 - 1)14.00^2}{15 + 12 - 2}} = 11.93$$

(Note that the pooled standard deviation of 11.93 is very close to the simple average of the standard deviations [10.00 + 14.00 = 24.00/2 = 12.00]. The larger the difference between the numbers of participants in the two groups and the larger the difference between the two standard deviations, the greater the difference between the pooled standard deviation and the simple average of the standard deviations.)

The usual formula for Cohen's d is the difference between the means divided by the pooled standard deviation, which is shown here in symbols:[1]

$$d = \frac{m_1 - m_2}{sd_{pooled}}$$

As a practical solution for consumers of research who do not want to engage in extensive calculations, a good *estimate* of d will usually be obtained by dividing the difference between the means by the *simple average* of the standard deviations. As you saw in the example above, the simple average of the standard deviations is 10.00 + 14.00 = 24.00/2 = 12.00. Divide the difference between the two means by 12.00 for an estimate. Another practical solution when conducting meta-analyses on experiments is to use only the standard deviation of the control group (and hence avoid averaging standard deviations altogether), as discussed in the next paragraph.

When analyzing the difference between an experimental group and a control group, some researchers prefer to divide the difference between the means by the standard deviation of the control group only (as opposed to the pooled standard deviation for both groups). The resulting statistic is widely known as Glass's delta (Δ), although it is sometimes also referred to as d in research literature. This is understandable because the value of d and the value of Δ are very similar when the two standard deviations are very similar. For example, in a perfect case in which the two standard deviations are identical, the standard deviation of the control group will equal the pooled standard deviation of the two groups, so d and Δ will have exactly the same value.

---

[1] Those of you who have taken statistics should note that the population value of the standard deviation (computed without the minus one [−1] in the denominator of the computational formula) should be used to obtain Cohen's d. If the sample standard deviation is used, the result is Hedge's g, which, for small samples, can differ noticeably from Cohen's d. Values of g can be converted to values of d using the following formula:

$$d = g\sqrt{N/df}$$

In Topic 54, the examples were *experiments* (with experimental and control groups). Cohen's *d* is also appropriate for describing the difference between two means in *nonexperimental studies*. For instance, we could survey a random sample of girls and a random sample of boys (without any physical treatments), compute a mean and standard deviation for each group, and compare the two groups using *d*. In such a study, it is usually best to subtract the smaller mean from the larger mean and divide by either the pooled standard deviation (for an exact value of *d*) or by the simple average of the two standard deviations (for an estimate of the value of *d*).

Also, in Topic 56, you learned that when examining a body of literature, it is sometimes helpful to be able to directly compare the effect sizes represented by values of *d* with effect sizes represented by values of *r*. The following formula will give a good approximation of the value of *d* corresponding to a value of *r*.

$$d = \frac{2r}{\sqrt{1 - r^2}}$$

The following formula is recommended for calculating the "effect size *r*" from a value of *d*. The subscript "es" for "effect size" is used here to distinguish the result from a value of *r* that is computed directly from raw scores (as opposed to being computed from a value of *d*).

$$r_{es} = \frac{d}{\sqrt{d^2 + 4}}$$

Table 1
Table of Random Numbers

Row #						
1	2 1 0	4 9 8	0 8 8	8 0 6	9 2 4	8 2 6
2	0 7 3	0 2 9	4 8 2	7 8 9	8 9 2	9 7 1
3	4 4 9	0 0 2	8 6 2	6 7 7	7 3 1	2 5 1
4	7 3 2	1 1 2	0 7 7	6 0 3	8 3 4	7 8 1
5	3 3 2	5 8 3	1 7 0	1 4 0	7 8 9	3 7 7
6	6 1 2	0 5 7	2 4 4	0 0 6	3 0 2	8 0 7
7	7 0 9	3 3 3	7 4 0	4 8 8	9 3 5	8 0 5
8	7 5 1	9 0 9	1 5 2	6 5 0	9 0 3	5 8 8
9	3 5 6	9 6 5	0 1 9	4 6 6	7 5 6	8 3 1
10	8 5 0	3 9 4	3 4 0	6 5 1	7 4 4	6 2 7
11	0 5 9	6 8 7	4 8 1	5 5 0	5 1 7	1 5 8
12	7 6 2	2 6 9	6 1 9	7 1 1	4 7 1	6 2 0
13	3 8 4	7 8 9	8 2 2	1 6 3	8 7 0	4 6 1
14	1 9 1	8 4 5	6 1 8	1 2 4	4 4 2	7 3 4
15	1 5 3	6 7 6	1 8 4	3 1 8	8 7 7	6 0 4
16	0 5 5	3 6 0	7 1 3	8 1 4	6 7 0	4 3 5
17	2 2 3	8 6 0	9 1 9	0 4 4	7 6 8	1 5 1
18	2 3 3	2 5 5	7 6 9	4 9 7	1 3 7	9 3 8
19	8 5 5	0 5 3	7 8 5	4 5 1	6 0 4	8 9 1
20	0 6 1	1 3 4	8 6 4	3 2 9	4 3 8	7 4 1
21	9 1 1	8 2 9	0 6 9	6 9 4	2 9 9	0 6 0
22	3 7 8	0 6 3	7 1 2	6 5 2	7 6 5	6 5 1
23	5 3 0	5 1 2	1 0 9	1 3 7	5 6 1	2 5 0
24	7 2 4	8 6 7	9 3 8	7 6 0	9 1 6	5 7 8
25	0 9 1	6 7 0	3 8 0	9 1 5	4 2 3	2 4 5
26	3 8 1	4 3 7	9 2 4	5 1 2	8 7 7	4 1 3

NOTES

Table 2

Table of Recommended Sample Sizes (*n*) for Populations (*N*) with Finite Sizes[1]

N	*n*	*N*	*n*	*N*	*n*
10	10	220	140	1,200	291
15	14	230	144	1,300	297
20	19	240	148	1,400	302
25	24	250	152	1,500	306
30	28	260	155	1,600	310
35	32	270	159	1,700	313
40	36	280	162	1,800	317
45	40	290	165	1,900	320
50	44	300	169	2,000	322
55	48	320	175	2,200	327
60	52	340	181	2,400	331
65	56	360	186	2,600	335
70	59	380	191	2,800	338
75	63	400	196	3,000	341
80	66	420	201	3,500	346
85	70	440	205	4,000	351
90	73	460	210	4,500	354
95	76	480	214	5,000	357
100	80	500	217	6,000	361
110	86	550	226	7,000	364
120	92	600	234	8,000	367
130	97	650	242	9,000	368
140	103	700	248	10,000	370
150	108	750	254	15,000	375
160	113	800	260	20,000	377
170	118	850	265	30,000	379
180	123	900	269	40,000	380
190	127	950	274	50,000	381
200	132	1,000	278	75,000	382
210	136	1,100	285	100,000	384

---

[1] Adapted from: Krejcie, R. V., & Morgan, D. W. (1970). Determining sample size for research activities. *Educational and Psychological Measurement, 30*, 607–610.

NOTES

INDEX

NOTES

NOTES